SPECIALIST

MICROSOFT® ACCESS 2003

NITA RUTKOSKY

**Pierce College at Puyallup
Puyallup, Washington**

EMCParadigm
PUBLISHING

Project Editor	Sonja Brown
Developmental Editor	James Patterson
Senior Designer	Leslie Anderson
Technical Reviewer	Desiree Faulkner
Cover Designer	Jennifer Wreisner
Copyeditor	Susan Capecchi
Desktop Production Specialists	Erica Tava, Lisa Beller
Proofreader	Joy McComb
Indexer	Nancy Fulton
Photo Researcher	Paul Spencer

Publishing Team—George Provol, Publisher; Janice Johnson, Director of Product Development and Instructional Design; Tony Galvin, Acquisitions Editor; Lori Landwer, Marketing Manager; Shelley Clubb, Electronic Design and Production Manager

Acknowledgments—The author and editors wish to thank the following instructors for their technical and academic contributions:

- Susan Lynn Bowen, Valdosta Technical College, Valdosta, GA, for testing the exercises and assessing instruction
- Ann Lewis, Ivy Tech State College, Evansville, IN, for creating the Chapter Challenge case studies and for preparing the IG materials
- Daphne Press, Ozarks Technical Community College, Springfield, MO, for preparing the Internet Projects and Job Study scenarios

Photo Credits: S1 (counterclockwise from top), William Gottlieb/CORBIS; CORBIS; CORBIS; Will & Deni McIntyre/CORBIS

Library of Congress Cataloging-in-Publication Data

Rutkosky, Nita Hewitt.
    Microsoft Access 2003 specialist certification / Nita Rutkosky.
        p. cm. -- (Benchmark series)
    Includes index.
    ISBN 0-7638-2041-5 (text)
1. Electronic data processing personnel--Certification. 2. Microsoft
software--Examinations--Study guides. 3. Microsoft Access. I. Title. II. Benchmark series
(Saint Paul, Minn.)

QA76.3.R894 2004
005.75'65--dc22

2003049473

Text: ISBN 0-7638-2041-5
Product Number 05614

© 2004 by Paradigm Publishing, Inc.
    Published by **EMC**Paradigm
    875 Montreal Way
    St. Paul, MN 55102

    (800) 535-6865
    E-mail: educate@emcp.com
    Web site: www.emcp.com

Printed in the United States of America
10 9 8 7 6 5 4 3 2

CONTENTS

WELCOME

You are about to begin working with a textbook that is part of the Benchmark Office 2003 Series. The word *Benchmark* in the title holds a special significance in terms of *what* you will learn and *how* you will learn. *Benchmark*, according to *Webster's Dictionary*, means "something that serves as a standard by which others may be measured or judged." In this text, you will learn the Microsoft Office Specialist skills required for certification on the Specialist and/or Expert level of one or more major applications within the Office 2003 suite. These skills are benchmarks by which you will be evaluated, should you choose to take one or more certification exams.

The design and teaching approach of this textbook also serve as a benchmark for instructional materials on software programs. Features and commands are presented in a clear, straightforward way, and each short section of instruction is followed by an exercise that lets you practice using the new feature. Gradually, as you move through each chapter, you will build your skills to the point of mastery. At the end of a chapter, you are offered the opportunity to demonstrate your newly acquired competencies—to prove you have met the benchmarks for using the Office suite or an individual program. At the completion of the text, you are well on your way to becoming a successful computer user.

EMC/Paradigm's Office 2003 Benchmark Series includes textbooks on Office 2003, Word 2003, Excel 2003, Access 2003 and PowerPoint 2003. Each book includes a Student CD, which contains documents and files required for completing the exercises. A CD icon and folder name displayed on the opening page of each chapter indicates that you need to copy a folder of files from the CD before beginning the chapter exercises. *(See the inside back cover for instructions on copying a folder.)*

Introducing Microsoft Office 2003

Microsoft Office 2003 is a suite of programs designed to improve productivity and efficiency in workplace, school, and home settings. A suite is a group of programs that are sold as a package and are designed to be used together, making it possible to exchange files among the programs. The major applications included in Office are Word, a word processing program; Excel, a spreadsheet program; Access, a database management program; and PowerPoint, a slide presentation program.

Using the Office suite offers significant advantages over working with individual programs developed by different software vendors. The programs in the Office suite use similar toolbars, buttons, icons, and menus, which means that once you learn the basic features of one program, you can use those same features in the other programs. This easy transfer of knowledge decreases the learning time and allows you to concentrate on the unique commands and options within each program. The compatibility of the programs creates seamless integration of data within and between programs and lets the operator use the program most appropriate for the required tasks.

New Features in Office 2003

Users of previous editions of Office will find that the essential features that have made Office popular still form the heart of the suite. New enhancements include improved templates for both business and personal use. The Smart Tags introduced in Office XP also have been enhanced in Office 2003 with special customization options. One of the most far-reaching changes is the introduction of XML (eXtensible Markup Language) capabilities. Some elements of this technology were essentially hidden behind the scenes in Office XP. Now XML has been brought to the forefront. XML enables data to be used more flexibly and stored regardless of the computer platform. It can be used between different languages, countries, and across the Internet. XML heralds a revolution in data exchange. At the same time, it makes efficient and effective use of internal data within a business.

Structure of the Benchmark Textbooks

Users of the Specialist Certification texts and the complete application textbooks may begin their course with an overview of computer hardware and software, offered in the *Getting Started* section at the beginning of the book. Your instructor may also ask you to complete the *Windows XP* and the *Internet Explorer* sections so you become familiar with the computer's operating system and the essential tools for using the Internet.

Instruction on the major programs within the Office suite is presented in units of four chapters each. Both the Specialist and Expert levels contain two units, which culminate with performance assessments to check your knowledge and skills. Each chapter contains the following sections:

- performance objectives that identify specifically what you are expected to learn
- instructional text that introduces and explains new concepts and features
- step-by-step, hands-on exercises following each section of instruction
- a chapter summary
- a knowledge self-check called Concepts Check
- skill assessment exercises called Skills Check
- a case study exercise called Chapter Challenge

Exercises offered at the end of units provide writing and research opportunities that will strengthen your performance in other college courses as well as on the job. The final activities simulate interesting projects you could encounter in the workplace.

Benchmark Series Ancillaries

The Benchmark Series includes some important resources that will help you succeed in your computer applications courses:

Snap Training and Assessment

A Web-based program designed to optimize skill-based learning for all of the programs of Microsoft Office 2003, Snap is comprised of:

- a learning management system that creates a virtual classroom on the Web, allowing the instructor to schedule tutorials and tests and to employ an electronic gradebook;
- over 200 interactive, multimedia tutorials, aligned to textbook chapters, that can be used for direct instruction or remediation;
- a test bank of over 1,800 performance skill items that simulate the operation of Microsoft Office and allow the instructor to assign pretests, to administer chapter posttests, and to create practice tests to help students prepare for Microsoft Office Specialist certification exams; and
- over 6,000 concept items that can be used in combined concepts/application courses to monitor student understanding of technical and computer literacy knowledge.

Online Resource Center

Internet Resource Centers hosted by EMC/Paradigm provide additional material for students and instructors using the Benchmark books. Online you will find Web links, updates to textbooks, study tips, quizzes and assignments, and supplementary projects.

Class Connection

Available for both WebCT and Blackboard, EMC/Paradigm's Class Connection is a course management tool for traditional and distance learning.

What does this logo mean?

It means this courseware has been approved by the Microsoft® Office Specialist program to be among the finest available for learning Microsoft Access 2003. It also means that upon completion of this courseware, you may be prepared to take an exam for Microsoft Office Specialist qualification.

What is a Microsoft Office Specialist?

A Microsoft Office Specialist is an individual who has passed exams for certifying his or her skills in one or more of the Microsoft Office desktop applications such as Microsoft Word, Microsoft Excel, Microsoft PowerPoint, Microsoft Outlook, Microsoft Access, or Microsoft Project. The Microsoft Office Specialist Program typically offers certification exams at the Specialist and Expert skill levels. The Microsoft Office Specialist Program is the only program in the world approved by Microsoft for testing proficiency in Microsoft Office desktop applications and Microsoft Project. This testing program can be a valuable asset in any job search or career advancement.

More Information

- To learn more about becoming a Microsoft Office Specialist, visit www.microsoft.com/officespecialist
- To learn about other Microsoft Office Specialist approved courseware from EMC/Paradigm Publishing, visit www.emcp.com

---

OFFICE *2003*

GETTING STARTED IN OFFICE 2003

In this textbook, you will learn to operate several microcomputer application programs that combine to make an application "suite." This suite of programs is called Microsoft Office 2003. The programs you will learn to operate are the *software*, which include instructions telling the computer what to do. Some of the software programs in the suite include a word processing program called *Word*, a spreadsheet program called *Excel*, a presentation program called *PowerPoint*, and a database program called *Access*.

Identifying Computer Hardware

The computer equipment you will use to operate the suite of programs is referred to as *hardware*. You will need access to a microcomputer system that should consist of the CPU, monitor, keyboard, printer, disk drives, and mouse. If you are not sure what equipment you will be operating, check with your instructor. The computer system displayed in Figure G.1 consists of six components. Each component is discussed separately in the material that follows.

FIGURE

G.1 *Microcomputer System*

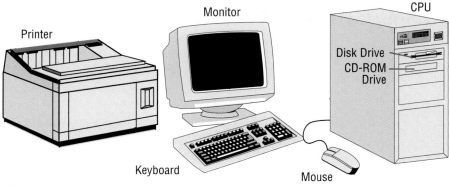

CPU

CPU stands for Central Processing Unit and it is the intelligence of the computer. All the processing occurs in the CPU. Silicon chips, which contain miniaturized circuitry, are placed on boards that are plugged into slots within the CPU. Whenever an instruction is given to the computer, that instruction is processed through circuitry in the CPU.

Monitor

The monitor is a piece of equipment that looks like a television screen. It displays the information of a program and the text being input at the keyboard. The quality of display for monitors varies depending on the type of monitor and the level of resolution. Monitors can also vary in size—generally from 14-inch size up to 21-inch size or larger.

Keyboard

The keyboard is used to input information into the computer. Keyboards for microcomputers vary in the number and location of the keys. Microcomputers have the alphabetic and numeric keys in the same location as the keys on a typewriter. The symbol keys, however, may be placed in a variety of locations, depending on the manufacturer. In addition to letters, numbers, and symbols, most microcomputer keyboards contain function keys, arrow keys, and a numeric keypad. Figure G.2 shows an enhanced keyboard.

FIGURE

G.2 *Microcomputer Enhanced Keyboard*

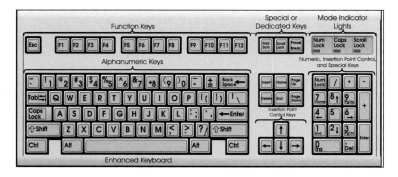

The 12 keys at the top of the enhanced keyboard, labeled with the letter F followed by a number, are called *function keys*. These keys can be used to perform functions within each of the suite programs. To the right of the regular keys is a group of *special* or *dedicated keys*. These keys are labeled with specific functions that will be performed when you press the key. Below the special keys are arrow keys. These keys are used to move the insertion point in the document screen.

In the upper right corner of the keyboard are three mode indicator lights. When certain modes have been selected, a light appears on the keyboard. For example, if you press the Caps Lock key, which disables the lowercase alphabet, a light appears next to Caps Lock. Similarly, pressing the Num Lock key will disable the special functions on the numeric keypad, which is located at the right side of the keyboard.

Disk Drives

Depending on the computer system you are using, Microsoft Office 2003 is installed on a hard drive or as part of a network system. Whether you are using

Office on a hard drive or network system, you will need to have available a CD drive and a floppy disk drive or other storage media. You will insert the CD (compact disk) that accompanies this textbook in the CD drive and then copy folders from the CD to a disk in the floppy disk drive. You will also save documents you complete at the computer to folders on your disk in the floppy drive.

Printer

When you create a document in Word, it is considered *soft copy*. If you want a *hard copy* of a document, you need to print it. To print documents you will need to access a printer, which will probably be either a laser printer or an ink-jet printer. A laser printer uses a laser beam combined with heat and pressure to print documents, while an ink-jet printer prints a document by spraying a fine mist of ink on the page.

Mouse

Many functions in the suite of programs are designed to operate more efficiently with a *mouse*. A mouse is an input device that sits on a flat surface next to the computer. A mouse can be operated with the left or the right hand. Moving the mouse on the flat surface causes a corresponding mouse pointer to move on the screen. Figure G.1 shows an illustration of a mouse.

Using the Mouse

The programs in the Microsoft Office suite can be operated using a keyboard or they can be operated with the keyboard and a mouse. The mouse may have two or three buttons on top, which are tapped to execute specific functions and commands. To use the mouse, rest it on a flat surface or a mouse pad. Put your hand over it with your palm resting on top of the mouse and your wrist resting on the table surface. As you move the mouse on the flat surface, a corresponding pointer moves on the screen.

When using the mouse, there are four terms you should understand—point, click, double-click, and drag. When operating the mouse, you may need to *point* to a specific command, button, or icon. Point means to position the mouse pointer on the desired item. With the mouse pointer positioned on the desired item, you may need to *click* a button on the mouse. Click means quickly tapping a button on the mouse once. To complete two steps at one time, such as choosing and then executing a function, *double-click* a mouse button. Double-click means to tap the left mouse button twice in quick succession. The term *drag* means to press and hold the left mouse button, move the mouse pointer to a specific location, and then release the button.

Using the Mouse Pointer

The mouse pointer will change appearance depending on the function being performed or where the pointer is positioned. The mouse pointer may appear as one of the following images:

The mouse pointer appears as an I-beam (called the *I-beam pointer*) in the document screen and can be used to move the insertion point or select text.

The mouse pointer appears as an arrow pointing up and to the left (called the *arrow pointer*) when it is moved to the Title bar, Menu bar, or one of the toolbars at the top of the screen or when a dialog box is displayed. For example, to open a new document with the mouse, you would move the I-beam pointer to the File option on the Menu bar. When the I-beam pointer is moved to the Menu bar, it turns into an arrow pointer. To make a selection, position the tip of the arrow pointer on the File option, and then click the left mouse button. At the drop-down menu that displays, make selections by positioning the arrow pointer on the desired option and then clicking the left mouse button.

The mouse pointer becomes a double-headed arrow (either pointing left and right, pointing up and down, or pointing diagonally) when performing certain functions such as changing the size of an object.

In certain situations, such as moving an object or image, the mouse pointer becomes a four-headed arrow. The four-headed arrow means that you can move the object left, right, up, or down.

When a request is being processed or when a program is being loaded, the mouse pointer may appear with an hourglass beside it. The hourglass image means "please wait." When the process is completed, the hourglass image is removed.

The mouse pointer displays as a hand with a pointing index finger in certain functions such as Help and indicates that more information is available about the item.

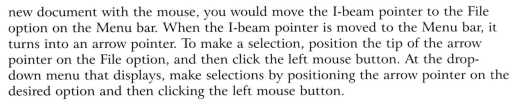

Choosing Commands

Once a program is open, several methods can be used in the program to choose commands. A command is an instruction that tells the program to do something. You can choose a command with one of the following methods:

- Click a toolbar button with the mouse
- Choose a command from a menu
- Use shortcut keys
- Use a shortcut menu

Choosing Commands on Toolbars

When a program such as Word or PowerPoint is open, several toolbars containing buttons for common tasks are available. In many of the suite programs, two toolbars are visible on the screen. One toolbar is called the Standard toolbar; the other is referred to as the Formatting toolbar. To choose a command from a toolbar, position the tip of the arrow pointer on a button, and then click the left mouse button. For example, to print the file currently displayed in the screen, position the tip of the arrow pointer on the Print button on the Standard toolbar, and then click the left mouse button.

Choosing Commands on the Menu Bar

Each of the suite programs contains a Menu bar that displays toward the top of the screen. This Menu bar contains a variety of options you can use to perform functions and commands on data. Functions are grouped logically into options, which display on the Menu bar. For example, features to work with files are grouped in the File option. Either the mouse or the keyboard can be used to make choices from the Menu bar or make a choice at a dialog box.

To use the mouse to make a choice from the Menu bar, move the I-beam pointer to the Menu bar. This causes the I-beam pointer to display as an arrow pointer. Position the tip of the arrow pointer on the desired option, and then click the left mouse button.

To use the keyboard, press the Alt key to make the Menu bar active. Options on the Menu bar display with an underline below one of the letters. To choose an option from the Menu bar, type the underlined letter of the desired option, or move the insertion point with the Left or Right Arrow keys to the option desired, and then press Enter. This causes a drop-down menu to display.

For example, to display the File drop-down menu in Word as shown in Figure G.3 using the mouse, position the arrow pointer on File on the Menu bar, and then click the left mouse button. To display the File drop-down menu with the keyboard, press the Alt key, and then type the letter F for File.

F I G U R E

| G.3 | *Word File Drop-Down Menu* |

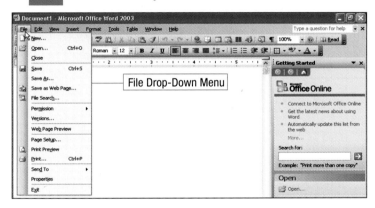

Choosing Commands from Drop-Down Menus

To choose a command from a drop-down menu with the mouse, position the arrow pointer on the desired option, and then click the left mouse button. At the drop-down menu that displays, move the arrow pointer down the menu to the desired option, and then click the left mouse button.

To make a selection from the drop-down menu with the keyboard, type the underlined letter of the desired option. Once the drop-down menu displays, you do not need to hold down the Alt key with the underlined letter. If you want to close a drop-down menu without making a choice, click in the screen outside the drop-down menu, or press the Esc key twice.

If an option can be accessed by clicking a button on a toolbar, the button is displayed preceding the option in the drop-down menu. For example, buttons display before the New, Open, Save, Save as Web Page, File Search, Print Preview, and Print options at the File drop-down menu (see Figure G.3).

Some menu options may be gray shaded (dimmed). When an option is dimmed, that option is currently not available. For example, if you choose the Table option on the Menu bar, the Table drop-down menu displays with dimmed options including Merge Cells, Split Cells, and Split Table.

Some menu options are preceded by a check mark. The check mark indicates that the option is currently active. To make an option inactive (turn it off) using the mouse, position the arrow pointer on the option, and then click the left mouse button. To make an option inactive with the keyboard, type the underlined letter of the option.

If an option from a drop-down menu displays followed by an ellipsis (...), a dialog box will display when that option is chosen. A dialog box provides a variety of options to let you specify how a command is to be carried out. For example, if you choose File and then Print from the PowerPoint Menu bar, the Print dialog box displays as shown in Figure G.4.

G.4 *PowerPoint Print Dialog Box*

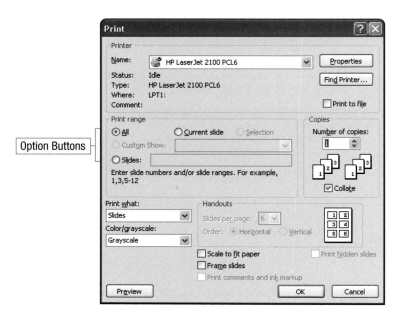

Or, if you choose Format and then Font from the Word Menu bar, the Font dialog box displays as shown in Figure G.5.

G.5 *Word Font Dialog Box*

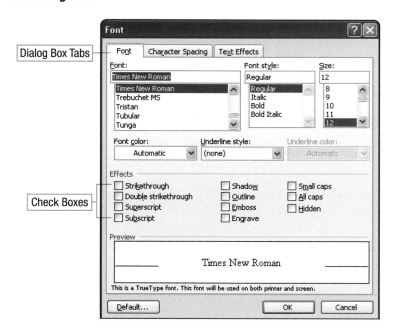

Some dialog boxes provide a set of options. These options are contained on separate tabs. For example, the Font dialog box shown in Figure G.5 contains a tab at the top of the dialog box with the word Font on it. Two other tabs display to the right of the Font tab—Character Spacing and Text Effects. The tab that displays in the front is the active tab. To make a tab active using the mouse, position the arrow pointer on the desired tab, and then click the left mouse button. If you are using the keyboard, press Ctrl + Tab or press Alt + the underlined letter on the desired tab. For example, to change the tab to Character Spacing in the Font dialog box, click Character Spacing, or press Ctrl + Tab, or press Alt + R.

To choose options from a dialog box with the mouse, position the arrow pointer on the desired option, and then click the left mouse button. If you are using the keyboard, press the Tab key to move the insertion point forward from option to option. Press Shift + Tab to move the insertion point backward from option to option. You can also hold down the Alt key and then press the underlined letter of the desired option. When an option is selected, it displays either in reverse video (white letters on a dark background) or surrounded by a dashed box called a *marquee*.

A dialog box contains one or more of the following elements: text boxes, list boxes, check boxes, option buttons, spin boxes, and command buttons.

Text Boxes

Some options in a dialog box require text to be entered. For example, the boxes below the *Find what* and *Replace with* options at the Excel Find and Replace dialog box shown in Figure G.6 are text boxes. In a text box, you type text or edit existing text. Edit text in a text box in the same manner as normal text. Use the Left and Right Arrow keys on the keyboard to move the insertion point without deleting text and use the Delete key or Backspace key to delete text.

FIGURE

G.6 *Excel Find and Replace Dialog Box*

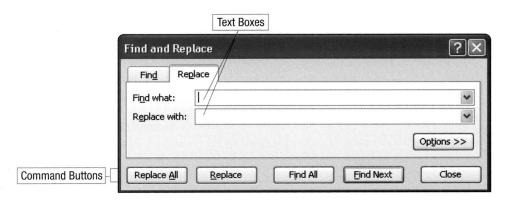

List Boxes

Some dialog boxes such as the Access Open dialog box shown in Figure G.7 may contain a list box. The list of files below the *Look in* option is contained in a list box. To make a selection from a list box with the mouse, move the arrow pointer to the desired option, and then click the left mouse button.

Some list boxes may contain a scroll bar. This scroll bar will display at the right side of the list box (a vertical scroll bar) or at the bottom of the list box (a horizontal scroll bar). Either a vertical scroll bar or a horizontal scroll bar can be used to move through the list if the list is longer than the box. To move down through a list on a vertical scroll bar, position the arrow pointer on the down scroll triangle and hold down the left mouse button. To scroll up through the list in a vertical scroll bar, position the arrow pointer on the up-pointing arrow and hold down the left mouse button. You can also move the arrow pointer above the scroll box and click the left mouse button to scroll up the list or move the arrow pointer below the scroll box and click the left mouse button to move down the list. To move through a list with a horizontal scroll bar, click the left-pointing arrow to scroll to the left of the list or click the right-pointing arrow to scroll to the right of the list.

To make a selection from a list using the keyboard, move the insertion point into the box by holding down the Alt key and pressing the underlined letter of the desired option. Press the Up and/or Down Arrow keys on the keyboard to move through the list.

In some dialog boxes where enough room is not available for a list box, lists of options are inserted in a drop-down list box. Options that contain a drop-down list box display with a down-pointing arrow. For example, the *Underline style* option at the Word Font dialog box shown in Figure G.5 contains a drop-down list. To display the list, click the down-pointing arrow to the right of the *Underline style* option box. If you are using the keyboard, press Alt + U.

Check Boxes

Some dialog boxes contain options preceded by a box. A check mark may or may not appear in the box. The Word Font dialog box shown in Figure G.5 displays a variety of check boxes within the *Effects* section. If a check mark appears in the box, the option is active (turned on). If there is no check mark in the check box, the option is inactive (turned off).

Any number of check boxes can be active. For example, in the Word Font dialog box, you can insert a check mark in any or all of the boxes in the *Effects* section and these options will be active.

To make a check box active or inactive with the mouse, position the tip of the arrow pointer in the check box, and then click the left mouse button. If you are using the keyboard, press Alt + the underlined letter of the desired option.

Option Buttons

In the PowerPoint Print dialog box shown in Figure G.4, the options in the *Print range* section are preceded by option buttons. Only one option button can be selected at any time. When an option button is selected, a green circle displays in the button.

To select an option button with the mouse, position the tip of the arrow pointer inside the option button, and then click the left mouse button. To make a selection with the keyboard, hold down the Alt key, and then press the underlined letter of the desired option.

Spin Boxes

Some options in a dialog box contain measurements or numbers that can be increased or decreased. These options are generally located in a spin box. For example, the Word Paragraph dialog box shown in Figure G.8 contains spin boxes located after the *Left, Right, Before,* and *After* options. To increase a number in a spin box, position the tip of the arrow pointer on the up-pointing arrow to the right of the desired option, and then click the left mouse button. To decrease the number, click the down-pointing arrow. If you are using the keyboard, press Alt + the underlined letter of the desired option, and then press the Up Arrow key to increase the number or the Down Arrow key to decrease the number.

FIGURE

G.8 **Word Paragraph Dialog Box**

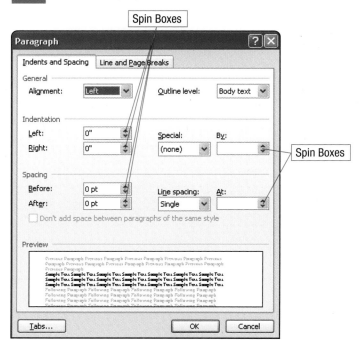

Command Buttons

In the Excel Find and Replace dialog box shown in Figure G.6, the boxes along the bottom of the dialog box are called **command buttons**. A command button is used to execute or cancel a command. Some command buttons display with an ellipsis (...). A command button that displays with an ellipsis will open another dialog box. To choose a command button with the mouse, position the arrow pointer on the desired button, and then click the left mouse button. To choose a command button with the keyboard, press the Tab key until the desired command button contains the marquee, and then press the Enter key.

Choosing Commands with Shortcut Keys

At the left side of a drop-down menu is a list of options. At the right side, shortcut keys for specific options may display. For example, the shortcut keys to save a document are Ctrl + S and are displayed to the right of the Save option at the File drop-down menu shown in Figure G.3. To use shortcut keys to choose a command, hold down the Ctrl key, type the letter for the command, and then release the Ctrl key.

Choosing Commands with Shortcut Menus

The software programs in the suite include menus that contain commands related to the item with which you are working. A shortcut menu appears right where you are working in the document. To display a shortcut menu, click the *right* mouse button or press Shift + F10.

For example, if the insertion point is positioned in a paragraph of text in a Word document, clicking the *right* mouse button or pressing Shift + F10 will cause the shortcut menu shown in Figure G.9 to display in the document screen.

F I G U R E

G.9 **Word Shortcut Menu**

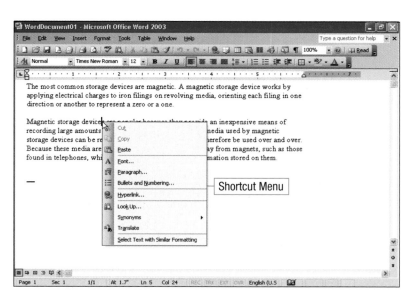

To select an option from a shortcut menu with the mouse, click the desired option. If you are using the keyboard, press the Up or Down Arrow key until the desired option is selected, and then press the Enter key. To close a shortcut menu without choosing an option, click anywhere outside the shortcut menu or press the Esc key.

Working with Multiple Programs

As you learn the various programs in the Microsoft Office suite, you will notice how executing commands in each is very similar. For example, the steps to save, close, and print are virtually the same whether you are working in Word, Excel, or PowerPoint. This consistency between programs greatly enhances a user's ability to easily transfer knowledge learned in one program to another within the suite.

Another appeal of Microsoft Office is the ability to have more than one program open at the same time. For example, you can open Word, create a document, and then open Excel, create a spreadsheet, and copy the spreadsheet into Word.

When a program is open, the name of the program, followed by the file name, displays in a button on the Taskbar. When another program is opened, the program name and file name display in a button that is positioned to the right of the first program button. Figure G.10 shows the Taskbar with Word, Excel, and PowerPoint open. To move from one program to another, all you need to do is click the button on the Taskbar representing the desired program file.

FIGURE

| G.10 | *Taskbar with Word, Excel, and PowerPoint Open* |

| start | Microsoft Office Wor... | Microsoft Office Excel... | Microsoft Office Pow... | 8:55 PM |

Completing Computer Exercises

Some computer exercises in this textbook require that you open an existing file. Exercise files are saved on the Student CD that accompanies this textbook. The files you need for each chapter are saved in individual folders. Before beginning a chapter, copy the necessary folder from the CD to a preformatted data disk. After completing exercises in a chapter, delete the chapter folder before copying the next chapter folder. (Check with your instructor before deleting a folder.)

The Student CD also contains model answers in PDF format for the exercises *within* (but not at the end of) each chapter so you can check your work. To access the PDF files, you will need to have Adobe Acrobat Reader installed on your computer's hard drive. The program and installation instructions are included on the Student CD in the AdobeAcrobatReader folder.

Copying a Folder

As you begin working in a chapter, copy the chapter folder from the CD to your disk. (Not every chapter contains a folder on the CD. For example, when completing exercises in the Access chapters, you will copy individual database files rather than individual chapter folders. Copy the chapter folder from the CD to your disk using the My Computer window by completing the following steps:

1. Insert the CD that accompanies this textbook in the CD drive.
2. Insert a formatted 3.5-inch disk in the disk drive.
3. At the Windows XP desktop, open the My Computer window by clicking the Start button and then clicking My Computer at the Start menu.
4. Double-click the CD drive in the contents pane (probably displays as *OFFICE2003_BENCH* followed by the drive letter).
5. Double-click the desired program folder name in the contents pane. (For example, if you are copying a folder for a Specialist Word chapter, double-click the *Word2003Specialist* folder.)
6. Click once on the desired chapter subfolder name to select it.
7. Click the Copy this folder hyperlink in the *File and Folder Tasks* section of the task pane.
8. At the Copy Items dialog box, click *3½ Floppy (A:)* in the list box and then click the Copy button.
9. After the folder is copied to your disk, close the My Computer window by clicking the Close button (white X on red background) that displays in the upper right corner of the window.

Deleting a Folder

Before copying a chapter folder onto your disk, delete any previous chapter folders. Do this in the My Computer window by completing the following steps:

1. Insert your disk in the disk drive.
2. At the Windows XP desktop, open the My Computer window by clicking the Start button and then clicking My Computer at the Start menu.
3. Double-click *3½ Floppy (A:)* in the contents pane.
4. Click the chapter folder in the list box.
5. Click the Delete this folder hyperlink in the *File and Folder Tasks* section of the task pane.
6. At the message asking if you want to remove the folder and all its contents, click the Yes button.
7. If a message displays asking if you want to delete a read-only file, click the Yes to All button.
8. Close the My Computer window by clicking the Close button (white X on red background) that displays in the upper right corner of the window.

Viewing or Printing the Exercise Model Answers

If you want to access the PDF model answer files, first make sure that Adobe Acrobat Reader is installed on your hard drive. (If it is not, installation instructions and the program file are available within the AdobeAcrobatReader folder on the Student CD.) Double-click the ExerciseModelAnswers(PDF) folder, double-click the desired chapter subfolder name, and double-click the appropriate file name to open the file. You can view and/or print the file to compare it with your own completed exercise file.

OFFICE *2003*

USING WINDOWS XP

A computer requires an operating system to provide necessary instructions on a multitude of processes including loading programs, managing data, directing the flow of information to peripheral equipment, and displaying information. Windows XP Professional is an operating system that provides functions of this type (along with much more) in a graphical environment. Windows is referred to as a **graphical user interface** (GUI—pronounced *gooey*) that provides a visual display of information with features such as icons (pictures) and buttons. In this introduction you will learn the basic features of Windows XP.

Historically, Microsoft has produced two editions of Windows—one edition for individual users (on desktop and laptop computers) and another edition for servers (on computers that provide service over networks). Windows XP is an upgrade and a merging of these two Windows editions and is available in two versions. The Windows XP Home Edition is designed for home use and Windows XP Professional is designed for small office and workstation use. Whether you are using Windows XP Home Edition or Windows XP Professional, you will be able to complete the steps in the exercises in this introduction.

Before using one of the software programs in the Microsoft Office suite, you will need to start the Windows XP operating system. To do this, turn on the computer. Depending on your computer equipment configuration, you may also need to turn on the monitor and printer. If you are using a computer that is part of a network system or if your computer is set up for multiple users, a screen will display showing the user accounts defined for your computer system. At this screen, click your user account name and, if necessary, type your password and then press the Enter key. The Windows XP operating system will start and, after a few moments, the desktop will display as shown in Figure W.1. (Your desktop may vary from what you see in Figure W.1.)

W.1 *Windows XP Desktop*

Icon

Recycle Bin

Taskbar *start* 8:56 PM

Exploring the Desktop

When Windows XP is loaded, the main portion of the screen is called the *desktop*. Think of the desktop in Windows as the top of a desk in an office. A business person places necessary tools—such as pencils, pens, paper, files, calculator—on the desktop to perform functions. Like the tools that are located on a desk, the desktop contains tools for operating the computer. These tools are logically grouped and placed in dialog boxes or panels that can be displayed using icons on the desktop. The desktop contains a variety of features for using your computer and software programs installed on the computer. The features available on the desktop are represented by icons and buttons.

Using Icons

Icons are visual symbols that represent programs, files, or folders. Figure W.1 identifies the *Recycle Bin* icon located on the Windows XP desktop. The Windows XP desktop on your computer may contain additional icons. Programs that have been installed on your computer may be represented by an icon on the desktop. Also, icons may display on your desktop representing files or folders. Double-click an icon and the program, file, or folder it represents opens on the desktop.

Using the Taskbar

The bar that displays at the bottom of the desktop (see Figure W.1) is called the *Taskbar*. The Taskbar, shown in Figure W.2, contains the Start button, a section that displays task buttons representing open programs, and the notification area.

FIGURE

FIGURE

W.2 *Windows XP Taskbar*

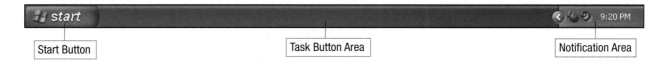

Start Button   Task Button Area   Notification Area

Click the Start button, located at the left side of the Taskbar, and the Start menu displays as shown in Figure W.3 (your Start menu may vary). You can also display the Start menu by pressing the Windows key on your keyboard or by pressing Ctrl + Esc. The left column of the Start menu contains pinned programs, which are programs that always appear in that particular location on the Start menu, and links to the most recently and frequently used programs. The right column contains links to folders, the Control Panel, online help, and the search feature.

FIGURE

W.3 *Start Menu*

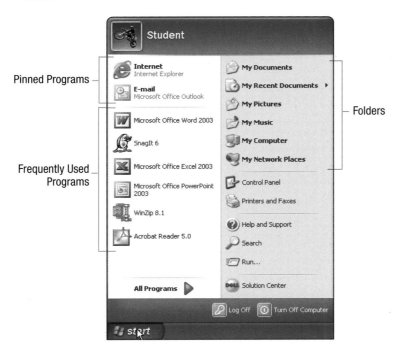

Pinned Programs

Frequently Used Programs

Folders

To choose an option from the Start menu, drag the arrow pointer to the desired option (referred to as ***pointing***), and then click the left mouse button. Pointing to options at the Start menu followed by a right-pointing arrow will cause a side menu to display with additional options. When a program is open, a task button representing the program appears on the Taskbar. If multiple programs are open, each program will appear as a task button on the Taskbar (a few specialized tools may not).

exercise 1

1. Open Windows XP. (To do this, turn on the computer and, if necessary, turn on the monitor and/or printer. If you are using a computer that is part of a network system or if your computer is set up for multiple users, you may need to click your user account name and, if necessary, type your password and then press the Enter key. Check with your instructor to determine if you need to complete any additional steps.)

2. When the Windows XP desktop displays, open Microsoft Word by completing the following steps:

    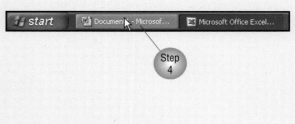

    Step 2d

    a. Position the arrow pointer on the Start button on the Taskbar and then click the left mouse button.
    b. At the Start menu, point to All Programs (a side menu displays) and then point to Microsoft Office (another side menu displays).
    c. Drag the arrow pointer to Microsoft Office Word 2003 in the side menu and then click the left mouse button.
    d. When the Microsoft Word program is open, notice that a task button representing Word displays on the Taskbar.

3. Open Microsoft Excel by completing the following steps:
    a. Position the arrow pointer on the Start button on the Taskbar and then click the left mouse button.
    b. At the Start menu, point to All Programs and then point to Microsoft Office.
    c. Drag the arrow pointer to Microsoft Office Excel 2003 in the side menu and then click the left mouse button.
    d. When the Microsoft Excel program is open, notice that a task button representing Excel displays on the Taskbar to the right of the task button representing Word.

    Step 4

4. Switch to the Word program by clicking the task button on the Taskbar representing Word.

5. Switch to the Excel program by clicking the task button on the Taskbar representing Excel.

    Step 6

6. Exit Excel by clicking the Close button that displays in the upper right corner of the Excel window. (The Close button contains a white *X* on a red background.)

7. Exit Word by clicking the Close button that displays in the upper right corner of the Word window.

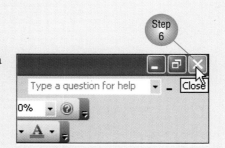

Exploring the Notification Area

The notification area is located at the right side of the Taskbar and contains the system clock along with small icons representing specialized programs that run in the background. Position the arrow pointer over the current time in the notification area of the Taskbar and today's date displays in a small yellow box above the time. Double-click the current time displayed on the Taskbar and the Date and Time Properties dialog box displays as shown in Figure W.4.

FIGURE

W.4   *Date and Time Properties Dialog Box*

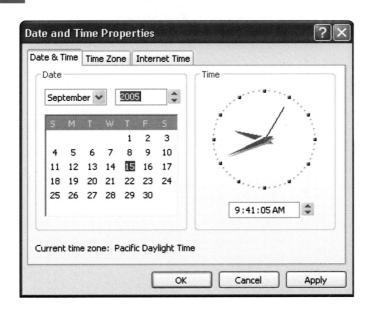

Change the date with options in the *Date* section of the dialog box. For example, to change the month, click the down-pointing arrow at the right side of the option box containing the current month and then click the desired month at the drop-down list. Change the year by clicking the up- or down-pointing arrow at the right side of the option box containing the current year until the desired year displays. To change the day, click the desired day in the monthly calendar that displays in the dialog box. To change the time, double-click either the hour, minute, or seconds and then type the appropriate time or use the up- and down-pointing arrows to adjust the time.

Some programs, when installed, will add an icon to the notification area of the Taskbar. Display the name of the icon by positioning the mouse pointer on the icon and, after approximately one second, the icon label displays in a small yellow box. Some icons may display information in the yellow box rather than the icon label. If more icons have been inserted in the notification area than can be viewed at one time, a left-pointing arrow button displays at the left side of the notification area. Click this left-pointing arrow button and the remaining icons display.

Setting Taskbar Properties

By default, the Taskbar is locked in its current position and size. You can change this default setting, along with other default settings, with options at the Taskbar and Start Menu Properties dialog box, shown in Figure W.5. To display this dialog box, position the arrow pointer on any empty spot on the Taskbar, and then click the *right* mouse button. At the shortcut menu that displays, click Properties.

FIGURE

W.5 **Taskbar and Start Menu Properties Dialog Box**

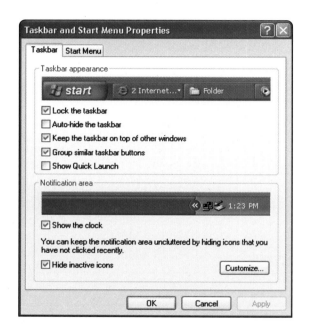

Each property is controlled by a check box. Property options containing a check mark are active. Click the option to remove the check mark and make the option inactive. If an option is inactive, clicking the option will insert a check mark in the check box and turn on the option (make it active).

exercise 2

CHANGING TASKBAR PROPERTIES

1. Make sure Windows XP is open and the desktop displays.
2. Hide the Taskbar and remove the display of the clock by completing the following steps:
   a. Position the arrow pointer on any empty area on the Taskbar and then click the *right* mouse button.
   b. At the shortcut menu that displays, click Properties.
   c. At the Taskbar and Start Menu Properties dialog box, click *Auto-hide the taskbar*. (This inserts a check mark in the check box.)
   d. Click *Show the clock*. (This removes the check mark from the check box.)

e. Click the Apply button.
f. Click OK to close the dialog box.
3. Display the Taskbar by positioning the mouse pointer at the bottom of the screen. When the Taskbar displays, notice that the time no longer displays at the right side of the Taskbar.
4. Return to the default settings for the Taskbar by completing the following steps:
   a. With the Taskbar displayed (if it does not display, position the mouse pointer at the bottom of the desktop), position the arrow pointer on any empty area on the Taskbar and then click the *right* mouse button.
   b. At the shortcut menu that displays, click Properties.
   c. At the Taskbar and Start Menu Properties dialog box, click *Auto-hide the taskbar*. (This removes the check mark from the check box.)
   d. Click *Show the clock*. (This inserts a check mark in the check box.)
   e. Click the Apply button.
   f. Click OK to close the dialog box.

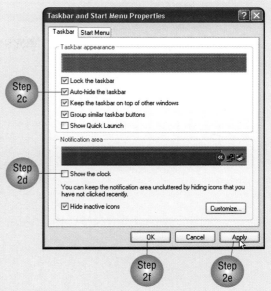

Step 2c
Step 2d
Step 2f
Step 2e

Turning Off the Computer

When you are finished working with your computer, you can choose to shut down the computer completely, shut down and then restart the computer, put the computer on standby, or tell the computer to hibernate. Do not turn off your computer until your screen goes blank. Important data is stored in memory while Windows XP is running and this data needs to be written to the hard drive before turning off the computer.

To shut down your computer, click the Start button on the Taskbar and then click *Turn Off Computer* at the Start menu. At the Turn off computer window, shown in Figure W.6, click the *Stand By* option and the computer switches to a low power state causing some devices such as the monitor and hard disks to turn off. With these devices off, the computer uses less power. Stand By is particularly useful for saving battery power for portable computers. Tell the computer to "hibernate" by holding down the Shift key while clicking the *Stand By* option. In hibernate mode, the computer saves everything in memory on disk, turns off the monitor and hard disk, and then turns off the computer. Click the *Turn Off* option if you want to shut down Windows XP and turn off all power to the computer. Click the *Restart* option if you want to restart the computer and restore the desktop exactly as you left it. You can generally restore your desktop from either standby or hibernate by pressing once on the computer's power button. Usually, bringing a computer out of hibernation takes a little longer than bringing a computer out of standby.

W.6 *Turn Off Computer Window*

Managing Files and Folders

As you begin working with programs in Windows XP, you will create files in which data (information) is saved. A file might contain a Word document, an Excel workbook, or a PowerPoint presentation. As you begin creating files, consider creating folders into which those files will be stored. File management tasks such as creating a folder and copying and moving files and folders can be completed at the My Computer window. To display the My Computer window shown in Figure W.7, click the Start button on the Taskbar and then click My Computer. The various components of the My Computer window are identified in Figure W.7.

W.7 *My Computer Window*

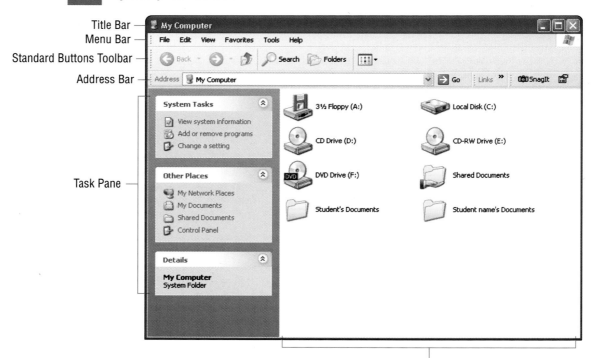

Copying, Moving, and Deleting Files/Folders

File and folder management activities might include copying and moving files or folders from a folder or drive to another or deleting files or folders. The My Computer window offers a variety of methods for copying, moving, and deleting files/folders. You can use options in the task pane, drop-down menu options, or shortcut menu options. This section will provide you with the steps for copying, moving, and deleting files/folders using options in the task pane.

To copy a file/folder to another folder or drive, first display the file in the contents pane by identifying the location of the file. If the file is located in the My Documents folder, click the My Documents hyperlink in the *Other Places* section of the task pane. If the file is located on the hard drive, double-click the desired drive in the contents pane and if the file is located on a floppy disk or CD, double-click the desired drive letter or CD letter. Next, click the folder or file name in the contents pane that you want to copy. This changes the options in the task pane to include management options such as renaming, moving, copying, and deleting folders or files. Click the Copy this folder (or Copy this file) hyperlink in the task pane and the Copy Items dialog box displays as shown in Figure W.8. At the Copy Items dialog box, click the desired folder or drive and then click the Copy button.

FIGURE

W.8   *Copy Items Dialog Box*

To move a file or folder to another folder or drive, select the file or folder and then click the Move this folder (or Move this file) hyperlink. At the Move Items dialog box, specify the location, and then click the Move button. Copying a file or folder leaves the file or folder in the original location and saves a copy at the new location, while moving removes the file or folder from the original location and moves it to the new location.

You can easily remove (delete) a file or folder from the My Computer window. To delete a file or folder, click the file or folder in the contents pane, and then click the <u>Delete this folder</u> (or <u>Delete this file</u>) hyperlink in the task pane. At the dialog box asking you to confirm the deletion, click Yes. A deleted file or folder is sent to the Recycle Bin. You will learn more about the Recycle Bin in the next section.

In Exercise 3, you will insert the CD that accompanies this book into the CD drive. When the CD is inserted, the drive may automatically activate and a dialog box may display on the screen telling you that the disk or device contains more than one type of content and asking what you want Windows to do. If this dialog box displays, click Cancel to remove the dialog box.

exercise 3

COPYING A FILE AND FOLDER AND DELETING A FILE

1. At the Windows XP desktop, insert the CD that accompanies this textbook into the CD drive. If a dialog box displays telling you that the disk or device contains more than one type of content and asking what you want Windows to do, click Cancel.
2. At the Windows XP desktop, open the My Computer window by clicking the Start button on the Taskbar and then clicking My Computer at the Start menu.
3. Copy a file from the CD that accompanies this textbook to a disk in drive A by completing the following steps:
   a. Insert a formatted 3.5-inch disk in drive A.
   b. In the contents pane, double-click the name of the drive containing the CD (probably displays as OFFICE2003_BENCH followed by a drive letter). (Make sure you double-click because you want the contents of the CD to display in the contents pane.)
   c. Double-click the *Windows* folder in the contents pane.
   d. Click *WordDocument01* in the contents pane to select it.
   e. Click the <u>Copy this file</u> hyperlink located in the *File and Folder Tasks* section of the task pane.
   f. At the Copy Items dialog box, click *3½ Floppy (A:)* in the dialog box list box.
   g. Click the Copy button.
4. Delete *WordDocument01* from drive A by completing the following steps:
   a. Click the <u>My Computer</u> hyperlink located in the *Other Places* section of the task pane.
   b. Double-click *3½ Floppy (A:)* in the contents pane.

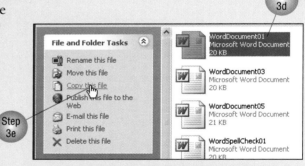

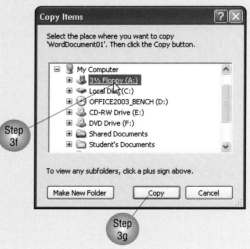

c. Click **WordDocument01**.

d. Click the <u>Delete this file</u> hyperlink in the *File and Folder Tasks* section of the task pane.

e. At the message asking you to confirm the deletion, click Yes.

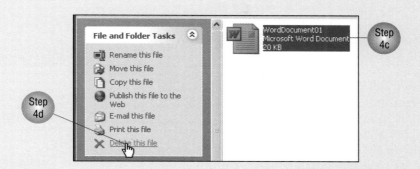

5. Copy the Windows folder from the CD drive to the disk in drive A by completing the following steps:

a. Click the <u>My Computer</u> hyperlink in the *Other Places* section of the task pane.

b. In the contents pane, double-click the name of the drive containing the CD (probably displays as OFFICE2003_BENCH followed by a drive letter).

c. Click the *Windows* folder in the contents pane to select it.

d. Click the <u>Copy this folder</u> hyperlink in the *File and Folder Tasks* section of the task pane.

e. At the Copy Items dialog box, click *3½ Floppy (A:)* in the list box.

f. Click the Copy button.

6. Close window by clicking the Close button (contains a white *X* on a red background) located in the upper right corner of the window. (You can also close the window by clicking File on the Menu bar and then clicking Close at the drop-down menu.)

Selecting Files/Folders

You can move, copy, or delete more than one file or folder at the same time. Before moving, copying, or deleting files/folders, select the desired files or folders. Selecting files/folders is easier when you change the display in the contents pane to List or Details. To change the display, open the My Computer window and then click the Views button on the Standard Buttons toolbar. At the drop-down list that displays, click the *List* option or the *Details* option.

To move adjacent files/folders, click the first file or folder and then hold down the Shift key and click the last file or folder. This selects and highlights all files/folders from the first file/folder you clicked to the last file/folder you clicked. With the adjacent files/folders selected, click the <u>Move the selected items</u> hyperlink in the *File and Folder Tasks* section of the task pane, and then specify the desired location at the Move Items dialog box. To select nonadjacent files/folders, click the first file/folder to select it, hold down the Ctrl key and then click any other files/folders you want to move or copy.

1. At the Windows XP desktop, open the My Computer window by clicking the Start button and then clicking My Computer at the Start menu.

2. Copy files from the CD that accompanies this textbook to a disk in drive A by completing the following steps:
    a. Make sure the CD that accompanies this textbook is inserted in the CD drive and a formatted 3.5-inch disk is inserted in drive A.
    b. Double-click the CD drive in the contents pane (probably displays as OFFICE2003_BENCH followed by the drive letter).
    c. Double-click the *Windows* folder in the contents pane.
    d. Change the display to Details by clicking the Views button on the Standard Buttons toolbar and then clicking *Details* at the drop-down list.
    e. Position the arrow pointer on **WordDocument01** in the contents pane and then click the left mouse button.
    f. Hold down the Shift key, click *WordDocument05*, and then release the Shift key. (This selects **WordDocument01**, **WordDocument02**, **WordDocument03**, **WordDocument04**, and **WordDocument05**.)
    g. Click the Copy the selected items hyperlink in the *File and Folder Tasks* section of the task pane.
    h. At the Copy Items dialog box, click *3½ Floppy (A:)* in the list box and then click the Copy button.

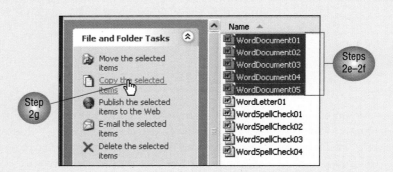

3. Display the files and folder saved on the disk in drive A by completing the following steps:
    a. Click the My Computer hyperlink in the *Other Places* section of the task pane.
    b. Double-click *3½ Floppy (A:)* in the contents pane.
4. Delete the files from drive A that you just copied by completing the following steps:
    a. Change the view by clicking the Views button on the Standard Buttons toolbar and then clicking *List* at the drop-down list.
    b. Click **WordDocument01** in the contents pane.

c. Hold down the Shift key, click **WordDocument05**, and then release the Shift key. (This selects **WordDocument01**, **WordDocument02**, **WordDocument03**, **WordDocument04**, and **WordDocument05**.)

d. Click the <u>Delete the selected items</u> hyperlink in the *File and Folder Tasks* section of the task pane.

e. At the message asking you to confirm the deletion, click Yes.

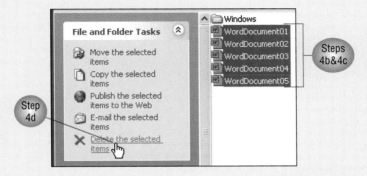

5. Close the window by clicking the Close button (white *X* on red background) that displays in the upper right corner of the window.

Manipulating and Creating Folders

As you begin working with and creating a number of files, consider creating folders in which you can logically group the files. To create a folder, display the My Computer window and then display in the contents pane the drive or disk on which you want to create the folder. Click the File option on the Menu bar, point to New, and then click Folder at the side menu. This inserts a folder icon in the contents pane and names the folder *New Folder*. Type the desired name for the new folder and then press Enter.

exercise 5

CREATING A NEW FOLDER

1. At the Windows XP desktop, open the My Computer window.
2. Create a new folder by completing the following steps:
   a. Make sure your disk is inserted in drive A (this disk contains the Windows folder you copied in Exercise 3).
   b. Double-click *3½ Floppy (A:)* in the contents pane.
   c. Double-click the *Windows* folder in the contents pane. (This opens the folder.)
   d. Click File on the Menu bar, point to New, and then click Folder.

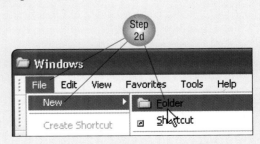

e. Type SpellCheckFiles and then press Enter. (This changes the name from *New Folder* to *SpellCheckFiles*.)

3. Copy **WordSpellCheck01**, **WordSpellCheck02**, **WordSpellCheck03**, and **WordSpellCheck04** into the SpellCheckFiles folder you just created by completing the following steps:

a. Click the Views button on the Standard Buttons toolbar and then click *List* at the drop-down list.

b. Click once on the file named **WordSpellCheck01** located in the contents pane.

c. Hold down the Shift key, click once on the file named ***WordSpellCheck04***, and then release the Shift key. (This selects **WordSpellCheck01**, **WordSpellCheck02**, **WordSpellCheck03**, and **WordSpellCheck04**.)

d. Click the <u>Copy the selected items</u> hyperlink in the *File and Folder Tasks* section of the task pane.

Step 2e

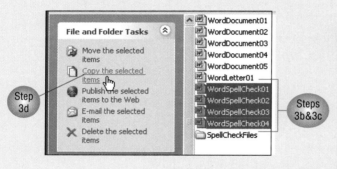

Step 3d

Steps 3b&3c

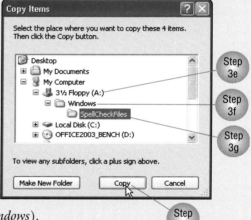

Step 3e

Step 3f

Step 3g

Step 3h

e. At the Copy Items dialog box, click *3½ Floppy (A:)* in the list box.

f. Click *Windows* (below *3½ Floppy (A:)*) in the list box.

g. Click *SpellCheckFiles* in the list box (below *Windows*).

h. Click the Copy button.

4. Display the files you just copied by double-clicking the *SpellCheckFiles* folder in the contents pane.

5. Delete the SpellCheckFiles folder and its contents by completing the following steps:

a. Click the Up button on the Standard Buttons toolbar. (This displays the contents of the Windows folder which is up one folder from the SpellCheckFiles folders.)

b. Click the *SpellCheckFiles* folder in the contents pane to select it.

c. Click the <u>Delete this folder</u> hyperlink in the *File and Folder Tasks* section of the task pane.

d. At the message asking you to confirm the deletion, click Yes.

6. Close the window by clicking the Close button located in the upper right corner of the window.

Step 5a

Step 5b

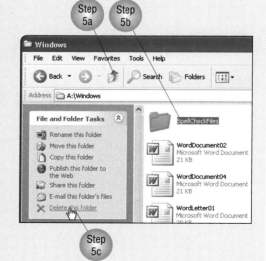

Step 5c

Using the Recycle Bin

Deleting the wrong file can be a disaster but Windows XP helps protect your work with the Recycle Bin. The Recycle Bin acts just like an office wastepaper basket; you can "throw away" (delete) unwanted files, but you can "reach in" (restore) to the Recycle Bin and take out a file if you threw it away by accident.

Deleting Files to the Recycle Bin

A file/folder or selected files/folders deleted from the hard drive are automatically sent to the Recycle Bin. Files/folders deleted from a disk are deleted permanently. (Recovery programs are available, however, that will help you recover deleted text. If you accidentally delete a file/folder from a disk, do not do anything more with the disk until you can run a recovery program.)

One method for deleting files is to display the My Computer window and then display in the contents pane the file(s) and/or folder(s) you want deleted. Click the file or folder or select multiple files or folders and then click the appropriate delete option in the task pane. At the message asking you to confirm the deletion, click Yes.

Another method for deleting a file is to drag the file to the *Recycle Bin* icon on the desktop. Drag a file icon to the Recycle Bin until the *Recycle Bin* icon is selected (displays with a blue background) and then release the mouse button. This drops the file you are dragging into the Recycle Bin.

Recovering Files from the Recycle Bin

You can easily restore a deleted file from the Recycle Bin. To restore a file, double-click the *Recycle Bin* icon on the desktop. This opens the Recycle Bin window shown in Figure W.9. (The contents of the Recycle Bin will vary.)

FIGURE

W.9 **Recycle Bin Window**

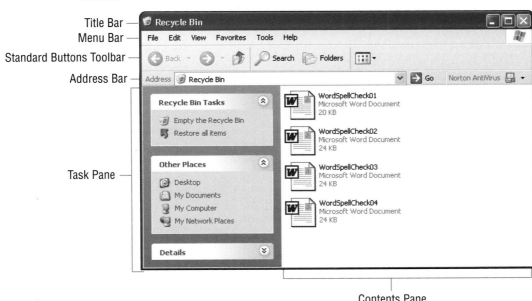

Contents Pane

To restore a file, click the file you want restored, and then click the <u>Restore this item</u> hyperlink in the *Recycle Bin Tasks* section of the task pane. This removes the file from the Recycle Bin and returns it to its original location. You can also restore a file by positioning the arrow pointer on the file, clicking the *right* mouse button, and then clicking Restore at the shortcut menu.

exercise 6

DELETING FILES TO AND RECOVERING FILES FROM THE RECYCLE BIN

(Before completing this exercise, check with your instructor to determine if you can copy files to the hard drive.)

1. At the Windows XP desktop, open the My Computer window.
2. Copy files from your disk in drive A to the My Documents folder on your hard drive by completing the following steps:
   a. Make sure your disk containing the Windows folder is inserted in drive A.
   b. Double-click *3½ Floppy (A:)* in the contents pane.
   c. Double-click the *Windows* folder in the contents pane.
   d. Click the Views button on the Standard Buttons toolbar and then click *List* at the drop-down list.
   e. Position the arrow pointer on **WordSpellCheck01** and then click the left mouse button.
   f. Hold down the Shift key, click **WordSpellCheck04**, and then release the Shift key.
   g. Click the <u>Copy the selected items</u> hyperlink in the *File and Folder Tasks* section of the task pane.
   h. At the Copy Items dialog box, click *My Documents* in the list box.
   i. Click the Copy button.

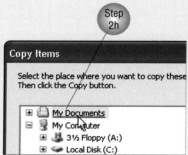

3. Click the <u>My Documents</u> hyperlink in the *Other Places* section of the task pane. (The files you copied, **WordSpellCheck01** through **WordSpellCheck04**, will display in the contents pane in alphabetical order.)
4. Delete **WordSpellCheck01** through **WordSpellCheck04** from the My Documents folder and send them to the Recycle Bin by completing the following steps:

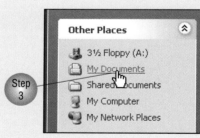

   a. Select **WordSpellCheck01** through **WordSpellCheck04** in the contents pane. (If these files are not visible, you will need to scroll down the list of files.)
   b. Click the <u>Delete the selected items</u> hyperlink in the *File and Folder Tasks* section of the task pane.
   c. At the message asking you to confirm the deletion to the Recycle Bin, click Yes.
5. Click the Close button to close the window.
6. At the desktop, display the contents of the Recycle Bin by double-clicking the *Recycle Bin* icon.

7. At the Recycle Bin window, restore **WordSpellCheck01** through **WordSpellCheck04** to the My Documents folder by completing the following steps:
   a. Select **WordSpellCheck01** through **WordSpellCheck04** in the contents pane of the Recycle Bin window. (If these files are not visible, you will need to scroll down the list of files.)
   b. With the files selected, click the <u>Restore the selected items</u> hyperlink in the *Recycle Bin Tasks* section of the task pane.

8. Close the Recycle Bin window by clicking the Close button located in the upper right corner of the window.
9. Display the My Computer window.
10. Click the <u>My Documents</u> hyperlink in the *Other Places* section of the task pane.
11. Delete the files you restored by completing the following steps:
    a. Select **WordSpellCheck01** through **WordSpellCheck04** in the contents pane. (If these files are not visible, you will need to scroll down the list of files. These are the files you recovered from the Recycle Bin.)
    b. Click the <u>Delete the selected items</u> hyperlink in the *File and Folder Tasks* section of the task pane.
    c. At the message asking you to confirm the deletion, click Yes.
12. Close the window.

Emptying the Recycle Bin

Just like a wastepaper basket, the Recycle Bin can get full. To empty the Recycle Bin, position the arrow pointer on the *Recycle Bin* icon on the desktop and then click the *right* mouse button. At the shortcut menu that displays, click Empty Recycle Bin. At the message asking you to confirm the deletion, click Yes. You can also empty the Recycle Bin by double-clicking the *Recycle Bin* icon. At the Recycle Bin window, click the <u>Empty the Recycle Bin</u> hyperlink in the *Recycle Bin Tasks* section of the task pane. At the message asking you to confirm the deletion, click Yes. (You can also empty the Recycle Bin by clicking File on the Menu bar and then clicking Empty Recycle Bin at the drop-down menu.)

Emptying the Recycle Bin deletes all files/folders. You can delete a specific file/folder from the Recycle Bin (rather than all files/folders). To do this, double-click the *Recycle Bin* icon on the desktop. At the Recycle Bin window, select the file/folder or files/folders you want to delete. Click File on the Menu bar and then click Delete at the drop-down menu. (You can also right-click a selected file/folder and then click Delete at the shortcut menu.) At the message asking you to confirm the deletion, click Yes.

exercise 7

(Before completing this exercise, check with your instructor to determine if you can delete files/folders from the Recycle Bin.)

1. At the Windows XP desktop, double-click the *Recycle Bin* icon.
2. At the Recycle Bin window, empty the contents of the Recycle Bin by completing the following steps:
   a. Click the Empty the Recycle Bin hyperlink in the *Recycle Bin Tasks* section of the task pane.
   b. At the message asking you to confirm the deletion, click Yes.
3. Close the Recycle Bin window by clicking the Close button located in the upper right corner of the window.

Step 2a

When the Recycle Bin is emptied, the files cannot be recovered by the Recycle Bin or by Windows XP. If you have to recover a file, you will need to use a file recovery program such as Norton Utilities. These utilities are separate programs, but might be worth their cost if you ever need them.

Creating a Shortcut

If you use a file or program on a consistent basis, consider creating a shortcut to the file or program. A shortcut is a specialized icon that represents very small files that point the operating system to the actual item, whether it is a file, a folder, or an application. For example, in Figure W.10, the *Shortcut to PracticeDocument* icon represents a path to a specific file in the Word 2003 program. The icon is not the actual file but a path to the file. Double-click the shortcut icon and Windows XP opens the Word 2003 program and also opens the file named PracticeDocument.

FIGURE

W.10 *PracticeDocument Shortcut Icon*

One method for creating a shortcut is to display the My Computer window and then display the drive or folder where the file is located. Right-click the desired file, point to Send To, and then click Desktop (create shortcut). You can easily delete a shortcut icon from the desktop by dragging the shortcut icon to the *Recycle Bin* icon. This deletes the shortcut icon but does not delete the file to which the shortcut pointed.

exercise 8

1. At the Windows XP desktop, display the My Computer window.
2. Make sure your disk is inserted in drive A.
3. Double-click *3½ Floppy (A:)* in the contents pane.
4. Double-click the *Windows* folder in the contents pane.
5. Change the display of files to a list by clicking the Views button on the Standard Buttons toolbar and then clicking *List* at the drop-down list.
6. Create a shortcut to the file named **WordLetter01** by right-clicking on *WordLetter01*, pointing to Send To, and then clicking Desktop (create shortcut).
7. Close the My Computer window by clicking the Close button located in the upper right corner of the window.
8. Open Word 2003 and the file named **WordLetter01** by double-clicking the **WordLetter01** shortcut icon on the desktop.
9. After viewing the file in Word, exit Word by clicking the Close button that displays in the upper right corner of the window.
10. Delete the **WordLetter01** shortcut icon by completing the following steps:
    a. At the desktop, position the mouse pointer on the **WordLetter01** shortcut icon.
    b. Hold down the left mouse button, drag the icon on top of the *Recycle Bin* icon, and then release the mouse button.

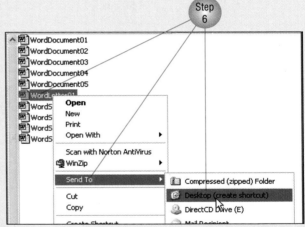

Customizing the Desktop

You can customize the Windows XP desktop to fit your particular needs and preferences. For example, you can choose a different theme, change the desktop background, add a screen saver, and apply a different appearance to windows, dialog boxes, and menus. To customize the desktop, position the arrow pointer on any empty location on the desktop and then click the *right* mouse button. At the shortcut menu that displays, click Properties. This displays the Display Properties dialog box with the Themes tab selected as shown in Figure W.11.

FIGURE

W.11 *Display Properties Dialog Box with Themes Tab Selected*

Changing the Theme

A Windows XP theme specifies a variety of formatting such as fonts, sounds, icons, colors, mouse pointers, background, and screen saver. Windows XP contains two themes—Windows XP (the default) and Windows Classic (which appears like earlier versions of Windows). Other themes are available as downloads from the Microsoft Web site. Change the theme with the *Theme* option at the Display Properties dialog box with the Themes tab selected.

Changing the Desktop

With options at the Display Properties dialog box with the Desktop tab selected, as shown in Figure W.12, you can choose a different desktop background and customize the desktop. Click any option in the *Background* list box and preview the results in the preview screen. With the *Position* option, you can specify that the background image is centered, tiled, or stretched on the desktop. Use the *Color* option to change the background color and click the Browse button to choose a background image from another location or Web site.

FIGURE

W.12 *Display Properties Dialog Box with Desktop Tab Selected*

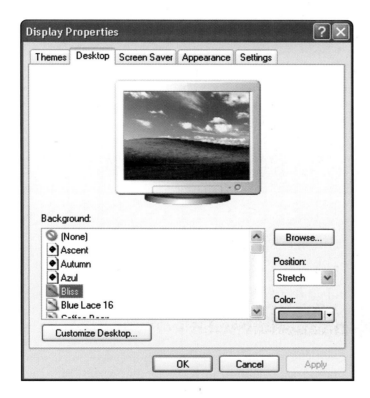

Adding a Screen Saver

If your computer sits idle for periods of time, consider adding a screen saver. A screen saver is a pattern that changes constantly, thus eliminating the problem of an image staying on the screen too long. To add a screen saver, display the Display Properties dialog box and then click the Screen Saver tab. This displays the dialog box as shown in Figure W.13.

W.13 *Display Properties Dialog Box with Screen Saver Tab Selected*

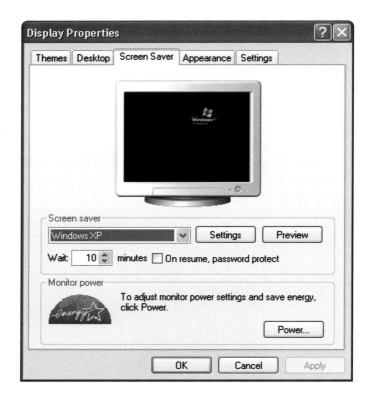

Click the down-pointing arrow at the right side of the *Screen saver* option box to display a list of installed screen savers. Click a screen saver and a preview displays in the monitor located toward the top of the dialog box. Click the Preview button and the dialog box is hidden and the screen saver displays on your monitor. Move the mouse or click a button on the mouse and the dialog box will reappear.

If your computer's hardware is Energy Star compatible, the *Monitor power* section is enabled. Click the Power button and a dialog box displays with options for choosing a power scheme appropriate to the way you use your computer. The dialog box also includes options for specifying how long the computer can be left unused before the monitor and hard disk are turned off and the system goes to standby or hibernate mode.

Changing Colors

Click the Appearance tab at the Display Properties dialog box and the dialog box displays as shown in Figure W.14. At this dialog box, you can change the desktop scheme. Schemes are predefined collections of colors used in windows, menus, title bars, and system fonts. Windows XP loads with the Windows XP style color scheme. Choose a different scheme with the *Windows and buttons* option and choose a specific color with the *Color scheme* option.

FIGURE

Display Properties Dialog Box with Appearance Tab Selected

Changing Settings

Click the Settings tab at the Display Properties dialog box and the dialog box displays as shown in Figure W.15. At this dialog box, you can set color and screen resolution.

FIGURE

Display Properties Dialog Box with Settings Tab Selected

The *Color quality* option determines how many colors your monitor displays. The more colors that are shown, the more realistic the images will appear. However, a lot of computer memory is required to show thousands of colors. Your exact choice is determined by the specific hardware you are using. The *Screen resolution* slide bar sets the screen's resolution. The higher the number, the more you can fit onto your screen. Again, your actual values depend on your particular hardware.

exercise 9

(Before completing this exercise, check with your instructor to determine if you can customize the desktop.)

1. At the Windows XP desktop, display the Display Properties dialog box by positioning the arrow pointer on an empty location on the desktop, clicking the *right* mouse button, and then clicking Properties at the shortcut menu.

2. At the Display Properties dialog box, change the desktop background by completing the following steps:
   a. Click the Desktop tab.
   b. If a background is selected in the *Background* list box (other than the *(None)* option), make a note of this background name.
   c. Click *Blue Lace 16* in the *Background* list box. (If this option is not available, choose another background.)
   d. Make sure *Tile* is selected in the *Position* list box.
   e. Click OK to close the dialog box.

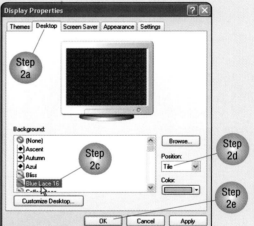

3. After viewing the desktop with the Blue Lace 16 background, remove the background image and change the background color by completing the following steps:
   a. Display the Display Properties dialog box.
   b. At the Display Properties dialog box, click the Desktop tab.
   c. Click *(None)* in the *Background* list box.
   d. Click the down-pointing arrow at the right side of the *Color* option and then click the dark red option at the color palette.
   e. Click OK to close the Display Properties dialog box.

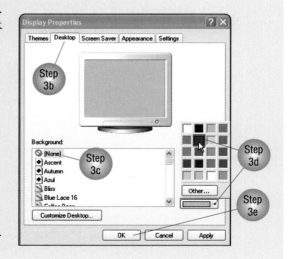

4. After viewing the desktop with the dark red background color, add a screen saver and change the wait time by completing the following steps:
   a. Display the Display Properties dialog box.

b. At the Display Properties dialog box, click the Screen Saver tab. (If a screen saver is already selected in the *Screen saver* option box, make a note of this screen saver name.)

c. Click the down-pointing arrow at the right side of the *Screen saver* option box.

d. At the drop-down list that displays, click a screen saver that interests you. (A preview of the screen saver displays in the screen located toward the top of the dialog box.)

e. Click a few other screen savers to see how they will display on the monitor.

f. Click OK to close the Display Properties dialog box. (At the desktop the screen saver will display, by default, after the monitor has sat idle for one minute.)

5. Return all settings back to the default by completing the following steps:

a. Display the Display Properties dialog box.

b. Click the Desktop tab.

c. If a background and color were selected when you began this exercise, click that background name in the *Background* list box and change the color back to the original color.

d. Click the Screen Saver tab.

e. At the Display Properties dialog box with the Screen Saver tab selected, click the down-pointing arrow at the right side of the *Screen saver* option box, and then click *(None)*. (If a screen saver was selected before completing this exercise, return to that screen saver.)

f. Click OK to close the Display Properties dialog box.

Exploring Windows XP Help and Support

Windows XP includes an on-screen reference guide providing information, explanations, and interactive help on learning Windows features. The on-screen reference guide contains complex files with hypertext used to access additional information by clicking a word or phrase.

Using the Help and Support Center Window

Display the Help and Support Center window shown in Figure W.16 by clicking the Start button on the Taskbar and then clicking Help and Support at the Start menu. The appearance of your Help and Support Center window may vary slightly from what you see in Figure W.16.

If you want to learn about a topic listed in the *Pick a Help topic* section of the window, click the desired topic and information about the topic displays in the window. Use the other options in the Help and Support Center window to get assistance or support from a remote computer or Windows XP newsgroups, pick a specific task, or learn about the additional help features. If you want help on a specific topic and do not see that topic listed in the *Pick a Help topic* section of the window, click inside the *Search* text box (generally located toward the top of the window), type the desired topic, and then press Enter or click the Start searching button (white arrow on a green background).

W.16 Help and Support Center Window

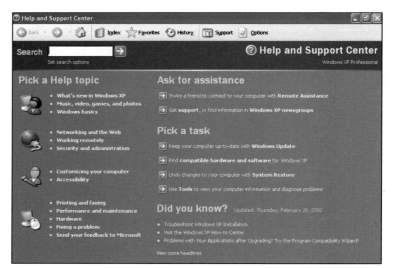

exercise 10

CUSTOMIZING THE DESKTOP

1. At the Windows XP desktop, use the Help and Support feature to learn about new Windows XP features by completing the following steps:

   a. Click the Start button on the Taskbar and then click Help and Support at the Start menu.

   b. At the Help and Support Center window, click the <u>What's new in Windows XP</u> hyperlink located in the *Pick a Help topic* section of the window.

   c. Click the <u>What's new topics</u> hyperlink located in the *What's new in Windows XP* section of the window. (This displays a list of Help options at the right side of the window.)

   d. Click the <u>What's new in Windows XP</u> hyperlink located at the right side of the window below the subheading *Overviews, Articles, and Tutorials*.

   e. Read the information about Windows XP that displays at the right side of the window.

   f. Print the information by completing the following steps:

      1) Click the Print button located on the toolbar that displays above the information titled *What's new in Windows XP Professional*.

      2) At the Print dialog box, make sure the correct printer is selected and then click the Print button.

2. Return to the opening Help and Support Center window by clicking the Home button located on the Help and Support Center toolbar.

3. Use the *Search* text box to search for information on deleting files by completing the following steps:

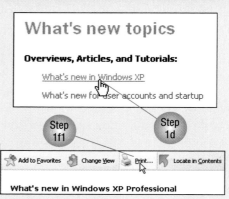

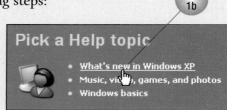

a. Click in the *Search* text box located toward the top of the Help and Support Center window.
b. Type deleting files and then press Enter.
c. Click the <u>Delete a file or folder</u> hyperlink that displays in the *Search Results* section of the window (below the *Pick a task* subheading).
d. Read the information about deleting a file or folder that displays at the right side of the window and then print the information by clicking the Print button on the toolbar and then clicking the Print button at the Print dialog box.
e. Click the <u>Delete or restore files in the Recycle Bin</u> hyperlink that displays in the *Search Results* section of the window.
f. Read the information that displays at the right side of the window about deleting and restoring files in the Recycle Bin and then print the information.

4. Close the Help and Support Center window by clicking the Close button located in the upper right corner of the window.

Displaying an Index of Help and Support Topics

Display a list of help topics available by clicking the Index button on the Help and Support Center window toolbar. This displays an index of help topics at the left side of the window as shown in Figure W.17. Scroll through this list until the desired topic displays and then double-click the topic. Information about the selected topic displays at the right side of the window. If you are looking for a specific topic or keyword, click in the *Type in the keyword to find* text box, type the desired topic or keyword, and then press Enter.

FIGURE

W.17 *Help and Support Center Window with Index Displayed*

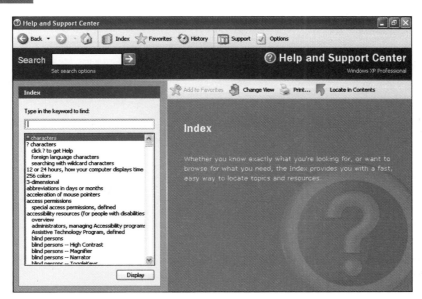

exercise 11

1. At the Windows XP desktop, use the Index to display information on accessing programs by completing the following steps:
   a. Click the Start button on the Taskbar and then click Help and Support at the Start menu.
   b. Click the Index button on the Help and Support Center window toolbar.
   c. Scroll down the list of Index topics until *accessing programs* is visible and then double-click the subheading *overview* that displays below *accessing programs*.
   d. Read the information that displays at the right side of the window and then print the information.

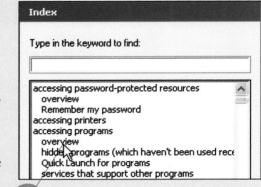

Step 1c

2. Find information on adding a shortcut to the desktop by completing the following steps:
   a. Select and delete the text *overview* that displays in the *Type in the keyword to find* text box and then type shortcuts.
   b. Double-click the subheading *for specific programs* that displays below the *shortcuts* heading.
   c. Read the information that displays at the right side of the window and then print the information.
3. Close the Help and Support Center window by clicking the Close button located in the upper right corner of the window.

Step 2a

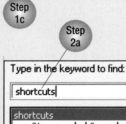

Step 2b

O F F I C E *2003*

BROWSING THE INTERNET USING INTERNET EXPLORER

Microsoft Internet Explorer is a Web browser program with options and features for displaying sites as well as navigating and searching for information on the Internet. The ***Internet*** is a network of computers connected around the world. Users access the Internet for several purposes: to communicate using e-mail, to subscribe to news groups, to transfer files, to socialize with other users around the globe in "chat" rooms, and largely to access virtually any kind of information imaginable.

Using the Internet, people can access a phenomenal amount of information for private or public use. To use the Internet, three things are generally required: an Internet Service Provider (ISP), a program to browse the Web (called a ***Web browser***), and a ***search engine***. In this section, you will learn how to use the Internet Explorer Web browser to browse Web sites, search for specific sites, and download a Web page and image.

Browsing the Internet

You will use the Microsoft Internet Explorer Web browser to locate information on the Internet. Uniform Resource Locators, referred to as URLs, are the method used to identify locations on the Internet. The steps for browsing the Internet vary but generally include: opening Internet Explorer, typing the URL for the desired site, navigating the various pages of the site, printing Web pages, and then closing Internet Explorer.

To launch Internet Explorer, double-click the *Internet Explorer* icon on the Windows desktop. Figure IE.1 identifies the elements of the Internet Explorer, version 6, window. The Web page that displays in your Internet Explorer window may vary from what you see in Figure IE.1.

IE.1 *Internet Explorer Window*

Title Bar
Menu Bar
Toolbar
Address Bar

Vertical Scroll Bar

If you know the URL for the desired Web site, click in the Address bar, type the URL, and then press Enter. In a few moments, the Web site opening page displays in the Internet Explorer window. URLs (Uniform Resource Locators) are the method used to identify locations on the Internet. The format of a URL is *http://server-name.path*. The first part of the URL, *http*, stands for HyperText Transfer Protocol, which is the protocol or language used to transfer data within the World Wide Web. The colon and slashes separate the protocol from the server name. The server name is the second component of the URL. For example, in the URL http://www.microsoft.com, the server name is *microsoft*. The last part of the URL specifies the domain to which the server belongs. For example, *.com* refers to "commercial" and establishes that the URL is a commercial company. Other examples of domains include *.edu* for "educational," *.gov* for "government," and *.mil* for "military."

exercise 1

BROWSING THE INTERNET WITH INTERNET EXPLORER

1. Make sure you are connected to the Internet through an Internet Service Provider and that the Windows desktop displays. (Check with your instructor to determine if you need to complete steps for accessing the Internet.)

2. Launch Microsoft Internet Explorer by double-clicking the *Internet Explorer* icon located on the Windows desktop.

3. At the Internet Explorer window, explore the Web site for Yosemite National Park by completing the following steps:

   a. Click in the Address bar, type www.nps.gov/yose and then press Enter.

Step 3a

b. Scroll down the Web site home page for Yosemite National Park by clicking the down-pointing arrow on the vertical scroll bar located at the right side of the Internet Explorer window.

c. Print the Web site home page by clicking the Print button located on the Internet Explorer toolbar.

4. Explore the Web site for Glacier National Park by completing the following steps:

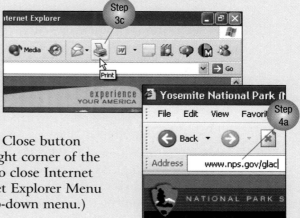

a. Click in the Address bar, type www.nps.gov/glac and then press Enter.

b. Print the Web site home page by clicking the Print button located on the Internet Explorer toolbar.

5. Close Internet Explorer by clicking the Close button (contains an *X*) located in the upper right corner of the Internet Explorer window. (You can also close Internet Explorer by clicking File on the Internet Explorer Menu bar and then clicking Close at the drop-down menu.)

Navigating Using Hyperlinks

Most Web pages contain "hyperlinks" that you click to connect to another page within the Web site or to another site on the Internet. Hyperlinks may display in a Web page as underlined text in a specific color or as images or icons. To use a hyperlink, position the mouse pointer on the desired hyperlink until the mouse pointer turns into a hand, and then click the left mouse button. Use hyperlinks to navigate within and between sites on the Internet. The Internet Explorer toolbar contains a Back button that, when clicked, will take you back to the previous Web page. If you click the Back button and then want to go back to the previous page, click the Forward button. By clicking the Back button, you can back your way out of hyperlinks and return to the Web site home page.

exercise 2

VISITING WEB SITES AND NAVIGATING USING HYPERLINKS

1. Make sure you are connected to the Internet and then double-click the *Internet Explorer* icon on the Windows desktop.

2. At the Internet Explorer window, display the White House Web page and navigate in the page by completing the following steps:

a. Click in the Address bar, type whitehouse.gov and then press Enter.

b. At the White House home Web page, position the mouse pointer on a hyperlink that interests you until the pointer turns into a hand, and then click the left mouse button.

c. At the Web page, click the Back button. (This returns you to the White House home page.)

d. At the White House home Web page, click the Forward button to return to the previous Web page.

e. Print the Web page by clicking the Print button on the Internet Explorer toolbar.

3. Display the Amazon.com Web site and navigate in the site by completing the following steps:

a. Click in the Address bar, type www.amazon.com and then press Enter.

b. At the Amazon.com home page, click a hyperlink related to books.

c. When a book Web page displays, click the Print button on the Internet Explorer toolbar.

4. Close Internet Explorer by clicking the Close button (contains an *X*) located in the upper right corner of the Internet Explorer window.

Searching for Specific Sites

If you do not know the URL for a specific site or you want to find information on the Internet but do not know what site to visit, complete a search with a search engine. A search engine is a software program created to search quickly and easily for desired information. A variety of search engines are available on the Internet, each offering the opportunity to search for specific information. One method for searching for information is to click the Search button on the Internet Explorer toolbar. This displays a Search Companion task pane, as shown in figure IE.2 (your task pane may vary) with options for completing a search. Another method for completing a search is to visit the Web site home page for a search engine and use options at the site.

FIGURE

IE.2 *Internet Explorer Search Companion Task Pane*

Search Companion Task Pane

exercise 3

1. Make sure you are connected to the Internet and then double-click the *Internet Explorer* icon on the Windows desktop.
2. At the Internet Explorer window, search for sites on bluegrass music by completing the following steps:
   a. Click the Search button on the Internet Explorer toolbar. (This displays the Search Companion task pane at the left side of the window.)
   b. Type Bluegrass music in the *What are you looking for?* text box and then press Enter.
   c. When a list of sites displays in the Search Companion task pane, click a site that interests you.
   d. When the Web site home page displays, click the Print button.

3. Click the Search button on the Internet Explorer toolbar to remove the Search Companion task pane.
4. Use the Yahoo search engine to find sites on bluegrass music by completing the following steps:
   a. Click in the Address bar, type www.yahoo.com and then press Enter.

   b. At the Yahoo Web site, click in the search text box, type Bluegrass music and then press Enter. (Notice that the sites displayed vary from the sites displayed in the earlier search.)
   c. Click hyperlinks until a Web site displays that interests you.
   d. When the site displays, click the Print button on the Internet Explorer toolbar.
5. Use the Google search engine to find sites on jazz music by completing the following steps:
   a. Click in the Address bar, type www.Google.com and then press Enter.
   b. When the Google Web site home page displays, click in the search text box, type Jazz music and then press Enter.
   c. Click a site that interests you.
   d. When the Web site home page displays, click the Print button on the Internet Explorer toolbar.
6. Close Internet Explorer.

Completing Advanced Searches for Specific Sites

The Internet contains a phenomenal amount of information. Depending on what you are searching for on the Internet and the search engine you use, some searches can result in several thousand "hits" (sites). Wading through a large number of sites can be very time-consuming and counterproductive. Narrowing a search to very specific criteria can greatly reduce the number of hits for a search. To narrow a search, use the advanced search options offered by the search engine.

exercise 4

NARROWING A SEARCH

1. Make sure you are connected to the Internet and then double-click the *Internet Explorer* icon on the Windows desktop.
2. Search for sites on skydiving in Oregon by completing the following steps:
   a. Click in the Address bar and then type www.yahoo.com.
   b. At the Yahoo Web site home page, click an advanced search hyperlink (this hyperlink may display as <u>Advanced</u> or <u>Advanced search</u>).
   c. At the advanced search page, click in the search text box specifying that you want all words you type to appear in the Web page (this text box may display as "all of these words").
   d. Type skydiving Oregon tandem static line. (This limits the search to Web pages containing all of the words typed in the search text box.)

e. Choose any other options at the advanced search Web page that will narrow your search.
   f. Click the Search button.
   g. When the list of Web sites displays, click a hyperlink that interests you.
   h. Click the Print button on the Internet Explorer toolbar to print the Web page.
   i. Click the Back button on the Internet Explorer toolbar until the Yahoo Search Options page displays.
3. Close Internet Explorer.

Downloading Images, Text, and Web Pages from the Internet

The image(s) and/or text that display when you open a Web page as well as the Web page itself can be saved as a separate file. This separate file can be viewed, printed, or inserted in another file. The information you want to save in a separate file is downloaded from the Internet by Internet Explorer and saved in a folder of your choosing with the name you specify. Copyright laws protect much of the information on the Internet. Before using information downloaded from the Internet, check the site for restrictions. If you do use information, make sure you properly cite the source.

exercise 5

1. Make sure you are connected to the Internet and then double-click the *Internet Explorer* icon on the Windows desktop.
2. Download a Web page and image from Banff National Park by completing the following steps:
   a. Use a search engine of your choosing to search for the Banff National Park Web site.
   b. From the list of sites that displays, choose a site that contains information about Banff National Park and at least one image of the park.
   c. Insert a formatted disk in drive A. (Check with your instructor to determine if you should save the Web page on a disk or save it into a folder on the hard drive or network.)
   d. Save the Web page as a separate file by clicking File on the Internet Explorer Menu bar and then clicking Save As at the drop-down menu.
   e. At the Save Web Page dialog box, click the down-pointing arrow at the right side of the *Save in* option and then click *3¹/₂ Floppy (A:)* at the drop-down list. (This step may vary depending on where your instructor wants you to save the Web page.)
   f. Click in the *File name* text box (this selects the text inside the box), type BanffWebPage and then press Enter.
3. Save the image as a separate file by completing the following steps:
   a. Right-click the image of the park. (The image that displays may vary from what you see to the right.)
   b. At the shortcut menu that displays, click Save Picture As.

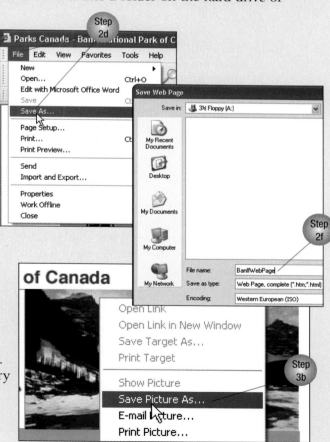

c. At the Save Picture dialog box, change the *Save in* option to drive A (or the location specified by your instructor).

d. Click in the *File name* text box, type BanffImage and then press Enter.

4. Close Internet Explorer.

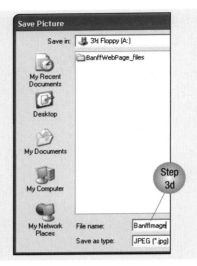

OPTIONAL
exercise

OPENING THE SAVED WEB PAGE AND IMAGE IN A WORD DOCUMENT

1. Open Microsoft Word by clicking the Start button on the Taskbar, pointing to *All Programs*, pointing to *Microsoft Office*, and then clicking *Microsoft Office Word 2003*.

2. With Microsoft Word open, insert the image in a document by completing the following steps:

    a. Click Insert on the Menu bar, point to Picture, and then click From File.

    b. At the Insert Picture dialog box, change the *Look in* option to drive A (or the location where you saved the Banff image) and then double-click ***BanffImage***.

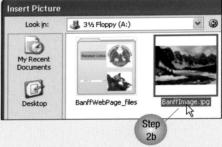

    c. When the image displays in the Word document, print the document by clicking the Print button on the Word Standard toolbar.

    d. Close the document by clicking File on the Menu bar and then clicking Close at the drop-down menu. At the message asking if you want to save the changes, click No.

3. Open the ***BanffWebPage*** file by completing the following steps:

    a. Click File on the Menu bar and then click Open at the drop-down menu.

    b. At the Open dialog box, change the *Look in* option to drive A (or the location where you saved the Web page), and then double-click ***BanffWebPage***.

    c. Print the Web page by clicking the Print button on the Word Standard toolbar.

    d. Close the **BanffWebPage** file by clicking File and then Close.

4. Close Word by clicking the Close button (contains an *X*) that displays in the upper right corner of the screen.

MICROSOFT® ACCESS

Each of us interacts with a database more often than we realize. Did you use a bank machine to get some cash today? Did you search the library's catalog for a book that you need? Did you browse an online retail catalog or flip through the pages of a printed catalog? If you did any of these activities, you were accessing and/or updating a database. Any time you look for something by accessing an organized file system you are probably using a database. Microsoft Access is the database management system included with Microsoft Office.

Organizing Information

Information in a database is organized into a collection of *tables* that can be related to each other for purposes of exchanging data. Each table is broken down into a series of columns (called *fields*) and rows (called *records*). If you are

Making ACCESS Work for YOU!

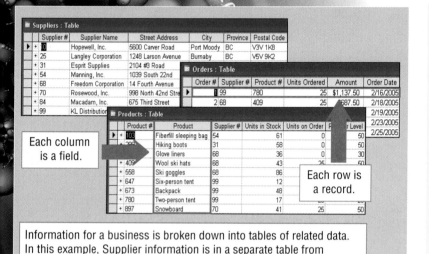

Suppliers : Table

	Supplier #	Supplier Name	Street Address	City	Province	Postal Code
+	10	Hopewell, Inc.	5600 Carver Road	Port Moody	BC	V3V 1K8
+	25	Langley Corporation	1248 Larson Avenue	Burnaby	BC	V5V 9K2
+	31	Esprit Supplies	2104 #3 Road			
+	54	Manning, Inc.	1039 South 22nd			
+	68	Freedom Corporation	14 Fourth Avenue			
+	70	Rosewood, Inc.	998 North 42nd Stre			
+	84	Macadam, Inc.	675 Third Street			
+	99	KL Distribution				

Orders : Table

	Order #	Supplier #	Product #	Units Ordered	Amount	Order Date
▶	1	99	780	25	$1,137.50	2/16/2005
	2	68	409	25	$687.50	2/18/2005
						2/19/2005
						2/23/2005
						2/25/2005

Products : Table

	Product #	Product	Supplier #	Units in Stock	Units on Order	Reorder Level
+	103	Fiberfill sleeping bag	54	61	0	50
+	299	Hiking boots	31	58	0	50
+	371	Glove liners	68	36	0	30
+	409	Wool ski hats	68	43	25	50
+	558	Ski goggles	68	86		
+	647	Six-person tent	99	12		
+	673	Backpack	99	48		
+	780	Two-person tent	99	17		
+	897	Snowboard	70	41	25	50

Each column is a field.

Each row is a record.

Information for a business is broken down into tables of related data. In this example, Supplier information is in a separate table from Product information and Order information.

familiar with a spreadsheet program such as Excel, you will be comfortable viewing a datasheet in Access. Much thought is put into the design of a database and its tables since all of the data a business collects in a database must be organized into logical groups.

Defining a *relationship* between two tables enables data from more than one table to be shared or exchanged for viewing, updating, or reporting purposes. Access allows for three kinds of relationships that can be created: one-to-one, one-to-many, and many-to-many.

Records within tables can be sorted and filtered numerous ways to allow the data to be reorganized to suit many needs. Sorting by one column and by multiple columns is accomplished with just a few mouse clicks. Temporarily hide records that don't meet your criteria by filtering the table. Edit, view and/or print as required and then redisplay the remaining records.

Forms allow those using a database to interact with the table by viewing and updating only one record at a time. Large tables clutter the screen, overwhelming the user

Products : Table

	Product #	Product	
+	103	Fiberfill sleeping bag	5
+	299	Hiking boots	3
+	371	Glove liners	6
+	409	Wool ski hats	6
+	558	Ski goggles	6
+	647	Six-person tent	99
+	673	Backpack	99
+	780	Two-person tent	99
+	897	Snowboard	70

Suppliers : Table

	Supplier #	Supplier Name	Street Address	City	Province	Postal Code
+	10	Hopewell, Inc.	5600 Carver Road	Port Moody	BC	V3V 1K8
+	25	Langley Corporation	1248 Larson Avenue	Burnaby	BC	V5V 9K2
+	31	Esprit Supplies	2104 #3 Road	Burnaby	BC	V5V 3K9
+	54	Manning, Inc.				
+	68	Freedom Corporation				
+	70	Rosewood,				
+	84	Macadam				
+	99	KL Distrib				

Orders : Table

	Order #	Supplier #	Product #	Units Ordered	Amount	Order Date
▶	1	99	780	25	$1,137.50	2/16/2005
	2	68	409	25	$687.50	2/18/2005
	3	68	558	50	$1,100.00	2/19/2005
	4	99	673	25	$1,906.25	2/23/2005
	5	70	897	25	$2,800.00	2/25/2005

	Product #	Product	Supplier Name	Units Ordered	Amount	Order Date
▶ +	103	Fiberfill sleeping bag	Hopewell, Inc.	25	$1,137.50	2/16/2005
+	299	Hiking boots	Langley Corporation	25	$687.50	2/18/2005
+	371	Glove liners	Esprit Supplies	50	$1,100.00	2/19/2005
+	409	Wool ski hats	Manning, Inc.	25	$1,906.25	2/23/2005
+	558					/25/2005

This view is created by selecting fields from all three tables which are related to each other.

City	Supplier Name	Street Address	Province	Postal Code
Burnaby	Esprit Supplies	2104 #3 Road	BC	V5V 3K9
Burnaby	Langley Corporation	1248 Larson Avenue	BC	V5V 9K2
Port Moody	Hopewe		C	V3V 1K8
Port Moody	KL Dist		C	V3V 3K8
Vancouver	Freedon		C	V2V 5K4
Vancouver	Macada		C	V2V 6K3
Vancouver	Manning, Inc.	1039 South 22nd	BC	V2V 5K9
Vancouver	Rosewood, Inc.	998 North 42nd Street	BC	V2V 8K1

Sorted by City and then by Supplier name

Supplier #	Supplier Name	Street Address	City			
10	Hopewell, Inc.	5600 Carver Road	Port Moody			
25	Langley Corporation	1248 Larson Avenue	Burnaby			
31	Esprit Supplies		Burnaby	BC	V5V 3K9	
54	Manning, Inc.		Vancouver	BC	V2V 5K9	
68	Freedom Corporation	14 Fourth Avenue	Vancouver	BC	V2V 5K4	
70	Rosewood, Inc.	998 North 42nd Street	Vancouver	BC	V2V 8K1	
84	Macadam, Inc.	675 Third Street	Vancouver	BC	V2V 6K3	
99	KL Distributions	402 Yukon Drive	Port Mood			

Original Table

Supplier Name	Street Address	City	Province	Postal Code
Freedom Corporation	14 Fourth Avenue	Vancouver	BC	V2V 5K4
Macadam, Inc.	675 Third Street	Vancouver	BC	V2V 6K3
Mann				
Rose				

Filtered to show only those suppliers in Vancouver and then sorted by Supplier Name

with data and requiring scrolling to view all of the fields. Creating a form solves this problem by presenting the table data in a more user-friendly interface. Additional explanatory text can be added to forms, providing information about using the form or following business practices.

Analyzing Information

Databases store a wealth of data that can be extracted in various ways. A *query* is one method for extracting information from tables. A basic query might simply list fields from several tables in one datasheet. This method is shown on the facing page, where individual fields from three tables are selected for viewing in one datasheet. In more complex queries, data can be selected for viewing based on meeting a single criterion or multiple criteria, and calculations can be performed on fields.

For more sophisticated analysis, tables can be grouped and then filtered on more than one field. Open a table or query and then switch to PivotTable View or PivotChart View. Access has simplified the task of creating pivot tables and pivot charts by incorporating a drag and drop technique in the view.

Interact with the pivot table or pivot chart by clicking one of the filter arrows, selecting or deselecting the items you want to view, and then click OK. The data in the view is instantly updated to reflect the new settings.

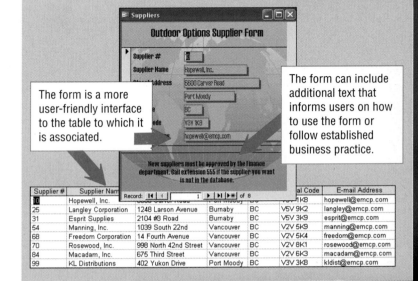

The form is a more user-friendly interface to the table to which it is associated.

The form can include additional text that informs users on how to use the form or follow established business practice.

Supplier #	Supplier Name				al Code	E-mail Address
10	Hopewell, Inc.				1K8	hopewell@emcp.com
25	Langley Corporation	1248 Larson Avenue	Burnaby	BC	V5V 9K2	langley@emcp.com
31	Esprit Supplies	2104 #3 Road	Burnaby	BC	V5V 3K9	esprit@emcp.com
54	Manning, Inc.	1039 South 22nd	Vancouver	BC	V2V 5K9	manning@emcp.com
68	Freedom Corporation	14 Fourth Avenue	Vancouver	BC	V2V 5K4	freedom@emcp.com
70	Rosewood, Inc.	998 North 42nd Street	Vancouver	BC	V2V 8K1	rosewood@emcp.com
84	Macadam, Inc.	675 Third Street	Vancouver	BC	V2V 6K3	macadam@emcp.com
99	KL Distributions	402 Yukon Drive	Port Moody	BC	V3V 3K8	kldist@emcp.com

Product #	Product	Supplier Name	Units in Stock	Units on Order	Reorder Level	Overstock
299	Hiking boots	Esprit Supplies	58	0	50	8
103	Fiberfill sleeping bag	Manning, Inc.	61	0	50	11
371	Glove liners	Freedom Corporation	36	0	30	6
409	Wool ski hats	Freedom Corporation	43	25	50	18
558					100	36
897					50	16
647						2
673						23
780						22

Overstock is a calculated column that adds the Units in Stock to the Units on Order and displays the amount that the sum is over the Reorder Level.

In this query only records with a value above zero in Units on Order to the supplier named Freedom Corporation are displayed.

Product #	Product	Supplier Name	Units in Stock	Units on Order
409	Wool ski hats	Freedom Corporation	43	25
558	Ski goggles	Freedom Corporation	86	50

Product #	Product	Supplier Name	Units Ordered	Amount	Order Date
780	Two-person tent	KL Distributions	25	$1,137.50	2/16/2005
409	Wool ski hats	Freedom Corporation	25	$687.50	2/18/200
558	Ski goggles	Freedom Corporation	50	$1,100.00	/2005
673	Backpack	KL Distributions	25	$1,9	2/23/2005
897	Snowboard	Rosewood, Inc.		,800.00	2/25/2005

Transform data in a table for analysis in a pivot table (left) or pivot chart (right).

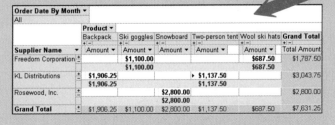

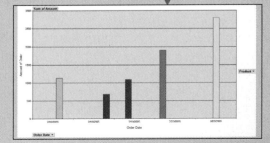

Product #	Product	Supplier Name	Units in Stock	Units on Order	Reorder Level	Overstock
299	Hiking boots	Esprit Supplies	58	0	50	8
103	Fiberfill sleeping bag	Manning, Inc.	61	0	50	11
371	Glove liners	Freedom Corporation	36	0	30	6
409	Wool ski hats	Freedom Corporation	43	25	50	18
558	Ski goggles	Freedom Corporation	86	50	100	36
897	Snowboard	Rosewood, Inc.	41	25	50	16
647	Six-person tent	KL Distributions	12	0	10	2
673	Backpack	KL Distributions	48	25	50	23
780	Two-person tent	KL Distributions	17	25	20	22

Create a report to produce high-quality output.

Overstock Report by Supplier Name

Supplier Name	Product	Product #	Units in Stock	Units on Order	Reorder Level	Overstock
Esprit Supplies						
	Hiking boots	299	58	0	50	8
				Total Overstock by Supplier Name:		8
Freedom Corporation						
	Glove liners	371	36	0	30	6
	Ski goggles	558	86	50	100	36
	Wool ski hats	409	43	25	50	18
				Total Overstock by Supplier Name:		60
KL Distributions						
	Backpack	673	48	25	50	23
	Six-person tent	647	12	0	10	2
	Two-person tent	780	17	25	20	22
				Total Overstock by Supplier Name:		47

Information in Access tables can be put on the Web by creating a data access page.

Order Entry Web Page

⊟ Supplier # 68

Order #: 2

Product #: 409

Units 25

Amount: $687.50

Order Date: 2/18/2005

Presenting Information

Having critical business information stored electronically and the ability to easily extract specific data from the database is a valuable asset to a business. However, there are still times when a printed report is a necessity. Reports in Access are used to create professional-looking, high-quality output. Reports can be grouped and sorted and can include calculations. Access includes the Report Wizard, which can be used to create a report such as the one shown at left by choosing the table or query for the source data, specifying a group or sort order, and choosing from predefined styles and layouts. Once the report is generated, you can easily modify its design by moving, resizing, adding, or deleting objects, changing the layout or sort order, adding a calculation, drawing lines, and so on.

In today's global workplaces, the Web is often the environment of choice for conducting business. Putting Access information on the Web is as easy as creating an object called a *data access page*. Data in tables can be linked to a data access page for easier viewing and updating by those not familiar with a database. Access includes the Page Wizard, which is similar to the Report Wizard and can be used to generate a Web page.

A business cannot survive without a well designed database that is easy to update and maintain. Microsoft Access is a database management system that is easy to learn and use. In just a few pages, you will be exploring the world of databases and learning how to access the technology that drives business success.

SPECIALIST

MICROSOFT®
ACCESS

Unit 1: Creating Database Tables, Queries, and Filters

➤ Maintaining Databases

➤ Customizing Databases

➤ Creating Queries, Forms, and Reports

➤ Enhancing Databases with Special Features

MICROSOFT ACCESS 2003

MICROSOFT OFFICE ACCESS 2003 SPECIALIST SKILLS – UNIT 1

Reference No.	Skill	Pages
AC03S-1	**Structuring Databases**	
AC03S-1-1	Create Access databases	S7-S20
AC03S-1-2	Create and modify tables	
	Create a table in design view	S8-S17
	Create a table using the Table Wizard	S67-S76
	Modify a table	S22-S27
AC03S-1-3	Define and create field types	
	Define, assign, and create field types	S8-S17
	Create Lookup field	S27-S32
AC03S-1-4	Modify field properties	
	Create input masks	S26-S32
	Change field data type	S9-S17
AC03S-1-5	Create and modify one-to-many relationships	
	Create a one-to-many relationship between tables	S41-S57
	Edit a one-to-many relationship	S57-S60
AC03S-1-6	**Enforce referential integrity**	**S49-S52**
AC03S-1-7	Create and modify queries	
	Create queries using the Simple Query Wizard	S93-S108
	Create queries with Aggregate Functions	S108-S112
	Create a Crosstab query	S113-S115
	Create a Find Duplicates query	S115-S119
	Create an Unmatched query	S119-S120
AC03S-2	**Entering Data**	
AC03S-2-1	Enter, edit and delete records	
	Enter data in a table	S17-S20
	Add and delete records	S24-S25
AC03S-2-2	Find and move among records	
	Find records with specific data and replace with other data	S77-S80
	Find duplicate records using the Find Duplicates query	S115-S119
AC03S-3	**Organizing Data**	
AC03S-3-1	Create and modify calculated fields and aggregate functions	S105-S112
AC03S-3-4	Format datasheets	S20-S23
AC03S-3-5	Sort records	
	Sort records in a table	S33-S34
	Sort fields in a query	S100-S101
AC03S-3-6	Filter records	
	Filter by selection	S120-S121
	Filter by form	S122-S124
AC03S-4	**Managing Databases**	
AC03S-4-3	Print database objects and data	
	Print a database table	S20-S23
	Print database relationships	S50-S54
AC03S-4-5	Back up a database	S81-S83
AC03S-4-6	Compact and repair databases	S81-S83

CREATING A DATABASE TABLE

PERFORMANCE OBJECTIVES

Upon successful completion of Chapter 1, you will be able to:

➤ **Design a database table**
➤ **Determine fields and assign data types in a database table**
➤ **Enter data in a database table**
➤ **Open, save, print, and close a database table**
➤ **Add and delete records in a database table**
➤ **Modify a database table by adding, deleting, or moving fields**
➤ **Use the Input Mask Wizard and the Lookup Wizard**

Managing information in a company is an integral part of operating a business. Information can come in a variety of forms, such as data on customers, including names, addresses, and telephone numbers; product data; purchasing and buying data; information on services performed for customers or clients; and much more. Most companies today manage data using a database management system software program. Microsoft Office Professional includes a database management system software program called *Access*. With Access, you can organize, store, maintain, retrieve, sort, and print all types of business data.

As an example of how Access might be used to manage data in an office, suppose a bookstore decides to send a mailer to all customers who have purchased a certain type of book in the past month (such as autobiographies). The bookstore uses Access and maintains data on customers, such as names, addresses, types of books purchased, and types of books ordered. With this data in Access, the manager of the bookstore can easily select those customers who have purchased or ordered autobiographies in the past month and send a mailer announcing a visit by an author who has just completed writing an autobiography. The bookstore could also use the information to determine what types of books have been ordered by customers in the past few months and use this information to determine what inventory to purchase.

Use the information in a database to perform a wide variety of functions. This chapter contains just a few ideas. With a properly designed and maintained database management system, a company can operate smoothly with logical,

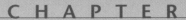

organized, and useful information. The Access program displays in the Start pop-up menu preceded by a picture of a key, and a key is displayed in the Taskbar when Access is open. The key symbolizes the importance of managing and maintaining data to a company's survival and success.

Organizing Data in a Database Table

HINT
Organize data in tables to minimize or eliminate duplication.

Data is not very useful to a company if it is not organized in a logical manner. Organizing data in a manageable and logical manner allows the data to be found and used for a variety of purposes.

Determining Fields

Microsoft Access is a database management system software program that allows you to design, create, input, maintain, manipulate, sort, and print data. Access is considered a relational database in which you organize data in related tables. In this chapter, you will be creating one table as part of a database file. In a later chapter, you will create a related table within the same database file.

HINT
A database table contains fields that describe a person, customer, client, object, place, idea, or event.

The first step in creating a table is to determine the fields. A field is one piece of information about a person, a place, or an item. For example, one field could be a customer's name, another field could be a customer's address, and another a customer number. All fields for one unit, such as a customer, are considered a record. For example, in Exercise 1, a record is all the information pertaining to one employee of Premium Health Services. A collection of records becomes a database table.

When designing a database table, determine fields for information to be included on the basis of how you plan to use the data. When organizing fields, be sure to consider not only current needs for the data but also any future needs. For example, a company may need to keep track of customer names, addresses, and telephone numbers for current mailing lists. In the future, the company may want to promote a new product to customers who purchase a specific type of product. For this situation, a field that identifies product type must be included in the database. When organizing fields, consider all potential needs for the data but also try to keep the fields logical and manageable.

After deciding what data you want included in a database table, you need to determine field names. Consider the following guidelines when naming fields in a database table:

- Each field must contain a unique name.
- The name must describe the contents of the field.
- A field name can contain up to 64 characters.
- A field name can contain letters, numbers, spaces, and symbols except the period (.), comma (,), exclamation point (!), square brackets ([]), and grave accent (`).
- A field name cannot begin with a space.

In Exercise 1, you will create a database table containing information on employees of a medical corporation. The fields in this table and the names you will give to each field are shown in Figure 1.1.

FIGURE

1.1 *Field Information and Names for Exercise 1*

Employee Information	Field Name
ID number	*Emp #*
Last name	*Last Name*
First name	*First Name*
Middle initial	*Middle Initial*
Street address	*Street Address*
City	*City*
State	*State*
ZIP Code	*ZIP Code*
Date of hire	*Hire Date*
Department code	*Dept Code*

Assigning a Data Type to Fields

Part of the process of designing a database table includes specifying or assigning a data type to each field. The data type specifies the type of data you can enter in a field. Assigning a data type to fields helps maintain and manage the data and helps identify for anyone entering information into the field what type of data is expected. The data types that are available in Access along with a description of each and the field size are shown in Table 1.1.

HINT

Assign a data type for each field that determines the values that can be entered for the field.

TABLE

1.1 *Data Types*

Assign this data type	To this type of field
Text	Assign to a field where text will be entered, such as names, addresses, and numbers that do not require calculations, such as telephone numbers, dates, Social Security numbers, and ZIP Codes. A maximum number of 255 characters can be stored in a text data field; 50 characters is the default.
Memo	Assign to a field where more than 255 characters are needed. Up to 64,000 characters can be stored in a memo data field.
Number	Assign to a field where positive and/or negative numbers are to be entered for mathematical calculations, except calculations that involve money or require a high degree of accuracy. A maximum of 15 digits can be stored in a number data field.

Continued on next page

Currency	Assign to a field where you do not want calculations rounded off during a calculation. A maximum of 15 digits can be stored in a currency data field.
Date/Time	Assign to a field where a date and/or time will be entered. Eight characters is the default.
AutoNumber	Create a field that automatically enters a number when a record is added. Three types of numbers can be generated—sequential numbers that change by one, random numbers, and replication ID numbers. A maximum of nine digits can be stored in an *AutoNumber* data field.
Yes/No	Assign to a field where data is to be limited to Yes or No, True or False, or On or Off.
OLE Object	Assign to an object such as an Excel spreadsheet or Word document linked to or embedded in an Access table. Up to 1 gigabyte of characters can be stored in the field.
Hyperlink	Assign to text or a combination of text and numbers stored as text and used as a hyperlink address. A hyperlink address can contain up to three parts and each part can contain up to 2,048 characters.
Lookup Wizard	Click this option to start the Lookup Wizard, which creates a *Lookup* field. When the wizard is completed, Access sets the data type based on the values selected during the wizard steps.

When designing a database table, determine the data type that is to be assigned to a field. The fields in Exercise 1 will be assigned the data types and field sizes shown in Figure 1.2.

FIGURE

1.2 *Data Types for Exercise 1*

Field Name	Data Type
Emp #	Text (Field Size = 5)
Last Name	Text (Field Size = 30)
First Name	Text (Field Size = 30)
Middle Initial	Text (Field Size = 2)
Street Address	Text (Field Size = 30)
City	Text (Field Size = 20)
State	Text (Field Size = 2)
ZIP Code	Text (Field Size = 5)
Dept Code	Text (Field Size = 2)
Hire Date	Date/Time

Data entered for some fields in Exercise 1, such as *ZIP Code,* will be numbers. These numbers, however, are not values and will not be used in calculations. This is why they are assigned the data type of Text (rather than Number or Currency).

During the process of creating the database table, field sizes are assigned. By default, a field is assigned the default number as described in Table 1.1. You can, however, specify a maximum field size. For example, a Text data type sets the field size at 50 characters by default. For a field in Exercise 1 such as the *ZIP Code,* a specific maximum number can be assigned, such as 5 (if you are only using the five-number ZIP Code). When assigning a field size, consider the data that will be entered in the field, and then shorten or lengthen the maximum number to accommodate any possible entries. For the *First Name* field or the *Last Name* field, for example, shortening the number to 30 would be appropriate, ensuring that all names would fit in the field. The two-letter state abbreviation will be used in the *State* field, so the number of characters is changed to 2.

Creating a Database Table

Once the fields, field names, and data types have been determined, you are ready to create the database table. To create a database table, you would follow these general steps:

1. Open Access. To do this, click the Start button on the Taskbar, point to *All Programs,* point to *Microsoft Office,* and then click *Microsoft Office Access 2003.* (These steps may vary.)

2. At the blank Access screen, click the New button located at the left side of the Database toolbar.

3. At the New File task pane, click the Blank database hyperlink. (The New File task pane displays at the right side of the window as shown in Figure 1.3.)

4. At the File New Database dialog box shown in Figure 1.4, change to the drive where your disk is located, type a name for the database in the *File name* text box, and then press Enter or click the Create button.

5. At the Database window shown in Figure 1.5, double-click *Create table in Design view* in the list box.

6. At the Table1 : Table window shown in Figure 1.6, type the first field name in the *Field Name* text box, and then press Tab. (This moves the insertion point to the *Data Type* text box and inserts the word *Text.*)

7. With the insertion point positioned in the *Data Type* text box and the word *Text* inserted in the box, press Tab to move the insertion point to *Description* or change the data type and then press Tab.

8. With the insertion point positioned in the *Description* text box, type a description of the field, and then press Tab.

9. Continue typing field names, assigning a data type to each field, and typing a description of all fields.

10. When all fields have been typed, click File and then Save, or click the Save button on the Table Design toolbar.

11. At the Save As dialog box shown in Figure 1.7, type a name for the table in the *Table Name* text box, and then press Enter or click OK.

12. A message displays telling you that no primary key is defined and asking if you want to create one. At this message, click No. (You will learn more about primary keys in Chapter 2.)

13. Click File and then Close to close the database table.

Create a Database Table
1. Click New button.
2. Click Blank database hyperlink.
3. Type file name.
4. Press Enter or click Create button.
5. Double-click *Create table in Design view.*
6. Type field names, specify types, and include descriptions.
7. Click Save button.
8. Type name for table.
9. Press Enter or click OK.

Provide full descriptions of fields in a database file if other users will be maintaining the database.

Save

1.3 *Microsoft Access Screen*

Title Bar

Menu Bar

Database Toolbar

Click the New button on the Database toolbar to display the New File task pane.

Click this hyperlink to display the File New Database dialog box.

New File Task Pane

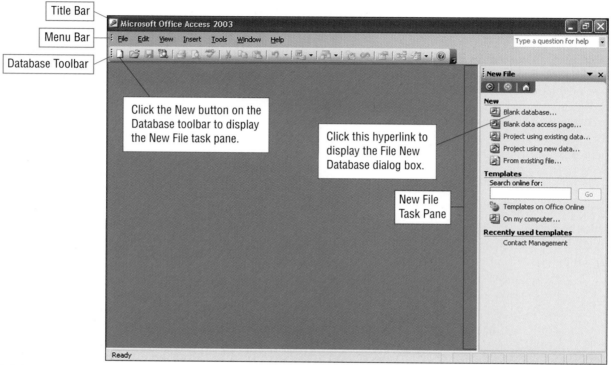

1.4 *File New Database Dialog Box*

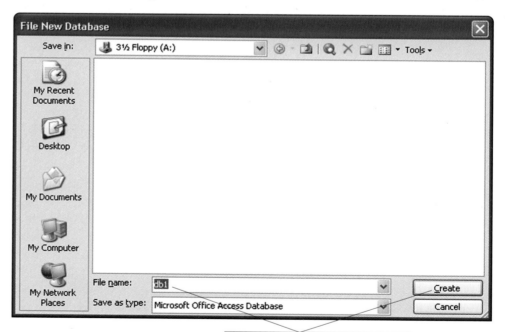

Type a name for the database in the *File name* text box and then press Enter or click the Create button.

FIGURE

1.5   **Database Window**

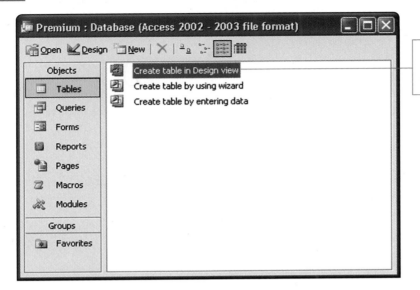

Double-click this option to create a table in Design view.

FIGURE

1.6   **Table1 : Table Window**

At this window, assign field names and data types; also provide a description.

FIGURE

1.7   **Save As Dialog Box**

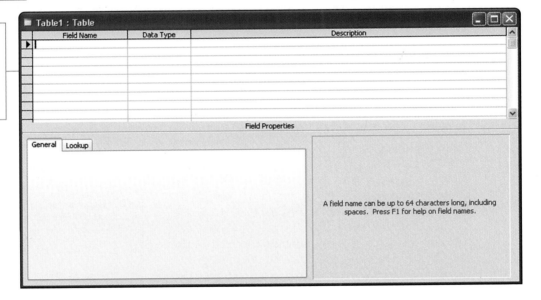

Type a name for the table in this text box.

At the Table window shown in Figure 1.6, field names are entered, data types are assigned, and descriptions are typed. When assigning a data type, Access displays information in the bottom portion of the window in a section with the General tab selected. Information in this section can be changed to customize a data type for a field. For example, you can specify that only a maximum of two characters can be entered in the *Middle Initial* field.

A database file can contain more than one table. Tables containing related data are saved in the same database. In Exercise 1, you will create a table named Employees that is part of the database file named Premium. In Exercise 2, you will create another table as part of the Premium database that includes payroll information.

CREATING AN EMPLOYEE DATABASE TABLE

(Note: Insert a blank formatted disk before beginning Exercise 1.)

1. Open Access by clicking Start button on the Taskbar, pointing to *All Programs*, pointing to *Microsoft Office*, and then clicking *Microsoft Office Access 2003*.
2. At the blank Access screen, click the New button (first button from the left) on the Database toolbar.
3. At the New File task pane, click the <u>Blank database</u> hyperlink located in the *New* section.
4. At the File New Database dialog box (see Figure 1.4), change to the drive where your disk is located, type Premium in the *File name* text box, and then press Enter or click the Create button.
5. At the Premium : Database window, double-click *Create table in Design view* in the list box.
6. At the Table1 : Table window, type the fields shown in Figure 1.8 by completing the following steps:
   a. Type Emp # in the *Field Name* text box and then press Tab.
   b. The word *Text* is automatically inserted in the *Data Type* text box. Change the field size from the default of 50 to 5. To do this, select *50* that displays after *Field Size* in the *Field Properties* section of the window and then type 5.
   c. Position the I-beam pointer in the *Description* text box (for the *Emp #* field), and then click the left mouse button. (You can also press F6 to switch to the top of the window, and then press Tab to move the insertion point to the *Description* text box.) Type Employee number in the *Description* text box and then press Tab.

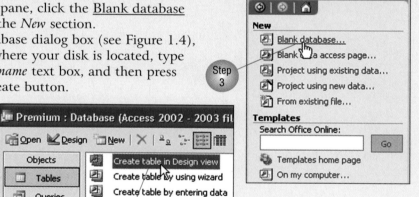

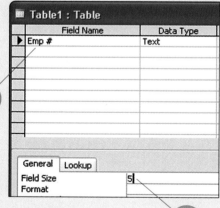

d. Type **Last Name** in the *Field Name* text box and then press Tab.
e. Change the field size to 30 and then click in the *Description* text box for the *Last Name* field (or press F6 and then press Tab). Type **Employee last name** and then press Tab.
f. Type **First Name** in the *Field Name* text box and then press Tab.
g. Change the field size to 30 and then click in the *Description* text box for the *First Name* field (or press F6 and then press Tab). Type **Employee first name** and then press Tab.
h. Continue typing the field names, data types, and descriptions as shown in Figure 1.8. Refer to Figure 1.2 for the text field sizes. To change the Data Type for the *Hire Date* field, click the down-pointing arrow after *Text* and then click *Date/Time* in the drop-down list.

7. When all of the fields are entered, save the database table by completing the following steps:
   a. Click the Save button on the Table Design toolbar.
   b. At the Save As dialog box, type **Employees** in the text box, and then press Enter or click OK.
   c. At the message telling you that no primary key is defined and asking if you want to create one, click No. (You will learn more about primary keys in Chapter 2.)

8. Close the Employees table by clicking File and then Close or clicking the Close button located in the upper right corner of the window.

9. Close the **Premium** database file by clicking File and then Close or clicking the Close button located at the right side of the Title bar.

FIGURE

1.8 *Exercise 1*

Field Name	Data Type	Description
Emp #	Text	Employee number
Last Name	Text	Employee last name
First Name	Text	Employee first name
Middle Initial	Text	Employee middle initial
Street Address	Text	Employee street address
City	Text	Employee city
State	Text	Employee state
Zip Code	Text	Employee Zip code
Dept Code	Text	Department code
Hire Date	Date/Time	Date of hire

Table1 : Table

In Exercise 1, you saved the table containing the fields with the name Employees and then closed the Premium database file. Access automatically saves an open (or active) database on a periodic basis and also when the database is closed. If you are working with a database that is saved on a disk, never remove the disk while the database is open because Access saves the database periodically. If the disk is not in the drive when Access tries to save it, problems will be encountered and you run the risk of damaging the database. Exit (close) Access by clicking the Close button located in the upper right corner of the Access Title bar (contains an *X*) or by clicking File and then Exit.

The Employees table contains a *Dept Code* field. This field will contain a two-letter code identifying the department within the company. In Exercise 2, you will create a table named Departments containing only two fields—the department code

HINT
The active database is saved automatically on a periodic basis and also when the database is closed.

HINT
If you are working with a database file saved on a floppy disk, never remove the disk while the database file is open. If you do, Access will have problems when trying to automatically save the database.

and the department name. Establishing a department code decreases the amount of data entered in the Employees table. For example, in an employee record, you type a two-letter code identifying the employee department rather than typing the entire department name. Imagine the time this saves when entering hundreds of employee records. This is an example of the power of a relational database.

(Note: If a Security warning message box appears when opening a database stating that unsafe expressions are not blocked, click Yes to confirm that you want to open the file. This message may or may not appear depending on the security level setting on the computer you are using. If the message appears, expect that it will reappear each time you open a database file.)

exercise 2

1. At the blank Access screen, click the Open button on the Database toolbar. (The Database toolbar displays directly below the Menu bar.)

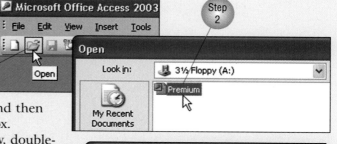

2. At the Open dialog box, make sure the drive is active where your disk is located and then double-click **Premium** in the list box.

3. At the Premium : Database window, double-click *Create table in Design view* in the list box.

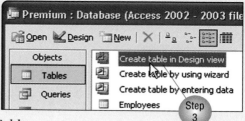

4. At the Table1 : Table window, type the fields shown in Figure 1.9 by completing the following steps:
   a. Type Dept Code in the *Field Name* text box and then press Tab.
   b. Change the field size to 2, and then click in the *Description* text box for the *Dept Code* field.
   c. Type Department code in the *Description* text box and then press the Tab key.
   d. Type Department in the *Field Name* text box and then press Tab.
   e. Change the field size to 30, and then click in the *Description* text box for the *Department* field.
   f. Type Department name in the *Description* text box.

5. When all of the fields are entered, save the database table by completing the following steps:
   a. Click the Save button on the Table Design toolbar.
   b. At the Save As dialog box, type Departments in the text box, and then press Enter or click OK.
   c. At the message telling you that no primary key is defined and asking if you want to create one, click No. (You will learn more about primary keys in Chapter 2.)

6. Close the Departments table by clicking File and then Close or clicking the Close button located in the upper right corner of the window.

7. Close the **Premium** database file by clicking File and then Close or clicking the Close button located at the right side of the Title bar.

1.9 *Exercise 2*

Field Name	Data Type	Description
Dept Code	Text	Department code
▶ Department	Text	Department name

Table1 : Table

Entering Data in a Table

After a database table has been designed with the necessary fields and has been created in Access, the next step is to input the data. One method for entering data into a database table is to change to the Datasheet view. A table datasheet displays the contents of a table in rows and columns in the same manner as a Word table or Excel worksheet. Each row in a datasheet represents one record. In the Employees table of the Premium database, one record will contain the information for one employee.

Opening a Database File

To open a database file, click the Open button on the Database toolbar or click File and then Open. At the Open dialog box, double-click the desired database file name in the Open dialog box list box.

Open

Opening a Table

Open a database file and a database window displays similar to the one shown in Figure 1.10. Open a specific table in the database file by double-clicking the table name in the list box.

HINT

Only one database file can be open at a time.

1.10 *Premium : Database Window*

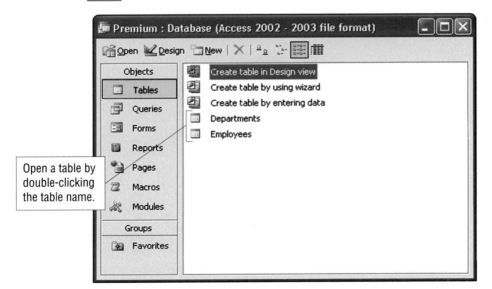

Open a table by double-clicking the table name.

Entering Data in a Database Table

Open a database table and the table displays in the Datasheet view. This is the view needed for entering data in the table. Type data for each field in the table, pressing Tab to move the insertion point from field to field. For example, the Employees database table in the Premium database file will display as shown in Figure 1.11. (Data has been entered in this database table.)

1.11 *Employees Table in Premium Database*

Emp #	Last Name	First Name	Middle Initial	Street Address	City	State	Zip Co
21043	Brown	Leland	C.	112 Kansas Ave	Missoula	MT	84311
19034	Guenther	Julia	A.	215 Bridge Wes	Lolo	MT	86308
27845	Oaklee	Thomas	E.	2310 Keating R	Missola	MT	84325
08921	Avery	Michael	W.	23155 Needhan	Florence	MT	85901
30091	Latora	Gina	M.	13221 138th Str	Missoula	MT	84302

QUICK STEPS

Enter Data in a Table
1. Click Open button.
2. Double-click database file name.
3. Double-click database table name.
4. Make sure table displays in Datasheet view.
5. Type data in fields.
6. Click Save button.

When you type data for the first field in the record, another row of cells is automatically inserted below the first row. Type the data for the first record, pressing Tab to move from field to field. The description you typed for each field when creating the database table displays at the left side of the Access Status bar. This description reminds you what data is expected in the field.

If you assigned the Yes/No data type to a field, a square displays in the field. This square can be left empty or a check mark can be inserted. If the field is asking a yes/no question, an empty box signifies "No" and a box with a check mark signifies "Yes." If the field is asking for a true/false answer, an empty box signifies "False" and a box with a check mark signifies "True." This field can also have an on/off response. An empty box signifies "Off" and a box with a check mark signifies "On." To insert a check mark in the box, tab to the field, and then press the spacebar.

When all records have been entered in the table, save the table again by clicking the Save button on the Table Datasheet toolbar. (The Table Datasheet toolbar displays directly below the Menu bar.)

exercise 3

ENTERING DATA IN THE EMPLOYEES AND THE DEPARTMENTS TABLES

1. At the blank Access screen, click the Open button on the Database toolbar.
2. At the Open dialog box, make sure the drive is active where your disk is located, and then double-click *Premium* in the list box.
3. At the Premium : Database window, double-click *Employees* in the list box.

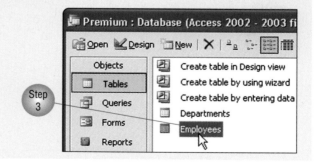

4. At the Employees : Table window, type the following data for five records in the specified fields. (Press Tab to move the insertion point to the next field or press Shift + Tab to move the insertion point to the previous field.) When typing data, not all of the data may be visible. You will adjust column widths in a later exercise.

Emp #	=	21043
Last Name	=	Brown
First Name	=	Leland
Middle Initial	=	C.
Street Address	=	112 Kansas Avenue
City	=	Missoula
State	=	MT
ZIP Code	=	84311
Dept Code	=	PA
Hire Date	=	11/5/1999

Emp #	=	19034
Last Name	=	Guenther
First Name	=	Julia
Middle Initial	=	A.
Street Address	=	215 Bridge West
City	=	Lolo
State	=	MT
ZIP Code	=	86308
Dept Code	=	MS
Hire Date	=	2/15/1994

Emp #	=	27845
Last Name	=	Oaklee
First Name	=	Thomas
Middle Initial	=	E.
Street Address	=	2310 Keating Road
City	=	Missoula
State	=	MT
ZIP Code	=	84325
Dept Code	=	HR
Hire Date	=	6/8/2000

Emp #	=	08921
Last Name	=	Avery
First Name	=	Michael
Middle Initial	=	W.
Street Address	=	23155 Neadham Avenue
City	=	Florence
State	=	MT
ZIP Code	=	85901
Dept Code	=	PA
Hire Date	=	11/5/1999

Emp #	=	30091
Last Name	=	Latora

First Name	=	Gina
Middle Initial	=	M.
Street Address	=	13221 138th Street
City	=	Missoula
State	=	MT
ZIP Code	=	84302
Dept Code	=	HR
Hire Date	=	9/16/2004

5. After typing the data, save the database table by clicking the Save button on the Table Datasheet toolbar.
6. Close the Employees table by clicking File and then Close or by clicking the Close button in the upper right corner of the window.
7. At the Premium : Database window, double-click *Departments* in the list box.
8. At the Departments : Table window, type the following data for four departments in the specified fields (press Tab to move the insertion point to the next field or press Shift + Tab to move the insertion point to the previous field):

| Dept Code | = | IS |
| Department Name | = | Information Services |

| Dept Code | = | HR |
| Department Name | = | Human Resources |

| Dept Code | = | MS |
| Department Name | = | Medical Services |

| Dept Code | = | PA |
| Department Name | = | Patient Accounts |

9. After typing the data, save the database table by clicking the Save button on the Table Datasheet toolbar.
10. Close the Departments table by clicking File and then Close or by clicking the Close button in the upper right corner of the window.
11. Close the **Premium** database file by clicking File and then Close or by clicking the Close button at the right side of the Title bar.

Printing a Database Table

Print

QUICK
STEPS

Print a Table
1. Open database file.
2. Open database table.
3. Click Print button.

Various methods are available for printing data in a database table. One method for printing is to open the database table and then click the Print button on the Table Datasheet toolbar. This sends the information directly to the printer without any formatting changes. In some fields created in the Employees database table, this means that you would not be able to see all printed text in a field if all of the text did not fit in the field. For example, when typing the data in Exercise 3, did you notice that the Street Address data was longer than the field column could accommodate? You can change the database table layout to ensure that all data is visible. You will first print the Employees and Departments tables with the default settings, learn about changing the layout, and then print the tables again.

exercise 4

1. At the blank Access screen, open the **Premium** database file.
2. Open the Employees table.
3. Click the Print button on the Table Datasheet toolbar.
4. Close the Employees table.
5. Open the Departments table.
6. Click the Print button on the Table Datasheet toolbar.
7. Close the Departments table.
8. Close the **Premium** database file.

Step 3

Look at the printing of the Employees table and notice how the order of records displays differently in the printing (and in the table) than the order in which the records were typed. Access automatically sorted the records by the ZIP Code in ascending order. Access automatically sorted the records in the Departments table alphabetically by department name. You will learn more about sorting later in this chapter.

Changing Page Setup

The Employees table printed on two pages in the Portrait orientation with default margins. The page orientation and page margins can be changed with options at the Page Setup dialog box with either the Margins or the Page tab selected. To display the Page Setup dialog box shown in Figure 1.12, you would open the Employees or Departments database table, click File, and then click Page Setup.

QUICK STEPS

Display Page Setup Dialog Box
1. Open database file.
2. Open database table.
3. Click File, Page Setup.

FIGURE

1.12 *Page Setup Dialog Box with Margins Tab Selected*

At the Page Setup dialog box with the Margins tab selected, notice that the default margins are 1 inch. Change these defaults by typing a different number in the desired margin text box. By default, the table name prints at the top center of the page. For example, when you printed the Employees table, *Employees* printed at the top of the page along with the current date (printed at the right side of the page). *Page 1* also printed at the bottom of the page. If you do not want the name of the table and the date as well as the page number printed, remove the check mark from the *Print Headings* option at the Page Setup dialog box with the Margins tab selected.

HINT
A table can be printed in landscape orientation.

Change the table orientation at the Page Setup dialog box with the Page tab selected as shown in Figure 1.13. To change to landscape orientation, click *Landscape*. You can also change the paper size with options in the *Paper* section of the dialog box and specify the printer with options in the *Printer for (table name)* section of the dialog box.

FIGURE

1.13 *Page Setup Dialog Box with Page Tab Selected*

HINT
Automatically adjust column widths in an Access database table in the same manner as adjusting column widths in an Excel worksheet.

QUICK STEPS

Changing Field Width
1. Open database table in Datasheet view.
2. Drag column boundary to desired position.

Changing Field Width

In the printing of the Employees table, not all of the data is visible in the *Street Address* field. You can remedy this situation by changing the width of the fields. Automatically adjust one field (column) in a database table to accommodate the longest entry in the field by positioning the arrow pointer on the column boundary at the right side of the column until it turns into a double-headed arrow pointing left and right with a line between and then double-clicking the left mouse button. Automatically adjust adjacent columns by selecting the columns first and then double-clicking on a column boundary.

exercise 5

1. Open the **Premium** database file and then open the Employees database table.
2. Change the page margins and orientation by completing the following steps:
   a. Click File and then Page Setup.
   b. At the Page Setup dialog box, click the Page tab.
   c. At the Page Setup dialog box with the Page tab selected, click *Landscape* in the *Orientation* section.

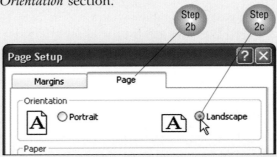

   d. Click the Margins tab.
   e. At the Page Setup dialog box with the Margins tab selected, select *1* in the *Top* text box, and then type *2*.
   f. Click OK to close the dialog box.
3. Automatically adjust all columns in the table to accommodate the longest entry by completing the following steps:
   a. Position the arrow pointer on the *Emp #* field name (the arrow pointer turns into a down-pointing black arrow).
   b. Hold down the left mouse button, drag the arrow pointer to the *Hire Date* field name, and then release the mouse button. (This selects all data in the table.)
   c. Position the arrow pointer on one of the column boundaries until it turns into a double-headed arrow pointing left and right with a line between, and then double-click the left mouse button. (If a column boundary is not visible, click the left scroll arrow at the left side of the horizontal scroll bar until a column boundary is visible.)

   d. Deselect the data by clicking in any field in the table.
4. Save the database table again by clicking the Save button on the Table Datasheet toolbar.
5. Send the table to the printer by clicking the Print button on the Table Datasheet toolbar.
6. Close the Employees database table and then close the **Premium** database file.

New Record   Delete Record

Maintaining a Database Table

Once a database table is created, more than likely it will require maintenance. For example, newly hired employees will need to be added to the Employees table. A system may be established for deleting an employee record when an employee leaves the company. The type of maintenance required on a database table is related to the type of data stored in the table.

Add a Record to a Table
1. Open database table in Datasheet view.
2. Click New Record button.

Adding a Record to a Table

Add a new record to an existing database table by clicking the New Record button on the Table Datasheet toolbar. Type the data in the appropriate fields and then save the table again.

QUICK STEPS

Delete a Record from a Table
1. Open database table in Datasheet view.
2. Click Delete Record button.

Deleting a Record in a Table

To delete an existing record in a database table, click in any field in the row you want to delete, and then click the Delete Record button on the Table Datasheet toolbar. A message displays telling you that you will not be able to undo the delete operation and asking if you want to continue. At this message, click Yes.

exercise 6

ADDING AND DELETING RECORDS IN THE EMPLOYEES TABLE

1. Open the **Premium** database file and then open the Employees database table.
2. Add two new records to the table by completing the following steps:
   a. Click the New Record button on the Table Datasheet toolbar.
   b. Type the following data in the specified fields:

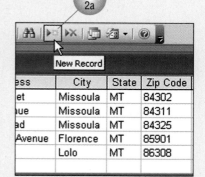

Step 2a

Emp #	=	30020
Last Name	=	Pang
First Name	=	Brian
Middle Initial	=	R.
Street Address	=	15512 Country Drive
City	=	Lolo
State	=	MT
ZIP Code	=	86308
Dept Code	=	IS
Hire Date	=	8/15/2005

   c. Click the New Record button on the Table Datasheet toolbar (or, just press the Tab key).
   d. Type the following data in the specified fields:

Emp #	=	30023
Last Name	=	Zajac
First Name	=	Elizabeth
Middle Initial	=	A.
Street Address	=	423 Corrin Avenue
City	=	Missoula

State	=	MT
ZIP Code	=	84325
Dept Code	=	HR
Hire Date	=	8/15/2005

3. Delete a record in the table by completing the following steps:
   a. Click anywhere in the last name *Guenther*.
   b. Click the Delete Record button on the Table Datasheet toolbar.
   c. At the message telling you that you will not be able to undo the delete operation and asking if you want to continue, click Yes.
4. Click the Save button on the Table Datasheet toolbar to save the Employees table.
5. Print the Employees database table in landscape orientation. (You will need to change to the *Landscape* orientation at the Page Setup dialog box with the Page tab selected.)
6. Close the Employees table and then close the **Premium** database file.

Step 3b

ity	State	Zip Code	Dep
soula	MT	84302	HR
soula	MT	84311	PA
soula	MT	84325	HR
ence	MT	85901	PA
	MT	86308	MS
	MT	86308	IS
soula	MT	84325	HR

Delete Record

Modifying a Table

Maintaining a database table involves adding and/or deleting records as needed. It can also involve adding, moving, changing, or deleting fields in the database table. These types of changes modify the structure of the database table and are done in the Design view. To display a database table in the Design view, open the database table, and then click the down-pointing arrow at the right side of the View button (first button from the left). When you click the down-pointing arrow, a drop-down list displays with two viewing choices—Design View and Datasheet View. Click Design View to change the display of the database table. In the Design view, *Field Name*, *Data Type*, and *Description* display at the top of the window and *Field Properties* displays toward the bottom of the window. In the Design view, you can add fields, remove fields, and change the order of fields.

View

In addition to clicking the down-pointing arrow at the right side of the View button, you can also just click the button. If the current view is the Datasheet view, clicking the button will change to the Design view. If the Design view is the current view, clicking the button will change to the Datasheet view.

Adding a Field

Situations change within a company, and a database table must be flexible to accommodate changes that occur with new situations. Adding a field is a change that may need to be made to an existing database table. For example, more information may be required to manage the data or an additional field may be needed for accounting purposes. Whatever the reason, being able to add a new field to an existing database table is a necessity.

QUICK STEPS

Add a Field to a Table
1. Open database table in Design view.
2. Click in row that will follow the new field.
3. Click Insert Rows button.

Insert   Undo
Rows

QUICK STEPS

Delete a Field from a Table
1. Open database table in Design view.
2. Click in row to be deleted.
3. Click Delete Rows button.

Delete Rows

QUICK STEPS

Use Input Mask
1. Open database table in Design view.
2. Type text in *Field Name* column.
3. Press Tab key.
4. Click Save button.
5. Click in Input Mask text box.
6. Click button containing three black dots.
7. At first Input Mask Wizard dialog box, click desired option.
8. Press Next.
9. At second Input Mask Wizard dialog box, make any desired changes.
10. Click Next.
11. At third Input Mask Wizard dialog box, make any desired changes.
12. Click Next.
13. Click Finish.

Add a row for a new field to an existing database table with a button on the Table Design toolbar, an option from the Insert drop-down menu, or a shortcut menu. To add a row for a new field, position the insertion point on any text in the row that will be immediately *below* the new field, and then click the Insert Rows button on the Table Design toolbar; click Insert and then Rows; or position the insertion point on any text in the row that will be immediately *below* the new field, click the *right* mouse button, and then click the left mouse button on Insert Rows. If you insert a row for a new field and then change your mind, immediately click the Undo button on the Table Design toolbar.

Deleting a Field

Delete a field in a database table and all data entered in that field is also deleted. When a field is deleted it cannot be undone with the Undo button. Delete a field only if you are sure you really want it and the data associated with it completely removed from the database table.

To delete a field, open the database table, and then change to the Design view. Position the insertion point in any text in the row containing the field you want deleted, and then click the Delete Rows button on the Table Design toolbar, or click Edit and then Delete Rows. At the message asking if you want to permanently delete the field and all of the data in the field, click Yes.

Using the Input Mask Wizard

For some fields, you may want to control the data entered in the field. For example, in a *ZIP Code* field, you may want the nine-digit ZIP Code entered (rather than the five-digit ZIP Code); or you may want the three-digit area code included in a telephone number. Use the *Input Mask* field property to set a pattern for how data is entered in a field. An input mask ensures that data in records conforms to a standard format. Access includes an Input Mask Wizard that guides you through creating an input mask.

Use the Input Mask Wizard when assigning a data type to a field. After specifying the *Field Size* in the *Field Properties* section of the Table window, click the *Input Mask* text box. Run the Input Mask Wizard by clicking the button containing the three black dots that appears to the right of the *Input Mask* text box. This displays the first Input Mask Wizard dialog box as shown in Figure 1.14. In the *Input Mask* list box, choose which input mask you want your data to look like, and then click the Next button. At the second Input Mask Wizard dialog box as shown in Figure 1.15, specify the appearance of the input mask and the desired placeholder character, and then click the Next button. At the third Input Mask Wizard dialog, specify whether you want the data stored with or without the symbol in the mask, and then click the Next button. At the fourth dialog box, click the Finish button.

1.14 *First Input Mask Wizard Dialog Box*

Choose the desired input mask from this list box.

1.15 *Second Input Mask Wizard Dialog Box*

Use this option to specify the placeholder character.

Using the Lookup Wizard

Like the Input Mask Wizard, you can use the Lookup Wizard to control the data entered in a field. Use the Lookup Wizard to confine the date entered into a field to a specific list of items. For example, in Exercise 7 you will use the Lookup Wizard to restrict the new *Employee Category* field to one of three choices—*Salaried*, *Hourly*, and *Temporary*. When the user clicks in the field in the datasheet, a down-pointing arrow displays. The user clicks this down-pointing arrow to display a drop-down list of available entries and then clicks the desired item.

QUICK STEPS

Use Lookup Wizard
1. Open table in Design view.
2. Type text in *Field Name* column.
3. Press Tab key.
4. Click down-pointing arrow.
5. Click *Lookup Wizard*.
6. At first Lookup Wizard dialog box, make desired changes.
7. Click Next.
8. At second Lookup Wizard dialog box, click in blank text box.
9. Type desired text.
10. Press Tab key.
11. Continue typing text and pressing Tab until all desired text is entered.
12. Click Next.
13. Click Finish.

Use the Lookup Wizard when assigning a data type to a field. Click in the *Data Type* text box and then click the down-pointing arrow that displays at the right side of the box. At the drop-down menu that displays, click *Lookup Wizard*. This displays the first Lookup Wizard dialog box as shown in Figure 1.16. At this dialog box, indicate that you want to enter the field choices by clicking the *I will type in the values that I want.* option, and then click the Next button. At the second Lookup Wizard dialog box shown in Figure 1.17, click in the blank text box below *Col1* and then type the first choice. Press the Tab key and then type the second choice. Continue in this manner until all desired choices are entered and then click the Next button. At the third Lookup Wizard dialog box, make sure the proper name displays in the *What label would you like for your lookup column?* text box, and then click the Finish button.

FIGURE

1.16 **First Lookup Wizard Dialog Box**

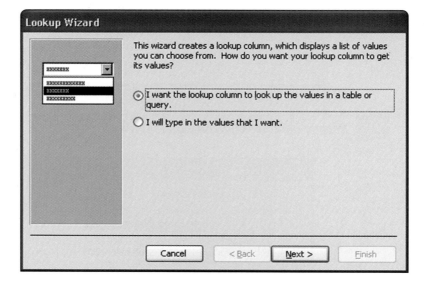

FIGURE

1.17 **Second Lookup Wizard Dialog Box**

Click in this text box, type the first choice, and then press Tab. Continue typing and pressing Tab until all desired text is entered.

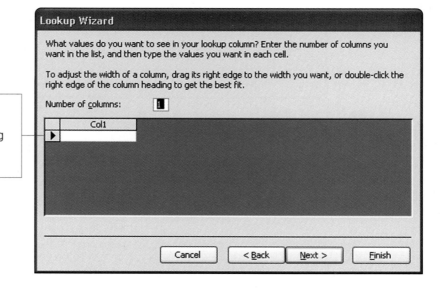

exercise 7

1. Open the **Premium** database file and then open the Employees database table.
2. Add the field *Telephone* to the table by completing the following steps:
   a. Click the down-pointing arrow at the right side of the View button on the Table Datasheet toolbar (first button from the left).
   b. At the drop-down list that displays, click *Design View*.
   c. Click anywhere in the text *Hire Date* that displays in the *Field Name* column. (You may need to scroll down the list to display this field.)
   d. Click the Insert Rows button on the Table Design toolbar.
   e. With the insertion point positioned in the new blank cell in the *Field Name* column, type **Telephone**.

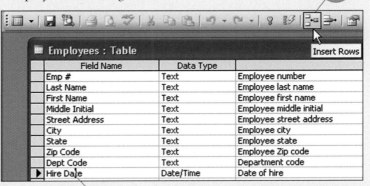

Step 2d

Insert Rows

Field Name	Data Type	
Emp #	Text	Employee number
Last Name	Text	Employee last name
First Name	Text	Employee first name
Middle Initial	Text	Employee middle initial
Street Address	Text	Employee street address
City	Text	Employee city
State	Text	Employee state
Zip Code	Text	Employee Zip code
Dept Code	Text	Department code
Hire Date	Date/Time	Date of hire

Step 2c

   f. Press Tab (this moves the insertion point to the *Data Type* column).
   g. Select *50* that displays in the *Field Size* text box in the *Field Properties* section of the window and then type **14**.
   h. Click the Save button to save the table. (You must save the table before using the Input Mask Wizard.)
   i. Click in the *Input Mask* text box in the *Field Properties* section of the window.
   j. Click the button containing the three black dots that displays to the right of the *Input Mask* text box.

Employees : Table

Field Name	D
Middle Initial	Text
Street Address	Text
City	Text
State	Text
Zip Code	Text
Dept Code	Text
Telephone	Text
Hire Date	Date/

Step 2e

General | Lookup

| Field Size | 14 |
| Format | |

Step 2g

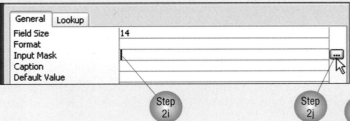

General | Lookup

Field Size	14
Format	
Input Mask	
Caption	
Default Value	

Step 2i   Step 2j   Step 2k

   k. At the first Input Mask Wizard dialog box, make sure *Phone Number* is selected in the *Input Mask* list box, and then click the Next button.

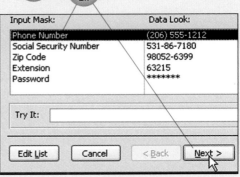

Input Mask:	Data Look:
Phone Number	(206) 555-1212
Social Security Number	531-86-7180
Zip Code	98052-6399
Extension	63215
Password	*******

Try It:

Edit List | Cancel | < Back | Next >

Creating a Database Table

l.   At the second Input Mask Wizard dialog box, click the down-pointing arrow at the right side of the *Placeholder character* text box, and then click # at the drop-down list.

m. Click the Next button.

n.   At the third Input Mask Wizard dialog box, click the *With the symbols in the mask, like this* option.

Step 2n

Step 2l

o.   Click the Next button.

p.   At the fourth Input Mask Wizard dialog box, click the Finish button.

q.   Click in the *Description* column in the *Telephone* row and then type Employee home telephone number.

3.   Delete the *Hire Date* row by completing the following steps:

a.   Click anywhere in the text *Hire Date* that displays in the *Field Name* column.

b.   Click the Delete Rows button on the Table Design toolbar.

Step 3b

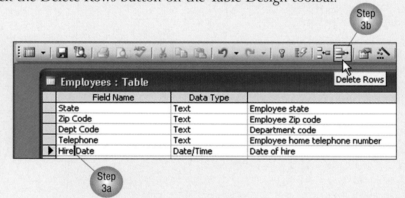

Step 3a

c.   At the message stating that the field will be permanently deleted, click Yes.

4.   Click the Save button on the Table Design toolbar to save the modified table.

5.   Add telephone numbers for the records in the Employees database table by completing the following steps:

a.   Change to the Datasheet view by clicking the down-pointing arrow at the right side of the View button on the Table Design toolbar and then clicking *Datasheet View*.

b.   Drag the scroll box on the horizontal scroll bar to the right until the *Telephone* field is visible.

c.   Position the arrow point at the left side of the first blank cell below the new *Telephone* field until the arrow pointer turns into a thick, white plus symbol and then click the left mouse button. (This selects the entire cell.)

d.   Type 4065556841 and then press the Down Arrow key. (This moves the insertion point to the next blank cell in the *Telephone* column.)

e.   Type 4065557454 and then press the Down Arrow key.

Step 5d

f. Type 4065553495 and then press the Down Arrow key.
g. Type 4065557732 and then press the Down Arrow key.
h. Type 4065550926 and then press the Down Arrow key.
i. Type 4065554509 and then press the Down Arrow key.
6. Click the Save button again on the Table Datasheet toolbar to save the database table.
7. Add the field *Employee Category* and use the Lookup Wizard to specify field choices by completing the following steps:
   a. Change to the Design view by clicking the down-pointing arrow at the right side of the View button on the Table Design toolbar and then clicking *Design View*.
   b. Click anywhere in the text *Dept Code* that displays in the *Field Name* column.
   c. Click the Insert Rows button on the Table Design toolbar.
   d. With the insertion point positioned in the new blank cell in the *Field Name* column, type Employee Category.
   e. Press Tab (this moves the insertion point to the *Data Type* column).
   f. Click the down-pointing arrow at the right side of the text box, and then click *Lookup Wizard* at the drop-down list.

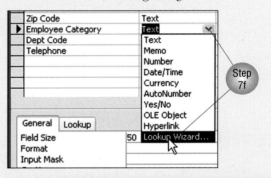

   g. At the first Lookup Wizard dialog box, click the *I will type in the values that I want* option, and then click the Next button.
   h. At the second Lookup Wizard dialog box, click in the blank text box below *Col1*, type Salaried, and then press Tab.
   i. Type Hourly and then press Tab.
   j. Type Temporary.
   k. Click the Next button.
   l. At the third Lookup Wizard dialog box, click the Finish button.

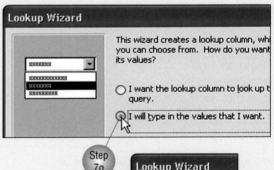

   m. Click in the *Description* column in the *Employee Category* row, and then type Employee category.
8. Click the Save button on the Table Design toolbar.
9. Insert information in the *Employee Category* for the records by completing the following steps:
   a. Change to the Datasheet view by clicking the down-pointing arrow at the right side of the View button on the Table Design toolbar and then clicking *Datasheet View*.
   b. Click in the first blank cell below the new *Employee Category* field.
   c. Click the down-pointing arrow at the right side of the cell and then click *Hourly* at the drop-down list.
   d. Click in next blank cell in the *Employee Category*, click the down-pointing arrow, and then click *Salaried* at the drop-down list.

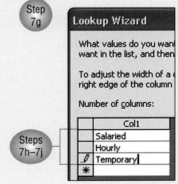

e. Continue entering information in the *Employee Category* by completing similar steps. Type the following in the specified records:

Third record	=	Hourly
Fourth record	=	Hourly
Fifth record	=	Temporary
Sixth record	=	Salaried

10. Click the Save button again on the Table Datasheet toolbar.
11. Print the table in landscape orientation with .5-inch left and right margins. (Change to the *Landscape* orientation at the Page Setup dialog box with the Page tab selected, and then change to .5-inch left and right margins at the Page Setup dialog box with the Margins tab selected. [You must make the changes in this order.])
12. Close the Employees table and then close the **Premium** database file.

Moving a Field

QUICK STEPS

Move a Field
1. Open table in Design view.
2. Select row to be moved.
3. Drag selected row to new position.

You can move a field in a database table to a different location. To do this, open the database table, and then change to the Design view. Position the arrow pointer on the gray button at the left side of the field you want moved until the arrow pointer turns into a right-pointing black arrow, and then click the left mouse button. This selects the entire row. Position the arrow pointer on the gray button at the left side of the selected row until it turns into the normal arrow pointer (white arrow pointing up and to the left). Hold down the left mouse button, drag the arrow pointer with the gray square attached until a thick gray line displays in the desired position, and then release the mouse button.

exercise 8

MOVING AND DELETING FIELDS IN THE EMPLOYEES TABLE

1. Open the **Premium** database file and then open the Employees database table.
2. Move the *Last Name* field immediately below the *Middle Initial* field by completing the following steps:
   a. Click the down-pointing arrow at the right of the View button on the Table Datasheet toolbar, and then click *Design View* at the drop-down list.
   b. Position the arrow pointer on the gray button (this color may vary) at the left side of the *Last Name* field until it turns into a right-pointing black arrow, and then click the left mouse button. (This selects the entire row.)
   c. Position the arrow pointer on the gray button at the left side of the selected row until it turns into the normal arrow pointer (white arrow pointing up and to the left).
   d. Hold down the left mouse button, drag the arrow pointer with the gray square attached until a thick gray line displays between the *Middle Initial* field and the *Street Address* field, and then release the mouse button.
3. Move the *Telephone* field above the *Dept Code* field by completing the following steps:
   a. Select the row containing the *Telephone* field.

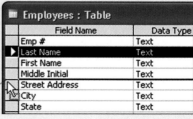

Step 2d

ACCESS

b. Position the arrow pointer on the gray button at the left side of the selected row until it turns into the normal arrow pointer (white arrow pointing up and to the left).

c. Hold down the left mouse button, drag the arrow pointer above the *Dept Code* field, and then release the mouse button.

4. Delete the *Middle Initial* field and the data in the field by completing the following steps:

a. Position the insertion point anywhere in the text *Middle Initial*.

b. Click the Delete Rows button on the Table Design toolbar.

c. At the message asking if you want to permanently delete the field and the data in the field, click Yes.

5. Click the Save button again on the Table Design toolbar to save the database table.

6. Click the View button on the Table Design toolbar to change to the Datasheet view.

7. Print the Employees database table in landscape orientation. (You will need to change to the *Landscape* orientation at the Page Setup dialog box with the Page tab selected.)

8. Close the Employees table and then close the **Premium** database file.

Sorting Records

The Table Datasheet toolbar contains two buttons you can use to sort data in records. Click the Sort Ascending button to sort from lowest to highest (or A-Z) on the field where the insertion point is located. Click the Sort Descending button to sort from highest to lowest (or Z-A).

QUICK STEPS

Sort Records
1. Open table in Datasheet view.
2. Click Sort Ascending button or Sort Descending button.

exercise 9

SORTING RECORDS IN THE EMPLOYEES TABLE

1. Open the **Premium** database file and then open the Employees database table.

2. Sort records in ascending order by city by completing the following steps:

a. Click in any city name in the database table.

b. Click the Sort Ascending button on the Table Datasheet toolbar.

c. Print the Employees database table in landscape orientation.

3. Sort records in descending order by employee number by completing the following steps:

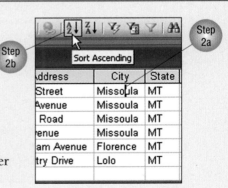

a. Click in any number in the *Emp #* field.
b. Click the Sort Descending button on the Table Datasheet toolbar.
c. Print the Employees database table in landscape orientation.

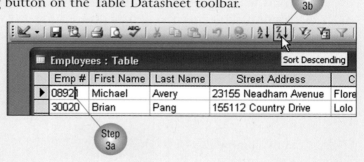

4. Click the Save button to save the database table.
5. Close the Employees table and then close the **Premium** database file.

CHAPTER summary

➤ Microsoft Access is a database management system software program that will organize, store, maintain, retrieve, sort, and print all types of business data.

➤ Organize data in Access in related database tables in a database file.

➤ The first step in organizing data for a database table is determining fields. A field is one piece of information about a person, place, or item. All fields for one unit, such as an employee or customer, are considered a record.

➤ A field name should be unique and describe the contents of the field. It can contain up to 64 characters including letters, numbers, spaces, and some symbols.

➤ Part of the process of designing a database table is assigning a data type to each field, which helps maintain and manage data and helps identify what type of data is expected for the field. Data types include Text, Memo, Number, Currency, Date/Time, AutoNumber, and Yes/No.

➤ When assigning a data type, specific field sizes can be assigned to a field.

➤ Access automatically saves a database file on a periodic basis and also when the database file is closed.

➤ Open a database file when starting Access or open a database file at the Open dialog box.

➤ Enter data in a database table in the Datasheet view. Type data in a field, pressing Tab to move to the next field or pressing Shift + Tab to move to the previous field.

➤ Print a database table by opening the table and then clicking the Print button on the Table Datasheet toolbar.

➤ Change margins in a database table at the Page Setup dialog box with the Margins tab selected.

➤ Change the page orientation and paper size and specify the printer with options at the Page Setup dialog box with the Page tab selected.

➤ Adjust field widths in a database table in the same manner as column widths in an Excel worksheet. Double-click a column boundary to automatically adjust the width to accommodate the longest entry.

➤ Maintaining a database table can include adding and/or deleting records.

➤ Modifying a database table can include adding, moving, or deleting a field.
➤ Use the Input Mask Wizard to set a pattern for how data is entered in a field.
➤ Use the Lookup Wizard to confine data entered in a field to a specific list of items.
➤ Sort records in a database table in ascending order with the Sort Ascending button on the Table Datasheet toolbar or in descending order with the Sort Descending button.

FEATURES summary

FEATURE	BUTTON	MENU	KEYBOARD
New File task pane		File, New	Ctrl + N
Save As dialog box		File, Save As	Ctrl + S
Close table		File, Close	
Open dialog box		File, Open	Ctrl + O
Print dialog box		File, Print	
Send table to printer			Ctrl + P
Page Setup dialog box		File, Page Setup	
Add record to table		Insert, New Record	Ctrl + +
Delete record from table		Edit, Delete Record	
Switch to Design view		View, Design View	
Switch to Datasheet view		View, Datasheet View	
Add a field to a table		Insert, Rows	
Delete a field from a table		Edit, Delete Rows	
Input Mask			
Sort records in Ascending order		Records, Sort, Sort Ascending	
Sort records in Descending order		Records, Sort, Sort Descending	

CONCEPTS check

Completion: On a blank sheet of paper, indicate the correct term, symbol, or number for each description.

1. All fields for one unit, such as a customer, are considered to be this.
2. A field name can contain up to this number of characters.
3. Assign this data type to a field where more than 255 characters are needed.
4. Assign this data type to a field where you do not want calculations rounded off during a calculation.
5. You would probably assign this data type to a field that will contain telephone numbers.
6. In a field assigned the Yes/No data type, a check mark in the box in the field asking a yes/no question signifies this.
7. This view is used in a database table to define field names and assign data types.
8. This is the view used in a database table to enter data in fields.
9. Display this dialog box to change the page orientation.
10. This is the default left and right margin measurements for a database table.
11. Add a new record to a database table in this view.
12. Add a new field to a database table in this view.
13. Use this wizard to set a pattern for how data is entered in a field.
14. Use this wizard to confine data entered in a field to a specific list of items.
15. Click the Sort Ascending button on this toolbar to sort records in ascending order.
16. Suppose you work for an insurance company and have been asked by your supervisor to design a database table to keep track of client claims. This database table should include the following information: client number (assigned in a separate database table), the date of the claim, type of claim, and the amount of claim. Determine the fields you would use in this database table and the data type you would assign to each and write out that information.

SKILLS check

Assessment 1

1. Use Access to create a database file for a store that sells vitamins and other health aids. The database table you create will keep track of what vitamins are ordered for the store. (This table assumes that the database file contains at least two other tables—one table containing information on suppliers and the other containing information on products. You will learn more about how tables are related in Chapter 2.) Use the name of the store, HealthPlus, as the database file name, and name the database table Orders. (The table does not contain a primary key.) Create the following fields in the Orders database table, and assign the data type shown (you determine the Description):

Field Name		Data Type
Order #	=	Text (field size = 3)
Product Code	=	Text (field size = 2)
Supplier #	=	Text (field size = 2)
Date of Order	=	Date/Time
Amount of Order	=	Currency

2. Save the database table and name it Orders.
3. Change to the Datasheet view and then enter the following data:

Order #	=	214
Product Code	=	MT
Supplier #	=	10
Date of Order	=	4/5/2005
Amount of Order	=	$875.50

Order #	=	223
Product Code	=	PA
Supplier #	=	27
Date of Order	=	4/6/2005
Amount of Order	=	$1,005.45

Order #	=	241
Product Code	=	GS
Supplier #	=	10
Date of Order	=	4/8/2005
Amount of Order	=	$441.95

Order #	=	259
Product Code	=	AV
Supplier #	=	18
Date of Order	=	4/8/2005
Amount of Order	=	$772.00

4. Automatically adjust the width of fields.
5. Save the Orders database table again.
6. Print and then close the Orders table.

Assessment 2

1. With the **HealthPlus** database file open, open the Orders table and then add the following records (remember to do this in the Datasheet view):

Order #	=	262
Product Code	=	BC
Supplier #	=	27
Date of Order	=	4/9/2005
Amount of Order	=	$258.65

Order #	=	265
Product Code	=	VC
Supplier #	=	18
Date of Order	=	4/13/2005
Amount of Order	=	$1,103.45

2. Delete the record for order number 241.
3. Save the Orders database table and then print the table with a top margin of 2 inches.
4. Close the Orders database table.

Assessment 3

1. With the **HealthPlus** database file open, create a new table named Suppliers with the following fields and assign the data type shown (you determine the Description):

Field Name		**Data Type**
Supplier #	=	Text (field size = 2)
Supplier Name	=	Text (field size = 20)
Street Address	=	Text (field size = 30)
City	=	Text (field size = 20)
State	=	Text (field size = 2)
ZIP Code	=	Text (field size = 10) Use the Input Mask Wizard to specify a nine-digit ZIP Code. *(Hint: At the first Input Mask Wizard dialog box, click **ZIP Code** in the **Input Mask** list box.)*

2. After creating and saving the database table with the fields shown above, enter the following data in the table (remember to do this in the Datasheet view):

Supplier #	=	10
Supplier Name	=	VitaHealth, Inc.
Street Address	=	12110 South 23rd
City	=	San Diego
State	=	CA
ZIP Code	=	97432-1567
Supplier #	=	18
Supplier Name	=	Mainstream Supplies
Street Address	=	312 Evergreen Building
City	=	Seattle
State	=	WA
ZIP Code	=	98220-2791
Supplier #	=	21
Supplier Name	=	LaVerde Products
Street Address	=	121 Vista Road
City	=	Phoenix
State	=	AZ
ZIP Code	=	86355-6014
Supplier #	=	27
Supplier Name	=	Redding Corporation
Street Address	=	554 Ninth Street
City	=	Portland
State	=	OR
ZIP Code	=	97466-3359

3. Automatically adjust the width of fields.
4. Save the Suppliers database table.
5. Change the page orientation to landscape and then print the table.
6. Close the Suppliers database table.

ACCESS

Assessment 4

1. With the **HealthPlus** database file open, open the Suppliers table.
2. Add the following fields and assign the data type as shown (remember to do this in the Design view):

Field Name		Data Type
Telephone	=	Text (field size = 14) Use the Input Mask Wizard to specify that the area code surrounded by parentheses is to be included in the telephone number.
E-mail Address	=	Text (field size = 30)
Supplier Type	=	Use the Lookup Wizard to create two categories for this field—*Wholesale* and *Retail*

3. Save the table, change to the Datasheet view, and then add the following information in the appropriate row (type the supplier telephone number, e-mail address, and insert the supplier type in the correct row).

Supplier	=	LaVerde Product
Telephone	=	(602) 555-6775
E-mail Address	=	laverdep@emcp.net
Supplier Type	=	*Wholesale*

Supplier	=	VitaHealth, Inc.
Telephone	=	(619) 555-2388
E-mail Address	=	vitahealth@emcp.net
Supplier Type	=	*Retail*

Supplier	=	Redding Corporation
Telephone	=	(503) 555-6679
E-mail Address	=	redding@emcp.net
Supplier Type	=	*Retail*

Supplier	=	Mainstream Supplies
Telephone	=	(206) 555-9005
E-mail Address	=	mainsupplies@emcp.net
Supplier Type	=	*Wholesale*

4. Automatically adjust the width of fields to accommodate the longest entry.
5. Save the Suppliers database table.
6. Change the page orientation to landscape and then print the table. (The table may print on two pages.)
7. Close the Suppliers database table.

Assessment 5

1. With the **HealthPlus** database file open, open the Orders table.
2. Change to the Design view and then move the fields around in the Orders database table so they are displayed in this order:

   Order #
   Date of Order
   Amount of Order
   Product Code
   Supplier #

3. Save the table, change to the Datasheet view, and then sort the records in ascending order by *Supplier #*.
4. Save, print, and then close the Orders database table.
5. Close the **HealthPlus** database file.

CHAPTER challenge

You are the manager of Miles Music Mania, a small music store that specializes in CDs, DVDs, and Laserdiscs. Recently, the small store has increased its volume of merchandise requiring better organization and easier retrieval of information. You decide to create a database named **MilesMusicMania** that contains a table named Inventory with information pertaining to the inventory of CDs, DVDs and Laserdiscs. Create at least five fields, using at least three different data types. Add five records to the table.

As the manager of Miles Music Mania, customers approach you and are interested in learning more about the artists or bands. For quick and reliable answers, you decide to add another field to the Inventory table that includes a hyperlink to the artist's or band's Web site. Use the Help feature to learn more about hyperlink fields. Add a hyperlink field to the Inventory table created in the first part of the Chapter Challenge. Add a hyperlink to at least one of the records in the Inventory table. Save the table again.

Export the Inventory table created in the first part of the Chapter Challenge to Word. Once in Word, the information can be used to create a flyer showing the various types of merchandise sold at Miles Music Mania store. Add additional formatting, graphics, and information in Word. Save the flyer in Word as **MilesMusicManiaFlyer** and then print it.

2

CREATING RELATIONSHIPS BETWEEN DATABASE TABLES

PERFORMANCE OBJECTIVES

Upon successful completion of Chapter 2, you will be able to:
- ➤ **Create a database table with a primary key and a foreign key**
- ➤ **Create a one-to-many relationship between database tables**

ACCESS

Access is a relational database program that allows you to create tables that have a relation or connection to each other within the same database file. In Chapter 1, you created a database table containing information on employees and another containing department information. With Access, you can connect these tables through a common field that appears in both tables.

In this chapter you will learn how to identify a primary key field in a database table that is unique to that table. In Access, data can be divided into logical groupings in database tables for easier manipulation and management. Duplicate information is generally minimized in database tables in the same database file. A link or relationship, however, should connect the database tables. In this chapter, you will define primary keys and define relationships between database tables.

Creating Related Tables

Generally, a database management system fits into one of two categories—either a file management system (also sometimes referred to as a *flat file database*) or a relational database management system. In a file management system, data is stored without indexing and sequential processing. This type of system lacks flexibility in manipulating data and requires the same data to be stored in more than one place.

In a relational database management system, like Access, relationships are defined between sets of data allowing greater flexibility in manipulating data and eliminating data redundancy (entering the same data in more than one place). In exercises in this chapter, you will define relationships between tables in the insurance company database file. Because these tables will be related, information on a client does not need to be repeated in a table on claims filed. If you used a file management system to maintain insurance records, you would need to repeat the client information for each claim filed.

Determining Relationships

Taking time to plan a database file is extremely important. Creating a database file with related tables takes even more consideration. You need to determine how to break down the required data and what tables to create to eliminate redundancies. One idea to help you determine the necessary tables in a database file is to think of the word "about." For example, an insurance company database will probably need a table "about" clients, another "about" the type of coverage, another "about" claims, and so on. A table should be about only one subject, such as a client, customer, department, or supplier.

Along with deciding on the necessary tables for a database file, you also need to determine the relationship between tables. The ability to relate, or "join," tables is part of what makes Access a relational database system. Figure 2.1 illustrates the tables and fields that either are or will become part of the SouthwestInsurance database file. Notice how each table is about only one subject—clients, type of insurance, claims, or coverage.

FIGURE

2.1 *SouthwestInsurance Database Tables*

Clients table

Client #

Client

Street Address

City

State

ZIP Code

Insurance table

License #

Client #

Insurance Code

Uninsured Motorist

Claims table

Claim #

Client #

License #

Date of Claim

Amount of Claim

Coverage table

Insurance Code

Type of Insurance

Some fields such as *Client #*, *License #*, and *Insurance Code* appear in more than one table. These fields are used to create a relationship between tables. For example, in Exercise 2 you will create a relationship between the Clients table and the Insurance table with the *Client #* field.

Creating relationships between tables tells Access how to bring the information in the database file back together again. With relationships defined, you can bring information together to create queries, forms, and reports. (You will learn about these features in future chapters.)

ACCESS

Creating a Primary Field

Before creating a relationship between tables, you need to define the primary key in a table. In a database table, at least one field must be unique so that one record can be distinguished from another. A field (or several fields) with a unique value is considered a *primary key*. When a primary key is defined, Access will not allow duplicate values in the primary field. For example, the *Client #* field in the Clients table must contain a unique number (you would not assign the same client number to two different clients). If you define this as the primary key field, Access will not allow you to type the same client number in two different records.

In a field specified as a primary key, Access expects a value in each record in the database table. This is referred to as *entity integrity*. If a value is not entered in a field, Access actually enters a *null value*. A null value cannot be given to a primary key field. Access will not let you close a database file containing a primary field with a null value.

To define a field as a primary key, open the database table, and then change to the Design view. Position the insertion point somewhere in the row containing the field you want as the primary key, and then click the Primary Key button on the Table Design toolbar. An image of a key is inserted at the beginning of the row identified as the primary key field. To define more than one field as a primary key, select the rows containing the fields you want as primary keys, and then click the Primary Key button on the Table Design toolbar.

Creating a Foreign Key

A primary key field in one table may be a foreign key in another. For example, if you define the *Client #* field in the Clients table as the primary key, the *Client #* field in the Insurance table will then be considered a *foreign key*. The primary key field and the foreign key field form a relationship between the two tables. In the Clients table, each entry in the *Client #* field will be unique (it is the primary key), but the same client number may appear more than once in the *Client #* field in the Insurance table (such as a situation where a client has insurance on more than one vehicle).

Each table in Figure 2.1 contains a unique field that will be defined as the primary key. Figure 2.2 identifies the primary keys and also foreign keys.

Specify a Primary Key
1. Open table in design view.
2. Click desired field.
3. Click Primary Key button.
4. Click Save button.

HINT

You must enter a value in the primary key field in every record.

Primary Key

FIGURE

| 2.2 | ***Primary and Foreign Keys*** |

Clients table
Client # *(primary key)*
Client
Street Address
City
State
ZIP Code

Insurance table
License # *(primary key)*
Client # *(foreign key)*
Insurance Code *(foreign key)*
Uninsured Motorist

Continued on next page

Claims table
Claim # *(primary key)*
Client # *(foreign key)*
License # *(foreign key)*
Date of Claim
Amount of Claim

Coverage table
Insurance Code *(primary key)*
Type of Insurance

In Exercise 1, you will create another table for the SouthwestInsurance database file, enter data, and then define primary keys for the tables. In the section following Exercise 1, you will learn how to create relationships between the tables.

exercise 1

CREATING A TABLE AND DEFINING PRIMARY KEYS

(Note: Delete from your disk any database files you created in Chapter 1. In Step 1, you will copy the SouthwestInsurance database file from the CD that accompanies this textbook to your disk. You will then remove the read-only attribute from the SouthwestInsurance database file on your disk. You need to remove this attribute before you can make changes to the database file.)

1. Copy the **SouthwestInsurance** database file on the CD that accompanies this textbook to your disk, remove the read-only attribute, and then open the database file by completing the following steps:
    a. Insert the CD that accompanies this textbook into the drive.
    b. Copy the **SouthwestInsurance** database file from the CD to your disk.
    c. Remove the read-only attribute from the **SouthwestInsurance** database located on your disk by completing the following steps:
        1) In Access, display the Open dialog box with the drive active containing your disk.
        2) Click once on the **SouthwestInsurance** database file name.
        3) Click the Tools button on the Open dialog box toolbar, and then click Properties at the drop-down menu.
        4) At the SouthwestInsurance Properties dialog box with the General tab selected, click *Read-only* in the *Attributes* section to remove the check mark.
        5) Click OK to close the SouthwestInsurance Properties dialog box.

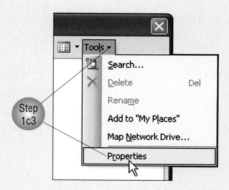

Step 1c3

    d. Open the **SouthwestInsurance** database file.
2. At the SouthwestInsurance : Database window, create a new table by completing the following steps:
    a. Double-click *Create table in Design view* in the list box.
    b. At the Table1 : Table window, type the fields, assign the data types, and type the descriptions as shown below (for assistance, refer to Chapter 1, Exercise 1):

Field Name	Data Type	Description
License #	Text (Field Size = 7)	Vehicle license number
Client #	Text (Field Size = 4)	Client number
Insurance Code	Text (Field Size = 1)	Insurance code
Uninsured Motorist	Yes/No	Uninsured motorist coverage

(Note: To create the Yes/No data type for the **Uninsured Motorist** *field, click the down-pointing arrow at the right side of the* **Data Type** *field, and then click* **Yes/No** *at the drop-down list.)*

c. Specify the *License #* as the primary key by completing the following steps:
   1) Click anywhere in the text *License #* (in the top row).
   2) Click the Primary Key button on the Table Design toolbar.

d. Save the database table by completing the following steps:
   1) Click the Save button on the Table Design toolbar.
   2) At the Save As dialog box, type **Insurance** in the *Table Name* text box, and then press Enter or click OK.

e. Close the Insurance table by clicking File and then Close or by clicking the Close button located in the upper right corner of the window.

3. Define primary keys for the other tables in the database file by completing the following steps:
   a. At the SouthwestInsurance : Database window, double-click *Claims* in the list box.
   b. With the Claims table open, click the View button on the Table Datasheet toolbar to switch to the Design view.
   c. Click anywhere in the text *Claim #,* and then click the Primary Key button on the Table Design toolbar.
   d. Click the Save button on the Table Design toolbar.
   e. Close the Claims table.
   f. At the SouthwestInsurance : Database window, double-click *Clients* in the list box.
   g. With the Clients table open, click the View button on the Table Datasheet toolbar to switch to the Design view.
   h. Click anywhere in the text *Client #,* and then click the Primary Key button on the Table Design toolbar.
   i. Click the Save button on the Table Design toolbar.
   j. Close the Clients table.
   k. At the SouthwestInsurance : Database window, double-click *Coverage* in the list box.
   l. With the Coverage table open, click the View button on the Table Datasheet toolbar to switch to the Design view.

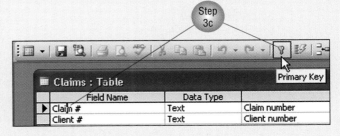

m. Click anywhere in the text *Insurance Code* and then click the Primary Key button on the Table Design toolbar.

n. Click the Save button on the Table Design toolbar.

o. Close the Coverage table.

4. Open the Insurance table and then type the following data in the specified fields: (If the *Uninsured Motorist* field is Yes, insert a check mark in the field by pressing the spacebar. If the field is No, leave the check box blank.)

Field Name	Data Type	
Insurance Code	Text	Insurance code
Type of Insurance	Text	Type of insurance

Coverage : Table — Step 3m — Primary Key

License #	=	341 VIT
Client #	=	3120
Insurance Code	=	F
Uninsured Motorist	=	Yes

License #	=	776 ERU
Client #	=	9383
Insurance Code	=	F
Uninsured Motorist	=	No

License #	=	984 CWS
Client #	=	7335
Insurance Code	=	L
Uninsured Motorist	=	Yes

License #	=	877 BNN
Client #	=	4300
Insurance Code	=	L
Uninsured Motorist	=	Yes

License #	=	310 YTV
Client #	=	3120
Insurance Code	=	F
Uninsured Motorist	=	Yes

5. Save and then close the Insurance table.

6. Close the **SouthwestInsurance** database file.

 Step 4

Insurance : Table

License #	Client #	Insurance Code	Uninsured Moto
341 VIT	3120	F	☑
776 ERU	9383	F	☐
984 CWS	7335	L	☑
877 BNN	4300	L	☑
310 YTV	3120	F	☑
*			☐

HINT

Defining a relationship between database tables is one of the most powerful features of a relational database management system.

Establishing a Relationship between Tables

In Access, one database table can be related to another, which is generally referred to as performing a *join*. When database tables with a common field are joined, data can be extracted from both tables as if they were one large table. Another reason for relating tables is to ensure the integrity of the data. For example, in Exercise 2, you will create a relationship between the Clients database table and the Claims database table. The relationship that is established will ensure that a client cannot be entered in the Claims database table without first being entered in the Clients database table. This ensures that a claim is not processed on a person who is not a client of the insurance company. This type of relationship is called a one-to-many relationship, which means that one record in the Clients table will match zero, one, or many records in the Claims database table.

In a one-to-many relationship, the table containing the "one" is referred to as the **primary table** and the table containing the "many" is referred to as the **related table**. Access follows a set of rules known as **referential integrity**, which enforces consistency between related tables. These rules are enforced when data is updated in related database tables. The referential integrity rules ensure that a record added to a related table has a matching record in the primary table.

Creating a One-to-Many Relationship

A relationship is specified between existing tables in a database file. To create a one-to-many relationship, you would complete these basic steps:

1. Open the database file containing the tables to be related.

2. Click the Relationships button that displays at the right side of the Database toolbar; or click Tools and then Relationships. This displays the Show Table dialog box, as shown in Figure 2.3.

3. At the Show Table dialog box, each table that will be related must be added to the Relationships window. To do this, click the first database table name to be included, and then click Add. Continue in this manner until all necessary database table names have been added to the Relationships window and then click the Close button.

4. At the Relationships window, such as the one shown in Figure 2.4, use the mouse to drag the common field from the primary table (the "one") to the related table (the "many"). This causes the Edit Relationships dialog box to display as shown in Figure 2.5.

5. At the Edit Relationships dialog box, check to make sure the correct field name displays in the *Table/Query* and *Related Table/Query* list boxes and the relationship type at the bottom of the dialog box displays as *One-To-Many*.

6. Specify the relationship options by choosing *Enforce Referential Integrity*, as well as *Cascade Update Related Fields* and/or *Cascade Delete Related Records*. (These options are explained in the text after these steps.)

7. Click the Create button. This causes the Edit Relationships dialog box to close and the Relationships window to display showing the relationship between the tables. In Figure 2.6, the Clients box displays with a black line attached along with the number *1* (signifying the "one" side of the relationship). The black line is connected to the Claims box along with the infinity symbol ∞ (signifying the "many" side of the relationship). The black line, called the **join line**, is thick at both ends if the enforce referential integrity option has been chosen. If this option is not chosen, the line is thin at both ends.

8. Click the Save button on the Relationship toolbar to save the relationship.

9. Close the Relationships window by clicking the Close button that displays at the right side of the Title bar.

Relationships

2.3 *Show Table Dialog Box*

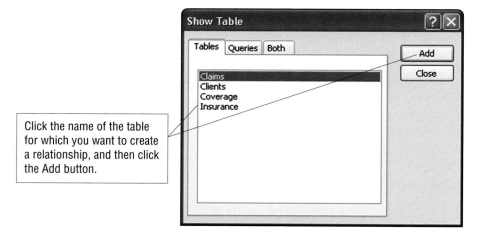

Show Table ? X

Tables | Queries | Both   Add

Claims   Close
Clients
Coverage
Insurance

> Click the name of the table
> for which you want to create
> a relationship, and then click
> the Add button.

FIGURE

2.4 *Relationships Window*

Relationships

> Insert in the
> Relationships
> window those
> tables for which
> you will create
> a relationship.

Clients
Client #
Client
Street Address
City
State

Claims
Claim #
Client #
License #
Date of Claim
Amount of Claim

Insurance
License #
Client #
Insurance Code
Uninsured Motoris

Coverage
Insurance Code
Type of Insuranc

2.5 *Edit Relationships Dialog Box*

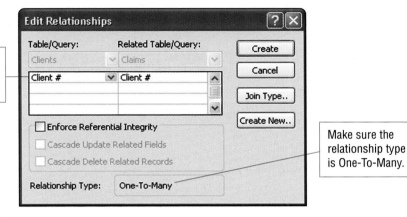

Make sure the correct field names display here.

Make sure the relationship type is One-To-Many.

2.6 *One-to-Many Relationship*

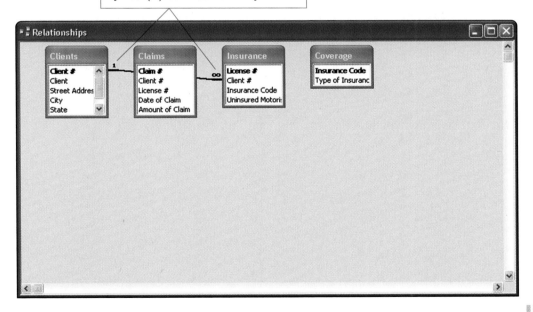

This is an example of a one-to-many relationship where 1 identifies the "one" side of the relationship and the infinity symbol (∞) identifies the "many" side.

Specifying Referential Integrity

In Step 6, the referential integrity of the relationship was established. Choose *Enforce Referential Integrity* at the Edit Relationships dialog box to ensure that the relationships between records in related tables are valid. Referential integrity can be set if the field from the primary table is a primary key and the related fields have the same data type. When referential integrity is established, a value for the primary key must first be entered in the primary table before it can be entered in the related table.

H I N T
Referential integrity makes sure that a record exists in the "one" database table before the record can be entered in the "many" database table.

If you select only *Enforce Referential Integrity* and the related table contains a record, you will not be able to change a primary key value or delete a primary key value in the primary table. If you choose *Cascade Update Related Fields*, you will be able to change a primary key value in the primary table and Access will automatically update the matching value in the related table. Choose *Cascade Delete Related Records* and you will be able to delete a record in the primary table and Access will delete any related records in the related table.

QUICK STEPS

Print Database Relationships
1. Open database.
2. Click Relationships button.
3. Click File, Print Relationships.
4. Click Print button.
5. Click Close button.

Print

Printing Database Relationships

Access contains a Print Relationships Wizard you can use to print a report displaying the relationships between tables. To print a report of relationships between tables in a database file, you would complete these steps:

1. Open the database.
2. Display the Relationships window by clicking the Relationships button on the Database toolbar.
3. At the Relationships window, click File and then Print Relationships. (This displays the Relationships report in Print Preview.)
4. Click the Print button on the Print Preview toolbar to send the report to the printer.
5. Click the Close button to close Print Preview.

Relating Tables in the SouthwestInsurance Database File

The SouthwestInsurance database file contains the four tables shown in Figure 2.1. Each table contains data about something—clients, insurance, claims, and coverage. You can relate these tables so that data can be extracted from more than one table as if they were all one large table. The relationships between the tables are identified in Figure 2.7.

FIGURE

2.7 *Relationships between SouthwestInsurance Database Tables*

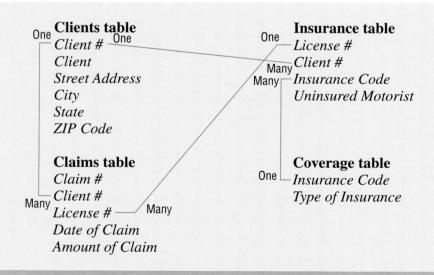

In the relationships shown in Figure 2.7, notice how the primary key is identified as the "one" and the foreign key is identified as the "many." Relate these tables so you can extract information from more than one table. For example, you can design a report about claims that contains information on claims as well as information on the clients submitting the claims.

exercise **2**

CREATING A ONE-TO-MANY RELATIONSHIP BETWEEN TWO DATABASE TABLES

1. Create a one-to-many relationship between the Clients table and the Claims table by completing the following steps:
   a. Open the **SouthwestInsurance** database file.
   b. Click the Relationships button that displays toward the right side of the Database toolbar.

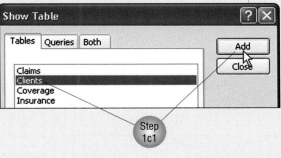

   c. At the Show Table dialog box, add the Clients and Claims tables to the Relationships window by completing the following steps:
      1) Click *Clients* in the list box and then click Add.
      2) Click *Claims* in the list box and then click Add.
   d. Click the Close button to close the Show Table dialog box.
   e. At the Relationships window, drag the *Client #* field from the Clients table to the Claims table by completing the following steps:
      1) Position the arrow pointer on the *Client #* field that displays in the Clients box.
      2) Hold down the left mouse button, drag the arrow pointer (with a field icon attached) to the *Client #* field in the *Claims* box, and then release the mouse button. (This causes the Edit Relationships dialog box to display.)

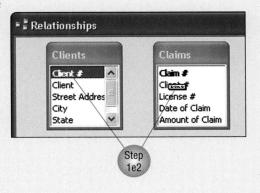

   f. At the Edit Relationships dialog box, make sure *Client #* displays in the *Table/Query* and *Related Table/Query* list boxes and the relationship type at the bottom of the dialog box displays as *One-To-Many*.
   g. Enforce the referential integrity of the relationship by completing the following steps:

1) Click *Enforce Referential Integrity*. (This makes the other two options available.)
2) Click *Cascade Update Related Fields*.
3) Click *Cascade Delete Related Records*.

h. Click the Create button. (This causes the Edit Relationships dialog box to close and the Relationships window to display showing a thick black line connecting Clients to Claims. At the Clients side, a *1* will appear and an infinity symbol ∞ will display at the Claims side of the thick black line.)

i. Click the Save button on the Relationship toolbar to save the relationship.

j. Print the relationships by completing the following steps:
1) At the Relationships window, click File and then Print Relationships. (This displays the Relationships report in Print Preview.)
2) Click the Print button on the Print Preview toolbar.
3) Click the Close button to close Print Preview.
4) At the Report dialog box, click the Close button (contains an *X*) located in the upper right corner of the dialog box.
5) At the message asking if you want to save changes to the design of the report, click No.

k. Close the Relationships window by clicking the Close button that displays at the right side of the Title bar.

2. Close the **SouthwestInsurance** database file.

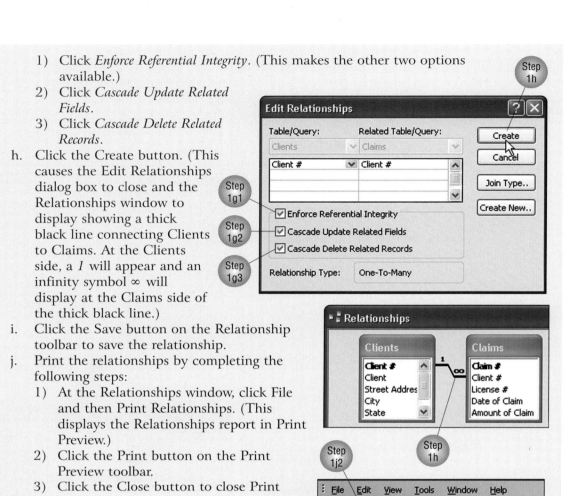

Once a relationship has been established between tables, clicking the Relationships button causes the Relationships window to display (rather than the Show Table dialog box). To create additional relationships, click Relationships on the Menu bar and then click Show Table. This displays the Show Table dialog box where you can specify the tables you need for creating another relationship.

exercise 3

1. Open the **SouthwestInsurance** database file.
2. Create a one-to-many relationship between the Clients table and the Insurance table by completing the following steps:

    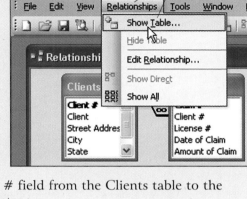

    a. Click the Relationships button that displays toward the right side of the Database toolbar.

    b. At the Relationships window, click Relationships on the Menu bar and then click Show Table at the drop-down menu.

    c. At the Show Table dialog box, click *Insurance* in the list box, and then click the Add button. (You do not need to add the Clients table because it was added in Exercise 2.)

    d. Click the Close button to close the Show Table dialog box.

    e. At the Relationships window, drag the *Client #* field from the Clients table to the Insurance table by completing the following steps:

       1) Position the arrow pointer on the *Client #* field that displays in the Clients box.

       2) Hold down the left mouse button, drag the arrow pointer (with a field icon attached), to the *Client # field in the Insurance box, and then release the mouse button. (This causes the Edit Relationships dialog box to display.)

    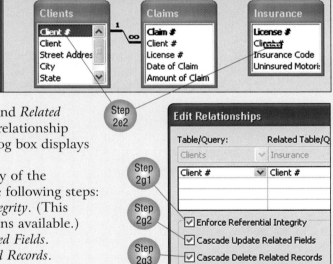

    f. At the Edit Relationships dialog box, make sure *Client # displays in the *Table/Query* and *Related Table/Query* list boxes and the relationship type at the bottom of the dialog box displays as *One-To-Many*.

    g. Enforce the referential integrity of the relationship by completing the following steps:

       1) Click *Enforce Referential Integrity*. (This makes the other two options available.)

       2) Click *Cascade Update Related Fields*.

       3) Click *Cascade Delete Related Records*.

    h. Click the Create button. (This causes the Edit Relationships dialog box to close and the Relationships window to display showing a thick black line connecting Clients to Insurance. At the Clients side, a *1* will appear and an infinity symbol ∞ will display at the Insurance side of the thick black line.)

    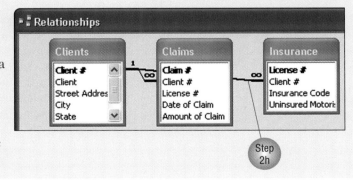

i. Click the Save button on the Relationship toolbar to save the relationship.
j. With the Relationships window still open, create the following one-to-many relationships by completing steps similar to those in Steps 2b through 2i:

1) Create a relationship between *License #* in the Insurance table and the Claims table. (*License #* in the Insurance table is the "one" and *License #* in the Claims table is the "many.") At the Edit Relationships dialog box, be sure to choose *Enforce Referential Integrity*, *Cascade Update Related Fields*, and *Cascade Delete Related Records*.

2) Add the Coverage table to the Relationships window and then create a relationship between *Insurance Code* in the Coverage table and the Insurance table. (*Insurance Code* in the Coverage table is the "one" and *Insurance Code* in the Insurance table is the "many.") At the Edit Relationships dialog box, be sure to choose *Enforce Referential Integrity*, *Cascade Update Related Fields*, and *Cascade Delete Related Records*.

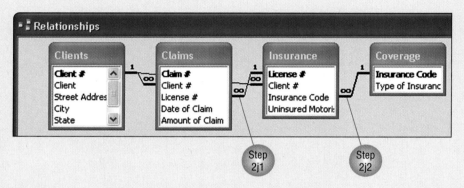

k. Click the Save button on the Relationship toolbar.
l. Print the relationships by completing the following steps:

1) At the Relationships window, click File and then Print Relationships. (This displays the Relationships report in Print Preview.)
2) Click the Print button on the Print Preview toolbar.
3) Click the Close button to close Print Preview.
4) At the Report dialog box, click the Close button (contains an *X*) located in the upper right corner of the dialog box.
5) At the message asking if you want to save changes to the design of the report, click No.

m. Close the Relationships window by clicking the Close button that displays at the right side of the Title bar.

3. Close the **SouthwestInsurance** database file.

In the relationship established in Exercise 2, a record must first be added to the Clients table before a related record can be added to the Claims table. This is because you chose the *Enforce Referential Integrity* option at the Edit Relationships dialog box. Because you chose the two options *Cascade Update Related Fields* and *Cascade Delete Related Records*, records in the Clients table (the primary table) can be updated and/or deleted and related records in the Claims table (related table) will automatically be updated or deleted.

exercise 4

1. Open the **SouthwestInsurance** database file.
2. Open the Clients table.
3. Change two client numbers in the Clients database (Access will automatically change it in the Claims table) by completing the following steps:
   a. Make sure the Clients : Table window displays in the Datasheet view.
   b. Click once in the *Client #* field for Paul Vuong containing the number *4300*.
   c. Change the number from *4300* to *4308*.
   d. Click once in the *Client #* field for Vernon Cook containing the number *7335*.
   e. Change the number from *7335* to *7325*.
   f. Click the Save button on the Table Datasheet toolbar.
   g. Close the Clients table.
   h. Open the Claims table. (Notice that the client numbers for Vernon Cook and Paul Vuong automatically changed.)
   i. Close the Claims table.
4. Open the Clients table, make sure the table displays in Datasheet view, and then add the following records at the end of the table:

Clients : Table (Step 3c / Step 3e)

	Client #	Client
+	3120	Spenser Winters
+	4308	Paul Vuong
+	7325	Vernon Cook
+	9383	Elaine Hueneka
*		

Claims : Table (Step 3h)

	Claim #	Client #	License #
▶	102394	9383	776 ERU
	104366	7325	984 CWS
	121039	4308	877 BNN
	153001	9383	776 ERU
*			

Client #	=	5508
Client	=	Martina Bentley
Street Address	=	6503 Taylor Street
City	=	Scottsdale
State	=	AZ
ZIP Code	=	85889

Client #	=	2511
Client	=	Keith Hammond
Street Address	=	21332 Janski Road
City	=	Glendale
State	=	AZ
ZIP Code	=	85310

Clients : Table (Step 4)

	Client #	Client	Street Address	City	State	Zip Code
+	3120	Spenser Winters	21329 132nd Street	Glendale	AZ	85310
+	4308	Paul Vuong	3451 South Varner	Glendale	AZ	85901
+	7325	Vernon Cook	22134 Cactus Drive	Phoenix	AZ	85344
+	9383	Elaine Hueneka	9088 Graham Road	Scottsdale	AZ	85889
+	5508	Martina Bentley	6503 Taylor Street	Scottsdale	AZ	85889
+	2511	Keith Hammond	21332 Janski Road	Glendale	AZ	85310
*						

5. With the Clients table still open, delete the record for Elaine Hueneka. At the message telling you that relationships that specify cascading deletes are about to cause records in this table and related tables to be deleted, click Yes.

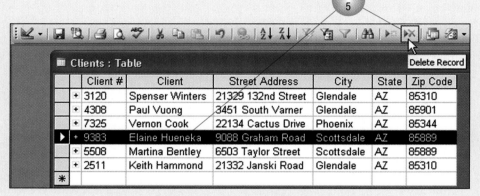

6. Save, print, and then close the Clients table.
7. Open the Insurance table, make sure the table displays in Datasheet view, and then add the following records at the end of the table:

License #	=	422 RTW
Client #	=	5508
Insurance Code	=	L
Uninsured Motorist	=	Yes

License #	=	130 YWR
Client #	=	5508
Insurance Code	=	F
Uninsured Motorist	=	No

License #	=	795 GRT
Client #	=	2511
Insurance Code	=	L
Uninsured Motorist	=	Yes

Insurance : Table

	License #	Client #	Insurance Code	Uninsured Moto
+	310 YTV	3120	F	☑
+	341 VIT	3120	F	☑
+	877 BNN	4308	L	☑
+	984 CWS	7325	L	☑
+	422 RTW	5508	L	☑
+	130 YWR	5508	F	☐
+	795 GRT	2511	L	☑
*				☐

Step 7

8. Save, print, and then close the Insurance table.

9. Open the Claims table, make sure the table displays in Datasheet view, and then add the following record:

Claim #	= 130057
Client #	= 2511
License #	= 795 GRT
Date of Claim	= 3/4/2005
Amount of Claim	= $186.40

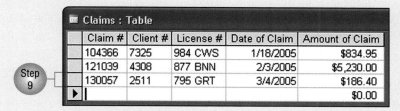

	Claim #	Client #	License #	Date of Claim	Amount of Claim
	104366	7325	984 CWS	1/18/2005	$834.95
	121039	4308	877 BNN	2/3/2005	$5,230.00
Step 9	130057	2511	795 GRT	3/4/2005	$186.40
▶					$0.00

10. Save and then print the Claims table.
11. With the Claims table still open, try to enter a record for a client who has not been entered in the Clients table by completing the following steps (Access will not allow this because of the one-to-many relationship that was established in Exercise 2):
    a. Add the following record to the Claims table:

Claim #	= 201221
Client #	= 5824
License #	= 640 TRS
Date of Claim	= 3/11/2005
Amount of Claim	= $895.25

    b. Click the Save button on the Table Datasheet toolbar.
    c. Click the Close button to close the Claims table. This causes a message to display telling you that the record cannot be added or changed because a related record is required in the Clients table. At this message, click OK.
    d. A message displays warning you that Access cannot save the table, that closing the object will cause the data changes you made to be lost, and asking if you want to close the database object. At this warning, click Yes.
12. Close the **SouthwestInsurance** database file.

Editing and Deleting a Relationship

Changes can be made to a relationship that has been established between database tables. The relationship can also be deleted. To edit a relationship, open the database file containing the tables with the relationship, and then click the Relationships button on the Database toolbar; or click Tools and then Relationships. This displays the Relationships window with the related database tables displayed in boxes. Position the arrow pointer on the thin portion of one of the black lines that connects the related tables and then click the *right* mouse button. This causes a shortcut menu to display. At this shortcut menu, click the left mouse button on Edit Relationship. This displays the Edit Relationships dialog box such as the one shown in Figure 2.5, where you can change the current relationship.

QUICK STEPS

Edit a Relationship
1. Open database file.
2. Click Relationships button.
3. Right-click on black line connecting related tables.
4. Click Edit Relationship.
5. At Edit Relationship dialog box, make desired changes.
6. Click OK.

To delete a relationship between tables, display the related tables in the Relationships window. Position the arrow pointer on the thin portion of the black line connecting the related tables, and then click the *right* mouse button. At the shortcut menu that displays, click the left mouse button on Delete. At the message asking if you are sure you want to permanently delete the selected relationship from your database, click Yes.

QUICK
STEPS

Delete a Relationship
1. Open database file.
2. Click Relationships button.
3. Right-click on black line connecting related tables.
4. Click Delete.
5. Click Yes.

Displaying Related Records in a Subdatasheet

When a relationship is established between tables, you can view and edit fields in related tables with a subdatasheet. Figure 2.8 displays the Clients database table with the subdatasheet displayed for the client Spenser Winters. The subdatasheet displays the fields in the Insurance table related to Spenser Winters. Use this subdatasheet to view information and also to edit information in the Clients table a well as the Insurance table. Changes made to fields in a subdatasheet affect the table and any related table.

A plus symbol (+) displays before each record in the Clients table shown in Figure 2.8. Access automatically inserts plus symbols before each record in a table that is joined to another table by a one-to-many relationship.

FIGURE

2.8 **Table with Subdatasheet Displayed**

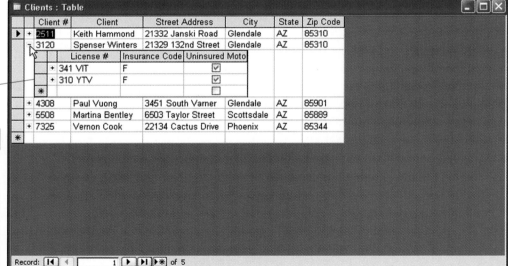

Subdatasheet

QUICK
STEPS

Display Subdatasheet
1. Open database table in Datasheet view.
2. Click plus symbol at left of desired record.
3. At Insert Subdatasheet dialog box, click desired table.
4. Click OK.

To create a subdatasheet, display the table that is the "one" in the one-to-many relationship. Click the plus symbol preceding the record for which you want to display fields in a related table. This displays the Insert Subdatasheet dialog box shown in Figure 2.9. At this dialog box, click the desired table in the list box, and then click OK. The subdatasheet is inserted below the record and contains fields from the related table. To remove the subdatasheet, click the minus sign preceding the record. (The plus symbol turns into the minus symbol when a subdatasheet displays.)

2.9   Insert Subdatasheet Dialog Box

Specify a different subdatasheet in a table by clicking the Insert option on the Menu bar and then clicking Subdatasheet. This displays the Insert Subdatasheet dialog box shown in Figure 2.9 where you can specify the desired table.

exercise 5

VIEWING AND EDITING A SUBDATASHEET

1. Open the **SouthwestInsurance** database file.
2. Open the Clients table.
3. Display a subdatasheet with fields in the Claims table by completing the following steps:
    a. Click the plus symbol that displays at the left side of the first row (the row for Keith Hammond).
    b. At the Insert Subdatasheet dialog box, click *Claims* in the list box, and then click OK.

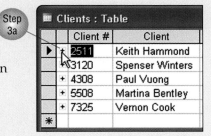

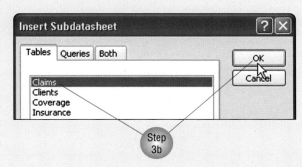

4. Display subdatasheets for each of the remaining records by clicking the plus symbol that displays before each of the remaining four rows.

5. Remove subdatasheets for each record by clicking the minus symbol that displays before each record.

6. Suppose that the client, Vernon Cook, has moved to a new address and purchased insurance for a new car. Display the Insurance subdatasheet and make changes to fields in the Clients table and the Insurance table by completing the following steps:

   a. Click Insert on the Menu bar, and then click Subdatasheet at the drop-down menu.

   b. At the Insert Subdatasheet dialog box, click *Insurance* in the list box, and then click OK.

   c. Click the plus symbol at the beginning of the row for Vernon Cook.

   d. Change his street address from *22135 Cactus Drive* to *1230 South Mesa*.

   e. Change his ZIP Code from *85344* to *86201*.

   f. Add the following information in the second row in the Insurance subdatasheet:

License #	= **430 DWT**
Insurance Code	= **F**
Uninsured Motorist	= **Yes**

   g. Click the Save button on the Table Datasheet toolbar.

   h. Close the Clients table.

7. Open the Clients table, print it, and then close it.

8. Open the Insurance table, print it, and then close it.

9. Close the **SouthwestInsurance** database table.

Step 6a

| | File | Edit | View | Insert | Format | Records | Tc |

Insert drop-down menu:
New Record Ctrl++
Column
Lookup Column...
Hyperlink Column
Subdatasheet...
Object...
Hyperlink... Ctrl+K

Clients : Ta

		Client #
▶	+	2511
	+	3120
	+	4308
	+	5508
	+	7325	Vernon Cook	22134 Ca
*		

Step 6d Step 6e

Clients : Table

		Client #	Client	Street Address	City	State	Zip Code
	+	2511	Keith Hammond	21332 Janski Road	Glendale	AZ	85310
	+	3120	Spenser Winters	21329 132nd Street	Glendale	AZ	85310
	+	4308	Paul Vuong	3451 South Varner	Glendale	AZ	85901
	+	5508	Martina Bentley	6503 Taylor Street	Scottsdale	AZ	85889
▶	-	7325	Vernon Cook	1230 South Mesa	Phoenix	AZ	86201

		License #	Insurance Code	Uninsured Moto
	+	984 CWS	L	☑
⬚	+	430 DWT	F	☑
*				☐

Step 6f

CHAPTER summary

➤ Access is a relational database software program where database tables can be created that have a relation or connection to one another.

➤ When planning a database table, take time to determine how to break down the required data and what relationships will need to be defined to eliminate data redundancies.

➤ In a database table there must be at least one field that is unique so that one record can be distinguished from another. A field with a unique value is considered a primary key.

➤ In a field defined as a primary key, duplicate values are not allowed in the primary field and Access also expects a value in each record in the primary key field.

➤ Define a primary key field with the Primary Key button on the Table Design toolbar.

➤ A primary key field included in another database table is referred to as a foreign key. Unlike a primary key field, a foreign key field can contain duplicate data.

➤ In Access, one database table can be related to another by performing a join. When database tables that have a common field are joined, data can be extracted from both tables as if they were one large table.

➤ A one-to-many relationship can be created between database tables in a database file. In this relationship, a record must be added to the "one" database table before it can be added to the "many" database table.

➤ A relationship between tables can be edited and/or deleted.

➤ Access contains a Print Relationships Wizard you can use to print a report displaying the relationships between tables.

➤ When a relationship is established between tables, you can view and edit fields in related tables with a subdatasheet.

➤ To display a subdatasheet, display the Insert Subdatasheet dialog box (by clicking the plus symbol at the beginning of a record or by clicking Insert and then Subdatasheet), click the desired table in the list box, and then click OK.

➤ Turn off the display of a subdatasheet by clicking the minus symbol at the beginning of a record.

FEATURES summary

FEATURE	BUTTON	MENU
Identify primary key	🔑	Edit, Primary Key
Relationships window	▤	Tools, Relationships
Edit Relationships dialog box		Relationships, Edit Relationships
Show Table dialog box		Relationships, Show Table
Print database relationships		File, Print Relationships, Print
Insert Subdatasheet dialog box		Insert, Subdatasheet

CONCEPTS check

Completion: On a blank sheet of paper, indicate the correct term, symbol, or character for each description.

1. A primary key field must contain unique data while this type of key field can contain duplicate data.
2. In Access, one database can be related to another, which is generally referred to as performing this.
3. In a one-to-many relationship, the table containing the "one" is referred to as this.
4. In a one-to-many relationship, the table containing the "many" is referred to as this.
5. In a one-to-many relationship, Access follows a set of rules that enforces consistency between related tables and is referred to as this.
6. In related tables, this number displays near the black line next to the primary table.
7. In related tables, this symbol displays near the black line next to the related table.
8. The black line that connects related tables is referred to as this.
9. Click this symbol at the beginning of a record in a related table to display the Insert Subdatasheet dialog box.
10. Turn off the display of a subdatasheet by clicking this symbol that displays at the beginning of the record.
11. Suppose you have created a database table named Committees within the database file named Members. The Committees table contains a field named *Member #* that you decide should be identified as the primary key field. List the steps you would complete to identify *Member #* as the primary key field (you are beginning at a blank Access screen).
12. List the steps you would complete to create a one-to-many relationship between the Member Information table and the Committees table in the Members database file. The primary key field in the Member Information table is *Member #*. (You are beginning at the Members : Database window.)

SKILLS check

Assessment 1

1. Use Access to create a database for keeping track of books. Name the database file **Books**. Name the first database table you create Author Information and include the following fields in the table (you determine the data type, field size, and description):

   Field Name
   Author # (primary key)
   First Name
   Last Name
   Middle Initial

2. After creating the database table with the fields shown above and defining the primary key, save the table. Switch to Datasheet view and then enter the following data in the table:

Author #	=	1
First Name	=	Branson
Last Name	=	Walters
Middle Initial	=	A.
Author #	=	2
First Name	=	Christiana
Last Name	=	Copeland
Middle Initial	=	M.
Author #	=	3
First Name	=	Shirley
Last Name	=	Romero
Middle Initial	=	E.
Author #	=	4
First Name	=	Jeffrey
Last Name	=	Fiedler
Middle Initial	=	R.

3. Automatically adjust the width of columns.
4. Save, print, and then close the Author Information table.
5. At the **Books** database file, create another table with book information with the following fields (you determine the data type, field size, and description):

> **Field Name**
> *ISBN* (primary key)
> *Author #*
> *Title*
> *Category Code*
> *Price*

6. After creating the database table with the fields shown above and defining the primary key, save the table and name it Book Information. Switch to Datasheet view and then enter the following data in the table:

ISBN	=	12-6543-9008-7
Author #	=	4
Title	=	Today's Telecommunications
Category Code	=	B
Price	=	$34.95
ISBN	=	09-5225-5466-6
Author #	=	2
Title	=	Marketing in the Global Economy
Category Code	=	M
Price	=	$42.50
ISBN	=	23-9822-7645-0
Author #	=	1
Title	=	International Business Strategies
Category Code	=	B
Price	=	$45.00

ISBN	=	08-4351-4890-3
Author #	=	3
Title	=	Technological Advances
Category Code	=	B
Price	=	$36.95

7. Automatically adjust the width of columns (to accommodate the longest entry).
8. Save, print, and then close the Book Information table.
9. At the **Books** database file, create another table with category information with the following fields (you determine the data type, field size, and description):

Field Name
Category Code (primary key)
Category

10. After creating the database table with the fields shown above and defining the primary key, save the table and name it Category. Switch to Datasheet view and then enter the following data in the table:

Category Code	=	B
Category	=	Business

Category Code	=	M
Category	=	Marketing

11. Save, print, and then close the Category table.
12. Close the **Books** database file.

Assessment 2

1. Open the **Books** database file and then create the following relationships:
   a. Create a one-to-many relationship with the *Author #* field in the Author Information table the "one" and the *Author #* field in the Book Information table the "many." (At the Edit Relationships dialog box, choose *Enforce Referential Integrity*, *Cascade Update Related Fields*, and *Cascade Delete Related Records*.)
   b. Create a one-to-many relationship with the *Category Code* field in the Category table the "one" and the *Category Code* field in the Book Information table the "many." (At the Edit Relationships dialog box, choose *Enforce Referential Integrity*, *Cascade Update Related Fields*, and *Cascade Delete Related Records*.)
2. Print the relationships.
3. After creating, saving, and printing the relationships, add the following record to the Author Information table:

Author #	=	5
First Name	=	Glenna
Last Name	=	Zener-Young
Middle Initial	=	A.

4. Adjust the column width for the *Last Name* field.
5. Save, print, and then close the Author Information table.
6. Add the following records to the Book Information table:

ISBN #	=	23-8931-0084-7
Author #	=	2
Title	=	Practical Marketing Strategies
Category	=	M
Price	=	$28.50

ISBN #	=	87-4009-7134-6
Author #	=	5
Title	=	Selling More
Category	=	M
Price	=	$40.25

7. Save, print, and then close the Book Information table.
8. Close the **Books** database file.

CHAPTER challenge

You are the librarian at Lacy's Literacy Center. To help maintain accurate records of the books and members, you decide to create a database named **Lacy'sLiteracyCenter**. The database will include two tables: one for book information (name of book, type of book, date checked out, etc.) and one for member information (member number, name, address, phone number, etc.). Include at least five fields for each table. Determine the appropriate data types and primary and foreign keys for each of the tables. Create a relationship between the two tables. Add two records to each of the tables.

Since many records will be added to each of the tables, creating a form will allow for easier and quicker data entry. Use the Help feature to learn how to create a form using the wizard. Use the member table in the database created in the first part of the Chapter Challenge to create a form that includes all of the fields in that table. Save the form as Member Form. Add three more records (members) using the Member Form.

In Word, create a short letter that will be sent to members informing them of the book signing that will take place next month. Use the members in the member table created in the first part of the Chapter Challenge and merge them with the letter created in Word. Save the main document as **BookSigning**. Merge and then print only one letter.

USING WIZARDS AND HELP

PERFORMANCE OBJECTIVES

Upon successful completion of Chapter 3, you will be able to:
- ➤ Create a database table using the Table Wizard
- ➤ Complete a spelling check on data in a table
- ➤ Find specific records in a table
- ➤ Find specific data in a table and replace with other data
- ➤ Back up a database file
- ➤ Compact and repair a database file
- ➤ Use the Help feature

ACCESS

Access, like other programs in the Microsoft Office suite, contains a variety of wizards you can use to design and create database tables, reports, forms, and so on. In this chapter, you will learn how to use the Table Wizard to prepare a database table. Access contains a spelling check feature as well as a find and replace feature. Use the spelling checker to find misspelled words in a table, and use the find and replace feature to find specific records in a table or find specific data in a table and replace with other data. As you continue working with a database file, consider compacting and repairing the file to optimize performance and back up the file to protect your data from accidental loss or hardware failure. Microsoft Office contains an on-screen reference manual containing information on features and commands for each program within the suite. In this chapter, you will learn to use the Help feature to display information about Access.

Creating a Database Table Using the Table Wizard

HINT

Before using the Table Wizard, you must create the database file into which you will save the table.

Access contains a Table Wizard you can use to design a database table. The wizard helps you design a table by offering possible field choices with data types already assigned. If the Table Wizard does not offer the exact field name you require, you can edit a field name to personalize it.

To use the Table Wizard, create a new database file. At the new database window, double-click the *Create table by using wizard* option in the list box. This displays the first Table Wizard dialog box shown in Figure 3.1. At this window, specify whether the table is designed for a business or personal use, choose a sample table from the *Sample Tables* list box, and choose the desired fields.

At the second Table Wizard dialog box, shown in Figure 3.2, type a name for the table and then specify if you want the wizard to set the primary key or if you want to set it. At the third Table Wizard dialog box, shown in Figure 3.3, specify what you want to do after the wizard creates the table—modify the table design, enter data directly into the table, or enter data into the table using a form the wizard creates.

FIGURE

3.1 *First Table Wizard Dialog Box*

Choose the desired sample table from this list box.

Choose the desired sample fields from this list box.

FIGURE

3.2 *Second Table Wizard Dialog Box*

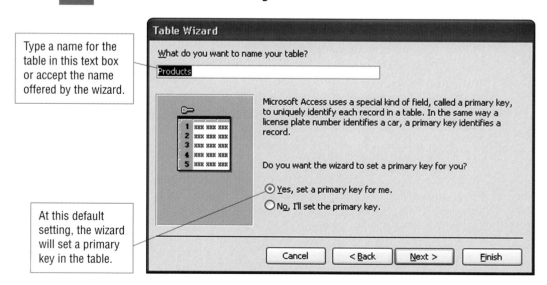

Type a name for the table in this text box or accept the name offered by the wizard.

At this default setting, the wizard will set a primary key in the table.

3.3 Third Table Wizard Dialog Box

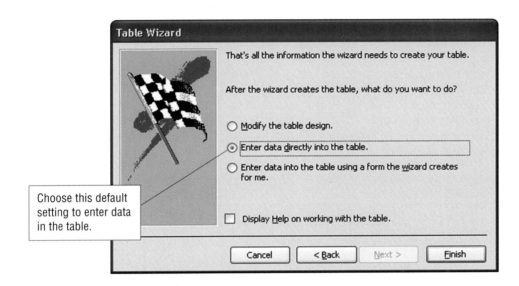

Choose this default setting to enter data in the table.

QUICK
STEPS

Create a Table Using the Table Wizard
1. At blank screen, click New button.
2. Click <u>Blank database</u> hyperlink.
3. Type database file name.
4. Press Enter.
5. Double-click *Create table by using wizard.*
6. Click desired sample table.
7. Insert desired fields in *Fields in my new table* list box.
8. Click Next button.
9. At second wizard dialog box, click Next.
10. At third wizard dialog box, click Finish.
11. Enter data into fields in table.

exercise 1

USING A TABLE WIZARD TO CREATE A DATABASE FILE

1. Create a database table for information on products used in MedSafe Clinic by completing the following steps:
   a. Start at the blank Access window and then click the New button on the Database toolbar or click File and then New. (This displays the New File task pane.)
   b. At the New File task pane, click the <u>Blank database</u> hyperlink.
   c. At the File New Database dialog box, make sure the proper drive is selected, type **MedSafeClinic** in the *File name* text box, and then press Enter or click the Create button.

   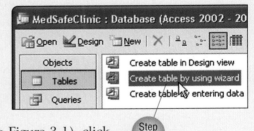

   d. At the MedSafeClinic : Database window, double-click *Create table by using wizard* in the list box.
   e. At the first Table Wizard dialog box (refer to Figure 3.1), click *Products* in the *Sample Tables* list box. (This changes the fields in the *Sample Fields* list box.)
   f. Choose some of the sample fields in the *Sample Fields* list box and add them to the *Fields in my new table* list box by completing the following steps:
      1) With *ProductID* already selected in the *Sample Fields* list box, click the button containing the greater than symbol (>) that displays between the *Sample Fields* list box and the *Fields in my new table* list box. (This inserts *ProductID* in the *Fields in my new table* list box and also selects *ProductName* in the *Sample Fields* list box.)

2) With *ProductName* selected in the *Sample Fields* list box, click the button containing the > symbol. (This adds *ProductName* to the *Fields in my new table* list box.)
3) Click once on *SupplierID* in the *Sample Fields* list box, and then click the button containing the > symbol.
4) Click once on *UnitsInStock* in the *Sample Fields* list box, and then click the button containing the > symbol.
5) With *UnitsOnOrder* already selected in the *Sample Fields* list box, click the button containing the > symbol.
6) With *UnitPrice* already selected in the *Sample Fields* list box, click the button containing the > symbol.
7) With *ReorderLevel* already selected in the *Sample Fields* list box, click the button containing the > symbol.

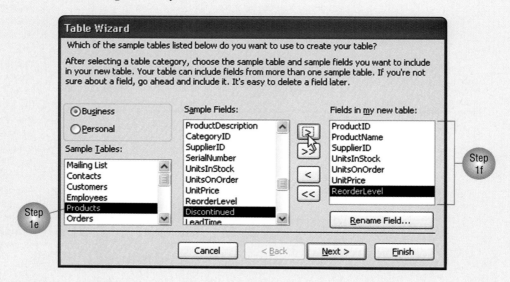

g.   Click the Next button located at the bottom of the dialog box.
h.   At the second Table Wizard dialog box (refer to Figure 3.2), the wizard offers the name *Products* for the table name and also will set a primary key for the table. These choices are appropriate so click the Next button at the bottom of the dialog box.
i.   At the third Table Wizard dialog box (refer to Figure 3.3), the wizard has already selected *Enter data directly into the table*. This is appropriate for this exercise, so click the Finish button that displays at the bottom right corner of the dialog box.
j.   At the Products : Table window shown in Figure 3.4, notice that *AutoNumber* automatically displays in the *Product ID* field. This is because the Table Wizard assigned the data type AutoNumber to the field. (Access will insert a *1* in this field as soon as you move to the second field in the *Product ID* field.) Press Tab to move the insertion point to the next field *(Product Name)*.
k.   Type the following in the specified fields (do not type anything in the *Product ID* field; simply press the Tab key and let Access insert the number):

Product Name	=	Latex gloves
Supplier ID	=	3
Units In Stock	=	243
Units On Order	=	0
Unit Price	=	0.50
Reorder Level	=	200

Product Name	=	Syringes
Supplier ID	=	1
Units In Stock	=	58
Units On Order	=	75
Unit Price	=	0.35
Reorder Level	=	75

Product Name	=	1-inch gauze pads
Supplier ID	=	4
Units In Stock	=	144
Units On Order	=	0
Unit Price	=	0.05
Reorder Level	=	125

Product Name	=	Tongue depressors
Supplier ID	=	1
Units In Stock	=	85
Units On Order	=	100
Unit Price	=	0.03
Reorder Level	=	100

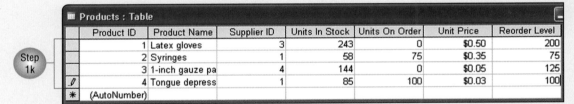

Products : Table

	Product ID	Product Name	Supplier ID	Units In Stock	Units On Order	Unit Price	Reorder Level
	1	Latex gloves	3	243	0	$0.50	200
	2	Syringes	1	58	75	$0.35	75
	3	1-inch gauze pa	4	144	0	$0.05	125
⬤	4	Tongue depress	1	85	100	$0.03	100
✱	(AutoNumber)						

Step 1k

    l.   Automatically adjust the column widths for all columns containing data.

    m. After entering the data and adjusting the column widths, click the Save button on the Table Datasheet toolbar.

   2. Change the page orientation to landscape, and then print the Products table.

   3. Close the Products table.

   4. Close the **MedSafeClinic** database file.

FIGURE

3.4 **Products : Table Window**

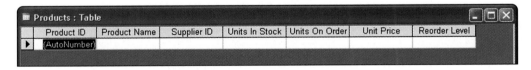

    In Exercise 1, Step 1f, you added fields to the *Fields in my new table* list box by selecting the desired field in the *Sample Fields* list box and then clicking the button containing the greater than symbol (>). Other buttons display by the button containing the greater than symbol. Click the button containing two greater than symbols (>>) and all fields in the *Sample Fields* list box are inserted in the *Fields in my new table* list box. If you want to remove a field from the *Fields in my new table* list box, select the field, and then click the button containing the less than symbol (<). Click the button containing two less than symbols (<<) to remove all fields from the *Fields in my new table* list box.

HINT
Rename a field by clicking the field in the *Fields in my new table* list box, clicking the Rename Field button, typing the new name, and then clicking OK.

The MedSafeClinic database file created in Exercise 1 contains only one table. Use the Table Wizard to create other tables within the same database file. In Exercise 2, you will use the Table Wizard to create a table containing information about suppliers used by MedSafeClinic.

When a second or subsequent table is created in a database file using the Table Wizard, a relationship can be created between database tables. In Exercise 2, you will be creating a one-to-many relationship using the Table Wizard. The Suppliers table you create in Exercise 2 will be identified as the "one" and the Products table you created in Exercise 1 will be identified as the "many."

exercise 2

CREATING ANOTHER TABLE AND RELATING TABLES USING THE TABLE WIZARD

1. Create a database table for suppliers used by MedSafeClinic by completing the following steps:
   a. At the blank Access window, click the Open button on the Database toolbar; or click File and then Open.
   b. At the Open dialog box, double-click **MedSafeClinic** in the list box.
   c. At the MedSafeClinic : Database window, double-click *Create table by using wizard* in the list box.
   d. At the first Table Wizard dialog box (refer to Figure 3.1), click *Suppliers* in the *Sample Tables* list box. (You will need to scroll down the list.)
   e. Add the following fields in the *Sample Fields* list box to the *Fields in my new table* list box (for help, refer to Exercise 1, Step 1f):

   SupplierID
   SupplierName
   Address
   City
   StateOrProvince
   PostalCode   *(Note: This is in a different order than shown in the* **Sample Fields** *list box.)*
   PhoneNumber
   EmailAddress

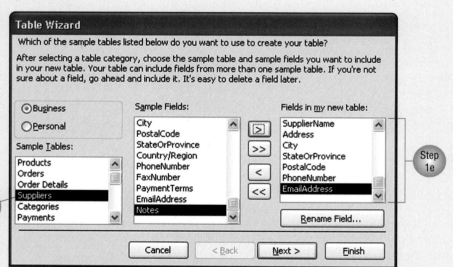

f. After inserting the fields above in the *Fields in my new table* list box, click the Next button located at the bottom of the dialog box.

g. At the second Table Wizard dialog box, the wizard offers the name *Suppliers* for the database table name and also will set a primary key for the table. These choices are appropriate so click the Next button at the bottom of the dialog box.

h. At the third Table Wizard dialog box shown in Figure 3.5, create a one-to-many relationship between Suppliers (the "one") and Products (the "many") by completing the following steps:

1) Click the Relationships button that displays toward the bottom right side of the dialog box.

2) At the Relationships dialog box shown in Figure 3.6, click the option button that displays before the *One record in the 'Suppliers' table will match many records in the 'Products' table* option.

Step 1h2

Relationships

How is your new 'Suppliers' table related to the 'Products' table?

○ The tables aren't related.

● One record in the 'Suppliers' table will match many records in the 'Products' table.

○ One record in the 'Products' table will match many records in the 'Suppliers' table.

3) Click OK to close the dialog box.

i. At the Table Wizard dialog box, click Next.

j. At the Table Wizard dialog box telling you that the wizard has all of the information it needs to create the table, make sure *Enter data directly into the table* is selected, and then click Finish.

k. At the Suppliers : Table window, type the following in the specified fields (the table wizard will automatically insert a number in the *Supplier ID* field):

Supplier Name	=	Robicheaux Suppliers
Address	=	3200 Linden Drive
City	=	Baton Rouge
State/Province	=	LA
Postal Code	=	70552
Phone Number	=	(318) 555-3411
E-mail Address	=	robi@emcp.net

Supplier Name	=	Quality Medical Supplies
Address	=	211 South Fourth Avenue
City	=	Tampa
State/Province	=	FL
Postal Code	=	33562
Phone Number	=	(813) 555-8900
E-mail Address	=	qms@emcp.net

Supplier Name	=	Peachtree Medical Supplies
Address	=	764 Harmon Way
City	=	Atlanta
State/Province	=	GA
Postal Code	=	73780
Phone Number	=	(404) 555-6474
E-mail Address	=	peachmed@emcp.net

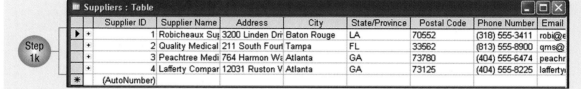

	Supplier Name	=	Lafferty Company
	Address	=	12031 Ruston Way
	City	=	Atlanta
	State/Province	=	GA
	Postal Code	=	73125
	Phone Number	=	(404) 555-8225
	E-mail Address	=	lafferty@emcp.net

Step 1k

		Supplier ID	Supplier Name	Address	City	State/Province	Postal Code	Phone Number	Email
▶	+	1	Robicheaux Sup	3200 Linden Dri	Baton Rouge	LA	70552	(318) 555-3411	robi@e
	+	2	Quality Medical	211 South Four	Tampa	FL	33562	(813) 555-8900	qms@
	+	3	Peachtree Medi	764 Harmon Wa	Atlanta	GA	73780	(404) 555-6474	peachr
	+	4	Lafferty Compar	12031 Ruston V	Atlanta	GA	73125	(404) 555-8225	laffertyı
*		(AutoNumber)							

Suppliers : Table

    l.   Automatically adjust the column widths for all columns containing data.
    m. Click the Save button on the Table Datasheet toolbar to save the Suppliers table.
2. Change the page orientation to landscape, change the left and right margins to .3 inch, and then print the Suppliers table. (Make sure you change the orientation before changing the margins.)
3. Close the Suppliers table.
4. Close the **MedSafeClinic** database file.

FIGURE

3.5 *Third Table Wizard Dialog Box*

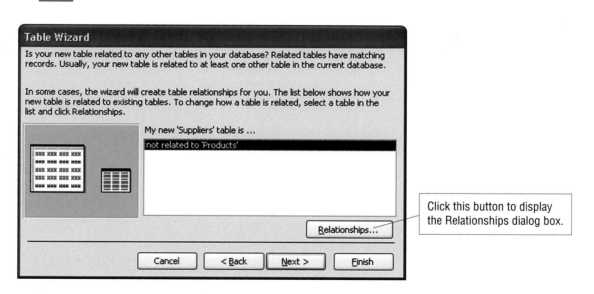

Click this button to display the Relationships dialog box.

Chapter Three

ACCESS

3.6 *Relationships Dialog Box*

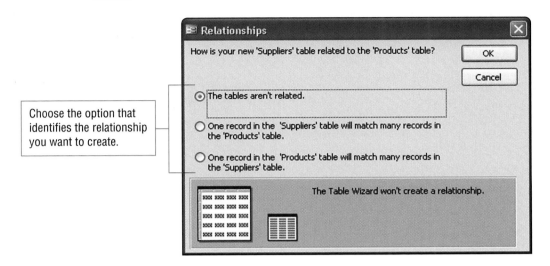

Choose the option that identifies the relationship you want to create.

In Exercise 2, a one-to-many relationship was created between the Suppliers and Products database tables. In this relationship, a record for a supplier must first be created in the Suppliers table before the supplier number can be used in a record in the Products table. In Exercise 3, you will add a new supplier to the Suppliers table and then use that supplier in a record in the Products table.

exercise 3

ADDING RECORDS TO THE SUPPLIERS AND PRODUCTS DATABASE TABLES

1. Open the **MedSafeClinic** database file.
2. Open the Suppliers table.
3. With Suppliers open in Datasheet view, add the following record at the end of the table:

Supplier Name =	National Products
Address =	2192 Second Street
City =	Little Rock
State/Province =	AR
Postal Code =	72203
Phone Number =	(501) 555-0551
E-mail Address =	natprod@emcp.net

Step 3

		Supplier ID	Supplier Name	Address	City	State/Province	Postal Code	Phone
▶	+	1	Robicheaux Suppliers	3200 Linden Drive	Baton Rouge	LA	70552	(318) 5
	+	2	Quality Medical Supplies	211 South Fourth Avenue	Tampa	FL	33562	(813) 5
	+	3	Peachtree Medical Supplies	764 Harmon Way	Atlanta	GA	73780	(404) 5
	+	4	Lafferty Company	12031 Ruston Way	Atlanta	GA	73125	(404) 5
	+	5	National Products	2192 Second Street	Little Rock	AR	72203	(501) 5
*		(AutoNumber)						

Suppliers : Table

4. Save the Suppliers table.

5. Change the page orientation to landscape, change the left and right margins to .3 inch, and then print the Suppliers table. (Make sure you change the orientation before changing the margins.)

6. Close the Suppliers table.

7. Open the Products table and then add the following records at the end of the table:

Product Name   =   Cotton swabs
Supplier ID   =   5
Units In Stock =   1345
Units On Order =   1000
Unit Price   =   0.03
Reorder Level =   1500

Product Name   =   Thermometer covers
Supplier ID   =   2
Units In Stock =   414
Units On Order =   250
Unit Price   =   0.02
Reorder Level =   450

8. Delete the record for tongue depressors.

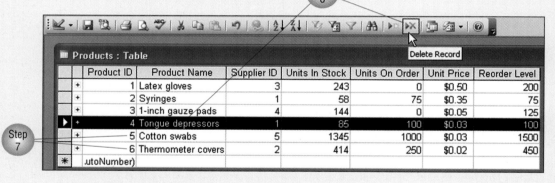

9. Adjust the column width for *Product Name*.
10. Save the Products table.
11. Change the page orientation to landscape and then print the Products table.
12. Close the Products table.
13. Close the **MedSafeClinic** database file.

Completing a Spelling Check

HINT

You can also begin spell checking by clicking Tools and then Spelling or by pressing F7.

Spelling

The spelling checker feature in Access finds misspelled words and offers replacement words. It also finds duplicate words and irregular capitalizations. When you spell check an object in a database file such as a table, the spelling checker compares the words in your table with the words in its dictionary. If a match is found, the word is passed over. If no match is found for the word, the spelling checker selects the word and offers replacement suggestions.

To complete a spelling check, open the desired database table in Datasheet view, and then click the Spelling button on the Table Datasheet toolbar. If the spelling checker does not find a match for a word in your table, the Spelling dialog box displays with replacement options. Figure 3.7 displays the Spelling dialog box with the word *Montain* selected and possible replacements displayed in the *Suggestions* list box. At the Spelling dialog box, you can choose to ignore the word (for example, if the spelling checker has selected a proper name), change to one of the replacement options, or add the word to the dictionary or AutoCorrect feature. You can also complete a spelling check on other objects in a database file such as a query, form, or report. (You will learn about these objects in future chapters.)

QUICK STEPS

Complete a Spelling Check
1. Open database table in Datasheet view.
2. Click Spelling button.
3. Change or ignore spelling as needed.
4. Click OK.

FIGURE

3.7 *Spelling Dialog Box*

The spelling checker selects this word in the table and offers this selection.

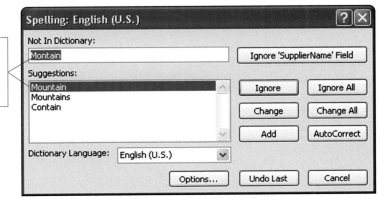

Finding and Replacing Data

If you need to find a specific entry in a field in a database table, consider using options at the Find and Replace dialog box with the Find tab selected as shown in Figure 3.8. Display this dialog box by clicking the Find button on the Table Datasheet toolbar or by clicking Edit and then Find. At the Find and Replace dialog box, enter the data for which you are searching in the *Find What* text box. By default, Access will look in the specific column where the insertion point is positioned. Click the Find Next button to find the next occurrence of the data or click the Cancel button to remove the Find and Replace dialog box.

QUICK STEPS

Find Data
1. Open database table in Datasheet view.
2. Click Find button.
3. Type data in *Find What* text box.
4. Click Find Next button.
5. Continue clicking Find Next button until entire table is searched.

Find

FIGURE

3.8 *Find and Replace Dialog Box with Find Tab Selected*

HINT

Press Ctrl + F to display the Find and Replace dialog box with the Find tab selected.

Enter the data for which you are searching in this text box.

The *Look In* option defaults to the column where the insertion point is positioned. You can choose to look in the entire table by clicking the down-pointing arrow at the right side of the option and then clicking the table name at the drop-down list. The *Match* option has a default setting of *Whole Field*. You can change this to *Any Part of Field* or *Start of Field*. The *Search* option has a default setting of *All*, which means that Access will search all data in a specific column. This can be changed to *Up* or *Down*. If you want to find data that contains specific uppercase and lowercase letters, insert a check mark in the *Match Case* check box. By default, Access will search fields as they are formatted.

You can use the Find and Replace dialog box with the Replace tab selected as shown in Figure 3.9 to search for specific data and replace with other data. Display this dialog box by clicking the Find button on the Table Datasheet toolbar and then clicking the Replace tab. Or you can display this dialog box by clicking Edit and then Replace.

FIGURE

3.9 *Find and Replace Dialog Box with Replace Tab Selected*

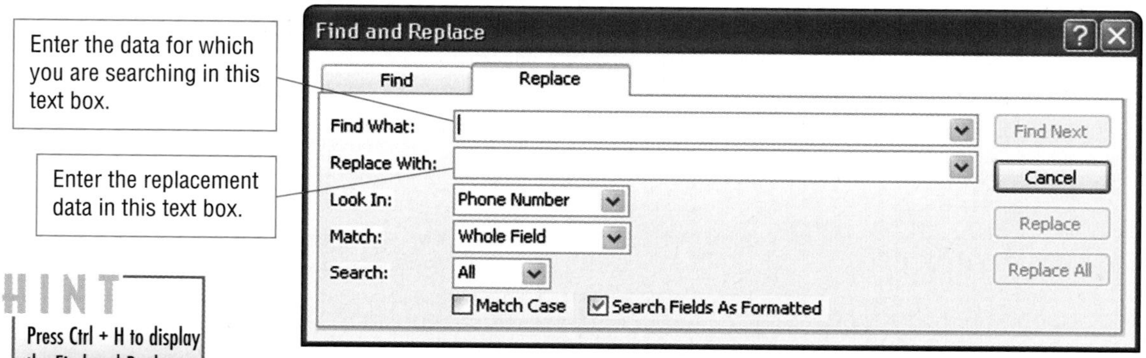

Enter the data for which you are searching in this text box.

Enter the replacement data in this text box.

HINT
Press Ctrl + H to display the Find and Replace dialog box with the Replace tab selected.

exercise 4

CHECKING THE SPELLING AND FINDING SPECIFIC DATA

1. Open the **MedSafeClinic** database file.
2. Open the Suppliers table.
3. With Suppliers open in Datasheet view, add the following record at the end of the table. (Type the misspelled words as shown below. You will correct the spelling in a later step.)

Supplier Name	=	Blue Montain Supplies
Address	=	9550 Unaversity Avenue
City	=	Little Rock
State/Province	=	AR
Postal Code	=	72209
Phone Number	=	(501) 555-4400
E-mail Address	=	bluemtn@emcp.net

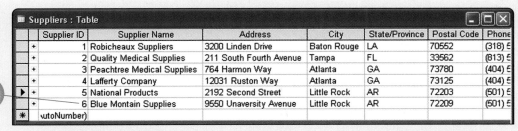

Step 3

		Supplier ID	Supplier Name	Address	City	State/Province	Postal Code	Phone
	+	1	Robicheaux Suppliers	3200 Linden Drive	Baton Rouge	LA	70552	(318) 5
	+	2	Quality Medical Supplies	211 South Fourth Avenue	Tampa	FL	33562	(813) 5
	+	3	Peachtree Medical Supplies	764 Harmon Way	Atlanta	GA	73780	(404) 5
	+	4	Lafferty Company	12031 Ruston Way	Atlanta	GA	73125	(404) 5
▶	+	5	National Products	2192 Second Street	Little Rock	AR	72203	(501) 5
	+	6	Blue Montain Supplies	9550 Unaversity Avenue	Little Rock	AR	72209	(501) 5
*		(AutoNumber)						

4. Save the Suppliers table.
5. Complete a spelling check on the table by completing the following steps:
   a. With the Suppliers table open in Datasheet view, click in the first entry in the *SupplierID* column.
   b. Click the Spelling button on the Table Datasheet toolbar.
   c. The spelling checker selects the name *Robicheaux*. This is a proper name, so click the Ignore button to tell the spelling checker to leave the name as written.

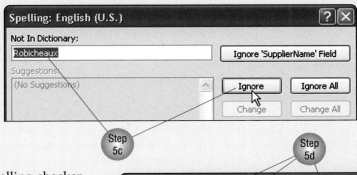

Step 5c

Step 5d

   d. The spelling checker selects *Montain*. The proper spelling *(Mountain)* is selected in the *Suggestions* list box, so click the Change button.
   e. The spelling checker selects *Unaversity*. The proper spelling *(University)* is selected in the *Suggestions* list box, so click the Change button.
   f. At the message telling you that the spelling check is complete, click the OK button.
6. Find any records containing the two-letter state abbreviation *GA* by completing the following steps:
   a. Click in the first entry in the *State/Province* column.
   b. Click the Find button on the Table Datasheet toolbar.

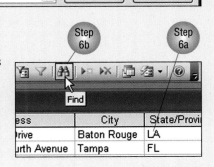

Step 6b

Step 6a

c. At the Find and Replace dialog box with the Find tab selected, type **GA** in the *Find What* text box.

d. Click the Find Next button. (Access finds and selects the first occurrence of *GA*. If the Find and Replace dialog box covers the data, drag the dialog box to a different location on the screen.)

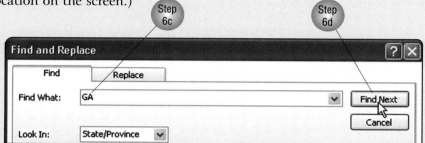

e. Continue clicking the Find What button until a message displays telling you that Access has finished searching the records. At this message, click OK.

f. Click the Cancel button to close the Find and Replace dialog box.

7. Suppose Quality Medical Supplies has changed its telephone number. Complete the following steps to find the current telephone number and replace it with the new telephone number:

a. Click in the first entry in the *Phone Number* column.

b. Click Edit and then Replace.

c. At the Find and Replace dialog box with the Replace tab selected, type (813) 555-8900 in the *Find What* text box.

d. Press the Tab key. (This moves the insertion point to the *Replace With* text box.)

e. Type (863) 555-2255 in the *Replace With* text box.

f. Click the Find Next button.

g. When Access selects the telephone number *(813) 555-8900*, click the Replace button.

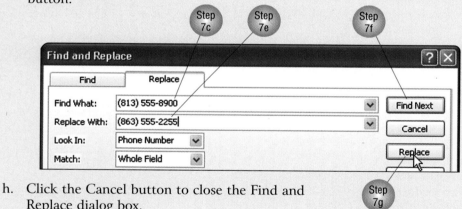

h. Click the Cancel button to close the Find and Replace dialog box.

8. Save the Suppliers table.

9. Change the page orientation to landscape, change the left and right margins to .3 inch, and then print the Suppliers table.

10. Close the Suppliers table.

11. Close the **MedSafeClinic** database file.

Backing Up a Database File

Back up a database file on a consistent basis to protect the data in the file from accidental loss or from any hardware failure. To back up a database file, click File and then Back Up Database. This displays the Save Backup As dialog box. At this dialog box, navigate to the desired folder or drive, type a name for the database file, and then press Enter or click the Save button.

Compacting and Repairing a Database File

To optimize performance of your database file, compact and repair the file on a consistent basis. As you work with a database file, data in the file can become fragmented causing the amount of space the database file takes on the disk or in the folder to be larger than necessary.

To compact and repair a database file, open the database file, click Tools, point to Database Utilities, and then click Compact and Repair Database. As the database file is compacting and repairing, a message displays on the Status bar indicating the progress of the procedure. When the procedure is completed, close the database file.

You can tell Access to compact and repair a database file each time you close the file. To do this, click Tools and then Options. At the Options dialog box, click the General tab and then click the *Compact on Close* option shown in Figure 3.10.

QUICK STEPS

Backup Database File
1. Open database file.
2. Click File, Back Up Database.
3. Type file name.
4. Click Save button.

HINT

Before compacting and repairing a database file in a multi-user environment, make sure that no other user has the database file open.

QUICK STEPS

Compact and Repair Database File
1. Open database file.
2. Click Tools, Database Utilities, Compact and Repair Database.

FIGURE

3.10 *Options Dialog Box with General Tab Selected*

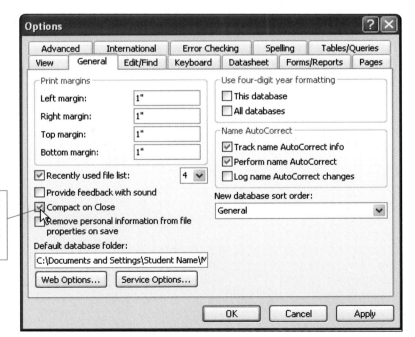

If you want Access to compact and repair a database file each time it is closed, insert a check mark in this check box.

exercise 5

1. Open the **MedSafeClinic** database file located on your disk.
2. Create a backup of the MedSafeClinic database file. To do this, complete the following steps:
   a. Click File and then Back Up Database.
   b. At the Save Backup As dialog box, type MSCBackup10-01-2005 in the *File name* text box. (This file name assumes that the date is October 1, 2005. You do not have to use the date in the file name but it does help when using the backup feature to archive database files.)
   c. Click the Save button.

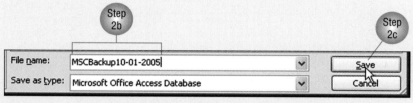

3. Close the **MedSafeClinic** database file.
4. Determine the current size of the **MedSafeClinic** database file (to compare to the size after compacting and repairing) by completing the following steps:
   a. At the blank Access screen, click the Open button on the Database toolbar.
   b. At the Open dialog box, click the down-pointing arrow at the right side of the Views button and then click *Details* at the drop-down list.
   c. Display the drive (or folder) where your **MedSafeClinic** database file is located and then check the size of the file.
   d. Close the Open dialog box.
5. Compact and repair the **MedSafeClinic** database file by completing the following steps:
   a. Open the **MedSafeClinic** database file.
   b. Click Tools, point to Database Utilities, and then click Compact and Repair Database.

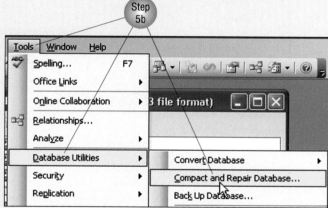

   c. When the compact and repair procedure is completed, close the **MedSafeClinic** database file.

6. Determine the size of the compacted and repaired **MedSafeClinic** database file by completing the following steps:

Step 6c

a. Click the Open button on the Database toolbar.
b. At the Open dialog box, make sure the details display in the list box and then look at the size of the **MedSafeClinic** database file and compare this size to the previous size. (Notice that the size of the compacted and repaired **MedSafeClinic** database file is the same size as the **MSCBackup10-01-2005** database file. The backup database file was automatically compacted and repaired when saved.)
c. Return the display back to a list by clicking the down-pointing arrow at the right side of the Views button and then clicking *List* at the drop-down list.
d. Close the Open dialog box.

Using Help

The Access Help feature is an on-screen reference manual containing information about all Access features and commands. The Access Help feature is similar to the Windows Help and the Help features in Word, PowerPoint, and Access. Get help using the *Ask a Question* text box on the Menu bar or with options at the Access Help task pane.

Ask a Question

Getting Help Using the *Ask a Question* Text Box

Click the text inside the *Ask a Question* text box located at the right side of the Menu bar (this removes the text), type a help question, and then press Enter. A list of topics matching key words in your question displays in the Search Results task pane.

Use Ask a Question Box
1. Click in *Ask a Question* text box.
2. Type help question.
3. Press Enter.

exercise 6

GETTING HELP USING THE *ASK A QUESTION* TEXT BOX

1. At a blank Access screen, click the text inside the *Ask a Question* text box located at the right side of the Menu bar.
2. Type How do I create an Input Mask?.
3. Press the Enter key.
4. At the Search Results task pane, click the <u>Create an input mask</u> hyperlink.
5. At the Microsoft Office Access Help window, click the <u>Create an input mask (MDB)</u> hyperlink.

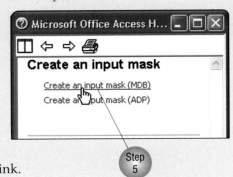
Step 5

Step 4

6. Click the <u>Create an input mask for a field in table Design view</u> hyperlink.
7. Click the <u>Show All</u> hyperlink that displays in the upper right corner of the window and then read the information that displays in the window.
8. Click the Close button (contains an *X*) located in the upper right corner of the Microsoft Office Access Help window.
9. Close the Search Results task pane.

Step 6

Microsoft Office Access Help

HINT

Press F1 to display the Access Help task pane.

Getting Help from the Access Help Task Pane

You can type a question in the *Ask a Question* text box or type a question or topic in the Access Help task pane. Display this task pane, shown in Figure 3.11, by clicking the Microsoft Office Access Help button on the Standard toolbar or by clicking Help on the Menu bar and then clicking Microsoft Office Access Help at the drop-down menu.

FIGURE

3.11   *Access Help Task Pane*

QUICK STEPS

Use Help Feature
1. Click Microsoft Office Access Help button.
2. Type help question.
3. Press Enter.

HINT

Click Help, About Microsoft Office Access, and then click the System Info button to display information about your computer such as your processor type, operating system, memory, and hard disk space.

Type in this text box the word, topic, or phrase on which you want help.

In the Access Help task pane, type a topic, feature, or question in the *Search for* text box and then press Enter or click the Start searching button (button containing white arrow on green background). Topics related to the topic, feature, or question display in the Search Results task pane. Click a topic in the results list box and information about that topic displays in the Microsoft Office Access Help window. If the window contains a <u>Show All</u> hyperlink in the upper right corner, click this hyperlink and the information expands to show all help information related to the topic. When you click the <u>Show All</u> hyperlink, it becomes the <u>Hide All</u> hyperlink.

(Note: If the Office Assistant displays when you click the Microsoft Office Access Help button, turn off the display of the Office Assistant. To do this, click the Options button in the yellow box above the Office Assistant. At the Office Assistant dialog box, click the Use the Office Assistant *option to remove the check mark from the check box, and then click OK.)*

exercise 7

GETTING HELP

1. At a blank Access screen, display information on increasing row height in a table. To begin, click the Microsoft Office Access Help button on the Standard toolbar. (This displays the Access Help task pane.)
2. Type **How do I increase the row height in a table datasheet?** in the *Search for* text box and then press Enter.
3. At the Search Results task pane, click the <u>Resize a column or row</u> hyperlink. (This displays the Microsoft Office Access Help window.)
4. Click the <u>Show All</u> hyperlink that displays in the upper right corner of the window.
5. Read the information about resizing a column or row. (You will need to scroll down the window to display all of the information.)
6. Click the Close button to close the Microsoft Office Access Help window.
7. Close the Search Results task pane.

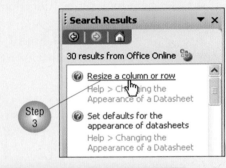

Step 3

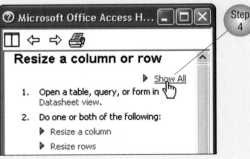

Step 4

CHAPTER summary

➤ Access contains a Table Wizard that helps create database tables.
➤ The Table Wizard offers possible field choices with data types already assigned.
➤ When a second or subsequent table is created in a database file using the Table Wizard, a relationship can be created between the tables.

- ➤ Use the spelling checker to find misspelled words in a table.
- ➤ The spelling checker compares the words in a table with words in its dictionary. If a match is found, the word is passed over. If no match is found, the spelling checker will select the word and offer possible replacements.
- ➤ Begin the spelling checker by clicking the Spelling button on the Table Datasheet toolbar.
- ➤ Use options at the Find and Replace dialog box with the Find tab selected to search for specific field entries in a table. Display this dialog box by clicking the Find button on the Table Datasheet toolbar or by clicking Edit and then Find.
- ➤ Use options at the Find and Replace dialog box with the Replace tab selected to search for specific data and replace with other data. Display this dialog box by clicking Edit and then Replace.
- ➤ Back up a database file on a consistent basis to protect the data in the file from accidental loss or from any hardware failure. To back up a database file, click File and then Back Up Database.
- ➤ Compact and repair a database file to optimize the performance of the file. Compact and repair a database file by clicking Tools, pointing to Database Utilities, and then clicking Compact and Repair Database.
- ➤ Get help by typing a question in the *Ask a Question* text box located at the right side of the Menu bar.
- ➤ Display the Access Help task pane by clicking the Microsoft Office Access Help button on the Standard toolbar or by clicking Help and then Microsoft Office Access Help.

FEATURES summary

FEATURE	BUTTON	MENU	KEYBOARD
Table Wizard		Insert, Table, Table Wizard	
Spelling checker		Tools, Spelling	F7
Find and Replace dialog box with Find tab selected		Edit, Find	Ctrl + F
Find and Replace dialog box with Replace tab selected		Edit, Replace	Ctrl + H
Save Backup As dialog box		File, Back Up Database	
Compact and repair database		Tools, Database Utilities, Compact and Repair Database	
Access Help task pane		Help, Microsoft Office Access Help	F1

Chapter Three

ACCESS

CONCEPTS check

Completion: On a blank sheet of paper, indicate the correct term, symbol, or character for each description.

1. Click this button at the first Table Wizard dialog box to add *all* of the selected fields in the *Sample Fields* list box to the *Fields in my new table* list box.
2. Click this button at the first Table Wizard dialog box to remove *all* of the fields in the *Fields in my new table* list box.
3. When a second or subsequent table is created in a database file using the Table Wizard, this can be created between the database tables.
4. Click this button on the Table Datasheet toolbar to begin the spelling checker.
5. Click this button on the Table Datasheet toolbar to display the Find and Replace dialog box with the Find tab selected.
6. Use options at the Find and Replace dialog box with this tab selected to search for specific data and replace with other data.
7. Click File and then Back Up Database and this dialog box displays.
8. To compact and repair a database file, click this option on the Menu bar, point to Database Utilities, and then click Compact and Repair Database.
9. Type a help question inside this box located at the right side of the Menu bar.
10. Click this hyperlink at the Microsoft Office Access Help window to display all information in the window.

SKILLS check

Assessment 1

1. Use the Table Wizard to create two tables in a database file named **LaffertyCompany**. Create the first table with the following specifications:
   a. At the first Table Wizard dialog box, click *Employees* in the *Sample Tables* list box.
   b. Insert the following fields located in the *Sample Fields* list box to the *Fields in my new table* list box:

      EmployeeID
      FirstName
      MiddleName
      LastName
      Title
      Extension

   c. At the second Table Wizard dialog box, accept the table name of *Employees* offered by the wizard and let the wizard set the primary key.
   d. At the third Table Wizard dialog box, leave *Enter data directly into the table* selected, and then click Finish.

e. Type the following data in the specified fields (the *Employee ID* field will automatically be assigned a number):

First Name	=	Samantha
Middle Name	=	Lee
Last Name	=	Murray
Title	=	Account Manager
Extension	=	412

First Name	=	Ralph
Middle Name	=	Edward
Last Name	=	Sorrell
Title	=	Director
Extension	=	432

First Name	=	Cheryl
Middle Name	=	Janet
Last Name	=	Plaschka
Title	=	Assistant Director
Extension	=	549

First Name	=	Brandon
Middle Name	=	Michael
Last Name	=	Perrault
Title	=	Administrative Assistant
Extension	=	653

First Name	=	Leland
Middle Name	=	John
Last Name	=	Nitsche
Title	=	Account Manager
Extension	=	894

f. Complete a spelling check on the table. (Assume proper names are spelled correctly.)
g. Adjust the column widths.
h. Save the Employees table.
i. Change the orientation to landscape and then print the table.
j. Close the Employees table.
2. Create a second table with the following specifications:
    a. At the first Table Wizard dialog box, click *Expenses* in the *Sample Tables* list box. (You will need to scroll down the list to display *Expenses*.)
    b. Insert the following fields located in the *Sample Fields* list box to the *Fields in my new table* list box:

    ExpenseID
    EmployeeID
    ExpenseType
    PurposeofExpense
    AmountSpent
    DateSubmitted

    c. At the second Table Wizard dialog box, accept the table name of *Expenses* offered by the wizard and let the wizard set the primary key.

d. At the third Table Wizard dialog box, create a one-to-many relationship where one record in the Employees table will match many records in the Expenses table. *(Hint: You must click the Relationships button at the third Table Wizard dialog box.)*

e. At the fourth Table Wizard dialog box, leave *Enter data directly into the table* selected, and then click Finish.

f. Type the following data in the specified fields (the *Expense ID* field will automatically be assigned a number):

Employee ID	=	1
Expense Type	=	Travel
Purpose of Expense	=	Marketing Conference
Amount Spent	=	$215.75
Date Submitted	=	2/4/05
Employee ID	=	2
Expense Type	=	Lodging
Purpose of Expense	=	Finance Conference
Amount Spent	=	$568.50
Date Submitted	=	2/10/05
Employee ID	=	3
Expense Type	=	Travel
Purpose of Expense	=	Management Workshop
Amount Spent	=	$422.70
Date Submitted	=	2/12/05
Employee ID	=	1
Expense Type	=	Business Dinner
Purpose of Expense	=	Customer Relations
Amount Spent	=	$124.90
Date Submitted	=	2/16/05
Employee ID	=	4
Expense Type	=	Printing
Purpose of Expense	=	Promotional Literature
Amount Spent	=	$96.00
Date Submitted	=	2/18/05
Employee ID	=	1
Expense Type	=	Travel
Purpose of Expense	=	Customer Contact
Amount Spent	=	$184.35
Date Submitted	=	2/19/05

g. Complete a spelling check on the table.
h. Adjust the column widths.
i. Save the Expenses table.
j. Change the orientation to landscape and then print the table.
k. Close the Expenses table.

Assessment 2

1. Open the **Employees** table in the LaffertyCompany database file and then add the following records:

First Name	=	Laurie
Middle Name	=	Jean
Last Name	=	Noviello
Title	=	Account Manager
Extension	=	568

First Name	=	Roderick
Middle Name	=	Earl
Last Name	=	Lobdell
Title	=	Assistant Director
Extension	=	553

2. Delete the record for Leland John Nitsche.
3. Save the Employees table and then print the table in landscape orientation.
4. Close the Employees table.
5. Open the Expenses table and then add the following records:

Employee ID	=	4
Expense Type	=	Printing
Purpose of Expense	=	Product Brochure
Amount Spent	=	$510.00
Date Submitted	=	2/22/05

Employee ID	=	5
Expense Type	=	Travel
Purpose of Expense	=	Customer Contact
Amount Spent	=	$75.20
Date Submitted	=	2/23/05

6. Save the Expenses table.
7. Print the Expenses table in landscape orientation.
8. Close the Expenses table.

Assessment 3

1. Open the Employees table in the **LaffertyCompany** database file.
2. Make the following changes:
   a. Click in the first entry of the *Last Name* column and then find the one occurrence of *Noviello* and replace with *Orson*.
   b. Click in the first entry of the *Title* column and then find all occurrences of *Account Manager* and replace with *Sales Director*.
3. Save the Employees table and then print the table in landscape orientation.
4. Close the Employees table.
5. Compact and repair the **LaffertyCompany** database file.
6. Close the **LaffertyCompany** database file.

Assessment 4

1. In Chapter 2, you learned to create a one-to-many relationship between database tables. In Access, a many-to-many relationship can also be created between database tables. Use the Access Help feature to read and print information on creating a many-to-many relationship between database tables.
2. After reading the information, open Microsoft Word, and then create a memo to your instructor and include the following:
    a. Description of a many-to-many relationship.
    b. Steps to create a many-to-many relationship.
    c. At least one example of a situation in which a many-to-many relationship would be useful.
3. Save the Word document and name it **sac3sc04**.
4. Print and then close **sac3sc04**.

CHAPTER challenge

Create a database named **(Yourlastname) Household** using a personal sample table from the wizard. Select your own fields from the sample field list. Set a primary key (if necessary). Use appropriate data types and input masks. Add at least five records to the table. Sort the table in ascending order. Save and print the table.

Once a table has been created, printing a copy of the table's design properties can be very beneficial. Use the Help feature to learn about printing the design characteristics of a table. Then print the design properties of the table that was created in the first part of the Chapter Challenge.

You have talked with your friend Judy about the database you created, and she would like to see what you have done in Access. Since she lives 500 miles away, you decide to e-mail her the table. Judy does not have Access, but does have a word processing application. Export the table created in the first part of the Chapter Challenge as an rtf file, so that Judy can view it with her application.

PERFORMING QUERIES AND FILTERING RECORDS

PERFORMANCE OBJECTIVES

Upon successful completion of Chapter 4, you will be able to:
➤ **Design a query to extract specific data from a database table**
➤ **Use the Simple Query Wizard to extract specific data from a database table**
➤ **Create a calculated field**
➤ **Use aggregate functions in queries**
➤ **Create crosstab, duplicate, and unmatched queries**
➤ **Filter data in records by selection and by form**

ACCESS

One of the primary uses of a database file is to extract specific information from the database. A company might need to know such information as: How much inventory is currently on hand? What products have been ordered? What accounts are past due? What customers live in a particular city? This type of information can be extracted from a database table by completing a query. You will learn how to perform a variety of queries on database tables in this chapter.

Access provides a Filter By Selection button and a Filter By Form button, which you can use to temporarily isolate specific records in a database table. Like a query, a filter lets you select specific field values from a database table. You will learn to use these two buttons to isolate specific data in tables.

Performing Queries

Being able to extract (pull out) specific data from a database table is one of the most important functions of a database. Extracting data in Access is referred to as performing a "query." The word *query* means to ask a question. Access provides several methods for performing a query. You can design your own query, use a Simple Query Wizard, or use complex query wizards. In this chapter, you will learn to design your own query, use the Simple Query Wizard, use aggregate functions in a query, and use the Crosstab, Find Duplicates, and Unmatched query wizards.

QUICK STEPS

Design a Query
1. Open database file.
2. Click Queries button.
3. Double-click *Create query in Design view*.
4. At Show Table dialog box, select table(s).
5. At select query window, drag fields to desired location.
6. Click Run button.
7. Save query.

Designing a Query

Designing a query consists of identifying the table from which you are gathering data, the field or fields from which the data will be drawn, and the criteria for selecting the data. To design a query and perform the query, you would follow these basic steps:

1. Open the database file.
2. At the database file dialog box, click the Queries button on the Objects bar shown in Figure 4.1.
3. Double-click *Create query in Design view* in the list box.
4. At the Show Table dialog box with the Tables tab selected as shown in Figure 4.2, select the table you want included in the query, and then click the Add button. Add any other tables required for the query. When all tables have been added, click the Close button.
5. At the Query1 : Select Query window shown in Figure 4.3, use the mouse to drag the first field to be included in the query from the table box in the top of the dialog box to the first empty *Field* text box. If more than one field is to be included in the query, continue dragging field names from the box in the top to the *Field* text boxes.
6. To establish a criterion, click inside the *Criteria* text box in the column containing the desired field name, and then type the criterion.
7. With the fields and criteria established, click the Run button located on the Query Design toolbar.
8. Access searches the specified table for records that match the criteria and then displays those records in the Query1 : Select Query window.
9. If the query will be used in the future, save the query and name it. If you do not need the query again, close the Query1 : Select Query window without saving it.

Run

HINT

Several types of queries can be created, with the select query being the most common.

FIGURE

4.1 *Objects Bar*

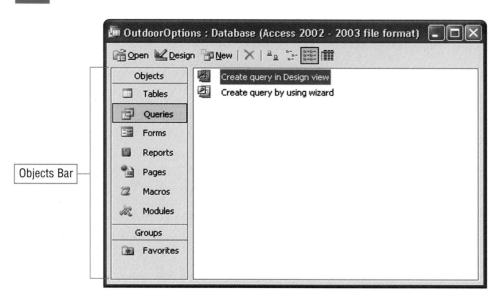

ACCESS

4.2 *Show Table Dialog Box*

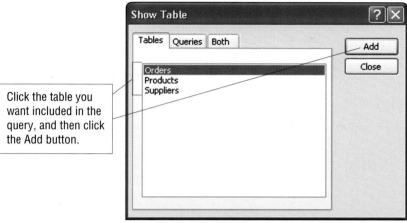

Click the table you want included in the query, and then click the Add button.

4.3 *Query1 : Select Query Window*

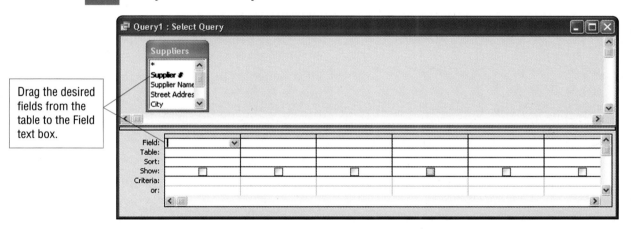

Drag the desired fields from the table to the Field text box.

In Step 4, the mouse is used to drag fields from the table box in the top of the dialog box to the first empty *Field* text box in the lower part of the dialog box. As an example, suppose you wanted to find out how many purchase orders were issued on a specific date. To do this, you would drag the *PurchaseOrderID* field from the table to the first *Field* text box, and then drag the *OrderDate* field from the table to the second *Field* text box. In this example, both fields are needed so the purchase order ID is displayed along with the specific order date. After dragging the fields, you would then insert the criterion. The criterion for this example would be something like *#1/15/2005#*. After the criterion is inserted, click the Run button on the Query Design toolbar and the results of the query are displayed on the screen.

Establishing Query Criteria

A query does not require that specific criteria are established. In the example described above, if the criterion for the date was not included, the query would "return" (*return* is the term used for the results of the query) all Purchase Order numbers with the dates. While this information may be helpful, you could easily

HINT

Limit the query results by specifying criteria.

HINT

Include only those fields in a query for which you want to enter criteria or fields which you want to display.

find this information in the table. The value of performing a query is to extract specific information from a table. To do this, you must insert a criterion like the one described in the example.

Access makes writing a criterion fairly simple because it inserts the necessary symbols in the criterion. If you type a city such as *Vancouver* in the *Criteria* text box and then press Enter, Access changes the criterion to *"Vancouver"*. The quotation marks are inserted by Access and are necessary for the query to run properly. You can either let Access put the proper symbols in the *Criteria* text box, or you can type the criterion with the symbols. Table 4.1 shows some criteria examples including what is typed and what is returned.

T A B L E

4.1 *Criteria Examples*

Typing this criterion	Returns this
"Smith"	Field value matching *Smith*
"Smith" or "Larson"	Field value matching either *Smith* or *Larson*
Not "Smith"	Field value that is not *Smith* (the opposite of "Smith")
"S*"	Field value that begins with *S* and ends in anything
"*s"	Field value that begins with anything and ends in *s*
"[A-D]*"	Field value that begins with *A* through *D* and ends in anything
#01/01/2005#	Field value matching the date 01/01/2005
< #04/01/2005#	Field value less than (before) 04/01/2005
> #04/01/2005#	Field value greater than (after) 04/01/2005
Between #01/01/2005 And #03/31/2005	Any date between 01/01/2005 and 03/31/2005

Establish Query Criteria

1. At select query window, click in desired *Criteria* text box.
2. Type criteria and then press Enter.
3. Click Run button.

In Table 4.1, notice the quotation marks surrounding field values (such as "Smith"). If you do not type the quotation marks when typing the criterion, Access will automatically insert them. The same is true for the pound symbol (#). Notice in Table 4.1 that the pound symbol (#) was used around dates. If you do not type the pound symbol around a date, Access will automatically insert the symbols. Access automatically inserts the correct symbol when you press the Enter key after typing the query criteria.

In the criteria examples, the asterisk was used as a wild card indicating any character. This is consistent with many other software applications where the asterisk is used as a wildcard character. The less than and greater than symbols were used in two of the criteria examples. These symbols can be used for fields containing numbers, values, dates, amounts, and so forth. In the next several exercises, you will be designing queries to extract specific information from different database tables in database files.

ACCESS

exercise 1

(Note: Delete from your disk any database files you created in Chapter 3.)

1. Copy the **OutdoorOptions** database file from the CD that accompanies this textbook to your disk. Remove the read-only attribute from the **OutdoorOptions** database file.
2. Open the **OutdoorOptions** database file.
3. Extract records of those suppliers located in Vancouver by completing the following steps:
   a. Click the Queries button on the Objects bar.
   b. Double-click *Create query in Design view* in the list box.

   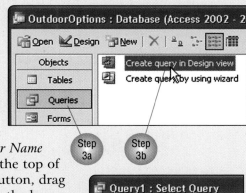

   Step 3a   Step 3b

   c. At the Show Table dialog box with the Tables tab selected (see Figure 4.2), click *Suppliers* in the list box, click the Add button, and then click the Close button.
   d. Drag fields from the table box to the *Field* text boxes by completing the following steps:
      1) Position the arrow pointer on the *Supplier Name* field in the table list box located toward the top of the window, hold down the left mouse button, drag the field icon to the first *Field* text box in the lower portion of the window, and then release the mouse button. (When you release the mouse button, Access automatically inserts the table name *Suppliers* in the *Table* text box and inserts a check mark in the *Show* check box.)

   Step 3d1

      2) Drag the *Street Address* field in the table list box to the next *Field* text box (to the right of *Supplier Name*).
      3) Drag the *City* field in the table list box to the next *Field* text box (to the right of *Street Address*).
      4) Drag the *Province* field in the table list box to the next *Field* text box (to the right of *City*).
      5) Drag the *Postal Code* field in the table list box to the next *Field* text box (to the right of *Province*).

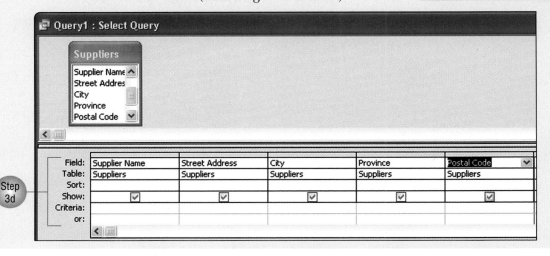

Step 3d

e. Insert the criterion text telling Access to display only those suppliers located in Vancouver by completing the following steps:

1) Position the I-beam pointer in the *Criteria* text box in the *City* column and then click the left mouse button. (This positions the insertion point inside the text box.)

2) Type **Vancouver** and then press Enter. (This changes the criteria to "Vancouver".)

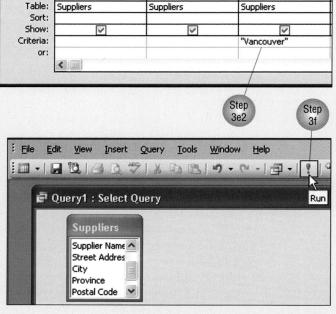

Field:	Supplier Name	Street Address	City
Table:	Suppliers	Suppliers	Suppliers
Sort:			
Show:	☑	☑	☑
Criteria:			"Vancouver"
or:			

Step 3e2

Step 3f

f. Return the results of the query by clicking the Run button on the Query Design toolbar.

g. Save the results of the query by completing the following steps:

1) Click the Save button on the Query Datasheet toolbar.

2) At the Save As dialog box, type **VancouverQuery** and then press Enter or click OK.

h. Print the results of the query by clicking the Print button on the Query Datasheet toolbar.

i. Close VancouverQuery.

4. Extract those product records with units on order greater than zero by completing the following steps:

a. At the OutdoorOptions : Database window, double-click *Create query in Design view*.

b. At the Show Table dialog box, click *Products* in the list box, click the Add button, and then click the Close button.

c. At the Query1 : Select Query window, drag the *Product* field from the table list box to the first *Field* text box.

d. Scroll down the table list box until *Units on Order* displays and then drag *Units on Order* to the second *Field* text box (to the right of *Product*).

e. Insert the query criteria by completing the following steps:

1) Position the I-beam pointer in the *Criteria* text box in the *Units on Order* column and then click the left mouse button. (This positions the insertion point inside the text box.)

2) Type **>0** and then press Enter. (Make sure you type a zero and not a capital *O*.)

f. Return the results of the query by clicking the Run button on the Query Design toolbar.

g. Save the query and name it UnitsOnOrderQuery.
h. Print the results of the query by clicking the Print button on the Query Datasheet toolbar.
i. Close UnitsOnOrderQuery.
5. Extract those orders greater than $1,500 by completing the following steps:
   a. At the OutdoorOptions : Database window, double-click *Create query in Design view*.
   b. At the Show Table dialog box, click *Orders* in the list box, click the Add button, and then click the Close button.
   c. At the Query1 : Select Query window, drag the *Order #* field from the table list box to the first *Field* text box.
   d. Drag the *Product #* field to the second *Field* text box (to the right of *Order #*).
   e. Scroll down the table list box until *Amount* is visible and then drag the *Amount* field to the third *Field* text box (to the right of *Product #*).
   f. Insert the query criteria by completing the following steps:
      1) Position the I-beam pointer in the *Criteria* text box in the *Amount* column and then click the left mouse button. (This positions the insertion point inside the text box.)
      2) Type >1500 and then press Enter. (Make sure you type zeros and not capital *O*s.)

Field:	Order #		Product #		Amount	
Table:	Orders		Orders		Orders	
Sort:						
Show:		☑		☑		☑
Criteria:					>1500	
or:						

   g. Return the results of the query by clicking the Run button on the Query Design toolbar.

Step 5f2

   h. Save the query and name it OrdersOver$1500Query.
   i. Print the results of the query by clicking the Print button on the Query Datasheet toolbar.
   j. Close OrdersOver$1500Query.
6. Close the **OutdoorOptions** database file.

In Exercise 1, you performed several queries on specific database tables. A query can also be performed on fields from more than one table. In Exercise 2, you will be performing queries on related database tables.

HINT
A query can be performed on two or more tables that are joined in a relationship.

exercise 2

PERFORMING A QUERY ON RELATED DATABASE TABLES

1. Open the **OutdoorOptions** database file.
2. Extract information on products ordered between February 20 and February 28, 2005, and include the supplier's name by completing the following steps:
   a. Click the Queries button on the Objects bar.
   b. Double-click *Create query in Design view*.
   c. At the Show Table dialog box, click *Products* in the list box and then click the Add button.
   d. Click *Suppliers* in the Show Table dialog box list box and then click the Add button.
   e. Click *Orders* in the list box, click the Add button, and then click the Close button.

f.   At the Query1 : Select Query window, drag the *Product* field from the Products table list box to the first *Field* text box.

g.   Drag the *Supplier Name* field from the Suppliers table list box to the second *Field* text box.

h.   Drag the *Order Date* field from the Orders table list box to the third *Field* text box. (You will need to scroll down the list box to display the *Order Date* field.)

i.   Insert the query criteria by completing the following steps:

1)   Position the I-beam pointer in the *Criteria* text box in the *Order Date* column and then click the left mouse button. (This positions the insertion point inside the text box.)

2)   Type **Between 2/20/2005 And 2/28/2005** and then press Enter. (Make sure you type zeros and not capital *O*s.)

j.   Return the results of the query by clicking the Run button on the Query Design toolbar.

k.   Save the query and name it Feb20-28OrdersQuery.

l.   Print and then close the query.

3.   Close the **OutdoorOptions** database file.

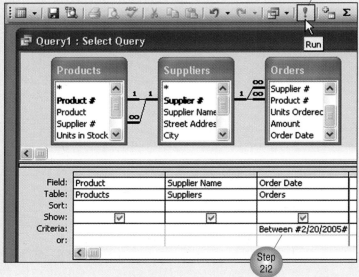

Step 2j

Step 2i2

QUICK STEPS

Sorting Fields in a Query

Sort Fields in Query
1. At select query window, click in *Sort* text box.
2. Click down arrow in *Sort* text box.
3. Click *Ascending* or *Descending*.

When designing a query, the sort order of a field or fields can be specified. Notice in Figure 4.3 that a *Sort* text box displays. Click inside one of the columns in the *Sort* text box and a down-pointing arrow displays at the right of the field. Click this down-pointing arrow and a drop-down list displays with the choices *Ascending*, *Descending*, and *(not sorted)*. Click Ascending to sort from lowest to highest or click Descending to sort from highest to lowest.

exercise 3

PERFORMING A QUERY ON RELATED TABLES AND SORTING IN ASCENDING ORDER

1.   Open the **OutdoorOptions** database file.
2.   Extract information on orders less than $1,500 by completing the following steps:

a.   Click the Queries button on the Objects bar.

b.   Double-click *Create query in Design view*.

c.   At the Show Table dialog box, click *Products* in the list box and then click the Add button.

d.   Click *Orders* in the list box, click the Add button, and then click the Close button.

e.   At the Query1 : Select Query window, drag the *Product #* field from the Products table list box to the first *Field* text box.

ACCESS

f. Drag the *Supplier #* field from the Products table list box to the second *Field* text box.
g. Drag the *Units Ordered* field from the Orders table list box to the third *Field* text box.
h. Drag the *Amount* field from the Orders table list box to the fourth *Field* text box.
i. Insert the query criterion by completing the following steps:
   1) Position the I-beam pointer in the *Criteria* text box in the *Amount* column and then click the left mouse button.
   2) Type <1500 and then press Enter. (Make sure you type a zero and not a capital *O*.)

Field:	Product #	Supplier #	Units Ordered	Amount
Table:	Products	Orders	Orders	Orders
Sort:				
Show:	☑	☑	☑	☑
Criteria:				<1500
or:				

Step 2i2

j. Sort the *Amount* field values from lowest to highest by completing the following steps:
   1) Position the insertion point in the *Sort* text box in the *Amount* column, and then click the left mouse button. (This will cause a down-pointing arrow to display at the right side of the text box.)
   2) Click the down-pointing arrow at the right side of the *Sort* text box and then click *Ascending*.

Step 2j1

Units Ordered	Amount
Orders	Orders
☑	Ascending
	Descending
	(not sorted)

Step 2j2

k. Return the results of the query by clicking the Run button on the Query Design toolbar.
l. Save the query and name it OrdersLessThan$1500Query.
m. Print and then close the query.
3. Close the **OutdoorOptions** database file.

Performing a Query with the Simple Query Wizard

The Simple Query Wizard provided by Access guides you through the steps for preparing a query. To use this wizard, open the database file, click the Queries button on the Objects bar, and then double-click the *Create query by using wizard* option in the list box. Or, click the New button and then, at the New Query dialog box, double-click *Simple Query Wizard* in the list box. At the first Simple Query Wizard dialog box, as shown in Figure 4.4, specify the database table(s) in the *Tables/Queries* list box. After specifying the database table, insert the fields you want included in the query in the *Selected Fields* list box, and then click the Next button.

4.4 *First Simple Query Wizard Dialog Box*

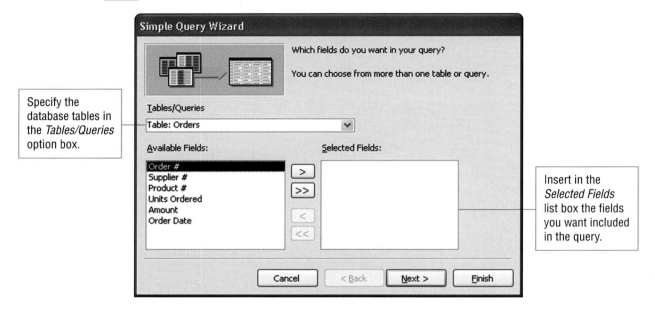

Specify the database tables in the *Tables/Queries* option box.

Insert in the *Selected Fields* list box the fields you want included in the query.

At the second Simple Query Wizard dialog box, specify whether you want a detail or summary query, and then click the Next button. At the third (and last) Simple Query Wizard dialog box, shown in Figure 4.5, type a name for the completed query or accept the name provided by the wizard. At this dialog box, you can also specify that you want to open the query to view the information or modify the query design. If you want to extract specific information, be sure to choose the *Modify the query design* option. After making any necessary changes, click the Finish button.

4.5 *Last Simple Query Wizard Dialog Box*

Type a name for the query in this text box or accept the name provided by the wizard.

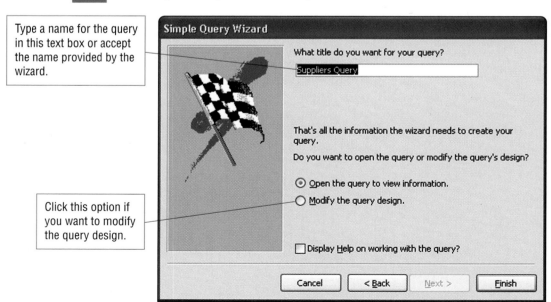

Click this option if you want to modify the query design.

If you do not modify the query design in the last Simple Query Wizard dialog box, the query displays all records for the fields identified in the first Simple Query Wizard dialog box. In Exercise 4 you will be performing a query without modifying the design, and in Exercise 5 you will be modifying the query design.

exercise 4

PERFORMING A QUERY WITH THE SIMPLE QUERY WIZARD

1. Open the **OutdoorOptions** database file.
2. Perform a query with the Simple Query Wizard by completing the following steps:
   a. Click the Queries button on the Objects bar.
   b. Double-click the *Create query by using wizard* option in the list box.
   c. At the first Simple Query Wizard dialog box, click the down-pointing arrow at the right of the *Tables/Queries* text box, and then click *Table: Suppliers*.

   Step 2c

   Simple Query Wizard

   Which fields do y

   You can choose f

   Tables/Queries

   Table: Orders ▾

Table: Orders
Table: Products
Table: Suppliers
Query: Feb20-28OrdersQuery
Query: OrdersLessThan$1500Query
Query: OrdersOver$1500Query
Query: UnitsOnOrderQuery
Query: VancouverQuery

   d. With *Supplier #* selected in the *Available Fields* list box, click the button containing the greater than symbol. (This inserts the *Supplier #* field in the *Selected Fields* list box.)
   e. With *Supplier Name* selected in the *Available Fields* list box, click the button containing the greater than symbol.
   f. Click the down-pointing arrow at the right of the *Tables/Queries* text box, and then click *Table: Orders*.
   g. Click *Product #* in the *Available Fields* list box, and then click the button containing the greater than symbol.
   h. Click *Amount* in the *Available Fields* list box, and then click the button containing the greater than symbol.

   Simple Query Wizard

   Which fields do you want in your query?

   You can choose from more than one table or query.

   Tables/Queries

   Table: Orders ▾

   Available Fields:

Order #
Supplier #
Units Ordered
Order Date

   [>]
   [>>]
   [<]
   [<<]

   Selected Fields:

Supplier #
Supplier Name
Product #
Amount

   Steps 2d–2h

   i. Click the Next button.
   j. At the second Simple Query Wizard dialog box, click the Next button.
   k. At the last Simple Query Wizard dialog box, click the Finish button. (The wizard will automatically save the query with the name Supplies Query.)
3. When the results of the query display, print the results.
4. Close the Suppliers Query : Select Query window.
5. Close the **OutdoorOptions** database file.

To extract specific information when using the Simple Query Wizard, tell the wizard that you want to modify the query design. This displays a dialog box where you can insert query criteria.

exercise 5

PERFORMING AND MODIFYING A QUERY WITH THE SIMPLE QUERY WIZARD

1. Open the **OutdoorOptions** database file.
2. Perform a query with the Simple Query Wizard and modify the query by completing the following steps:
   a. Click the Queries button on the Objects bar.
   b. Double-click the *Create query by using wizard* option in the list box.
   c. At the first Simple Query Wizard dialog box, click the down-pointing arrow at the right of the *Tables/Queries* text box, and then click *Table: Suppliers*.
   d. Insert the following fields in the *Selected Fields* list box:

   > *Supplier Name*
   > *Street Address*
   > *City*
   > *Province*
   > *Postal Code*

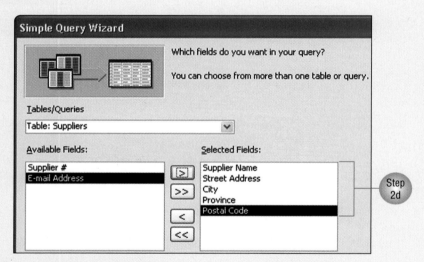

   e. Click the Next button.
   f. At the second Simple Query Wizard dialog box, type **SuppliersNotVancouver** in the *What title do you want for your query?* text box, click the *Modify the query design* option, and then click the Finish button.
   g. At the SuppliersNotVancouver : Select Query window, insert the query criterion by completing the following steps:
      1) Click in the *Criteria* text box in the *City* column.
      2) Type **Not Vancouver** and then press Enter.
   h. Specify that the fields are to be sorted in ascending order by Postal Code by completing the following steps:
      1) Click in the *Sort* text box in the *Postal Code* column (you may need to scroll to see this column).
      2) Click the down-pointing arrow that displays at the right side of the text box and then click *Ascending*.

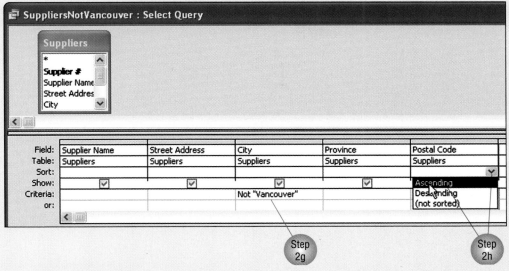

Step
2g

Step
2h

i. Click the Run button on the Query Design toolbar. (Those suppliers not situated in Vancouver will display and the records will display in ascending order by Postal Code.)
j. With the results of the query displayed, print the query.
k. Click the Save button to save the query.
l. Close the query.
3. Close the **OutdoorOptions** database file.

Creating a Calculated Field

A calculated control uses a mathematical equation to determine the contents that are displayed in the control object. In a query, you can insert a calculated field that performs mathematical equations. Insert a calculated field in the *Fields* text box when designing a query. To insert a calculated field, click in the desired *Field* text box. Type the desired field name followed by a colon and then type the equation. For example, to multiply Unit Price by Units Ordered and name the field *Total Amount*, you would type Total Amount:[Unit Price]*[Units Ordered] in the *Field* text box.

exercise 6

CREATING A CALCULATED FIELD IN A QUERY

1. Open the **OutdoorOptions** database file.
2. Perform a query with the Simple Query Wizard and modify the query by completing the following steps:
   a. Click the Queries button on the Objects bar.
   b. Double-click the *Create query by using wizard* option in the list box.
   c. At the first Simple Query Wizard dialog box, click the down-pointing arrow at the right of the *Tables/Queries* text box, and then click *Table: Suppliers*.

d. Insert the *Supplier Name* field in the *Selected Fields* list box.
e. Click the down-pointing arrow at the right of the *Tables/Queries* text box, click *Table: Products*, and then insert the following fields in the *Selected Fields* list box:

> *Product*
> *Units in Stock*
> *Units on Order*

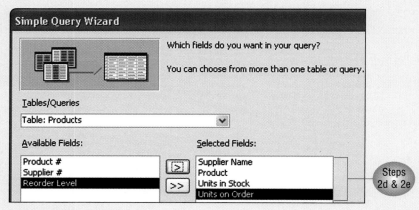

Steps
2d & 2e

f. Click the Next button.
g. At the second Simple Query Wizard dialog box, click the Next button.
h. At the last Simple Query Wizard dialog box, type StockTotals in the *What title do you want for your query?* text box, click the *Modify the query design* option, and then click the Finish button.
i. At the StockTotals : Select Query window, insert a calculated field that calculates the total number of units by completing the following steps:
    1) Click in the fifth *Field* text box.
    2) Type Total:[Units in Stock]+[Units on Order] and then press Enter.

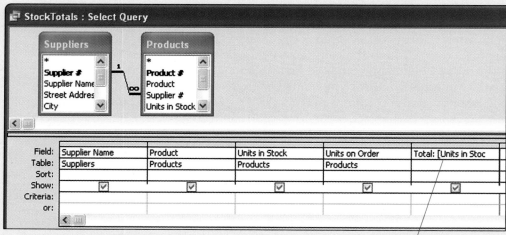

j. Click the Run button on the Query Design toolbar. (All records will display with the total of the units in stock and on order displayed.)

Step
2i

k. With the results of the query displayed, print the query.
l. Click the Save button to save the query.
m. Close the query.
3. Close the **OutdoorOptions** database file.

exercise 7

1. Open the **OutdoorOptions** database file.
2. Perform a query with the Simple Query Wizard and modify the query by completing the following steps:
   a. Click the Queries button on the Objects bar.
   b. Double-click the *Create query by using wizard* option in the list box.
   c. At the first Simple Query Wizard dialog box, click the down-pointing arrow at the right of the *Tables/Queries* text box, and then click *Table: Suppliers*.
   d. Insert the *Supplier Name* field in the *Selected Fields* list box.
   e. Click the down-pointing arrow at the right of the *Tables/Queries* text box, click *Table: Orders*, and then insert the following fields in the *Selected Fields* list box:

   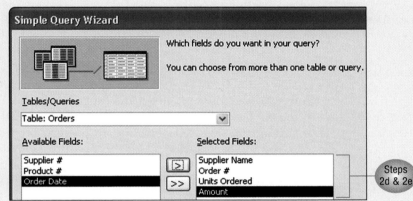

   Steps 2d & 2e

   > *Order #*
   > *Units Ordered*
   > *Amount*

   f. Click the Next button.
   g. At the second Simple Query Wizard dialog box, click the Next button.
   h. At the last Simple Query Wizard dialog box, type **UnitPrices** in the *What title do you want for your query?* text box, click the *Modify the query design* option, and then click the Finish button.
   i. At the UnitPrices : Select Query window, insert a calculated field that calculates the unit price by completing the following steps:
      1) Click in the fifth *Field* text box.
      2) Type **Unit Price:[Amount]/[Units Ordered]** and then press Enter.

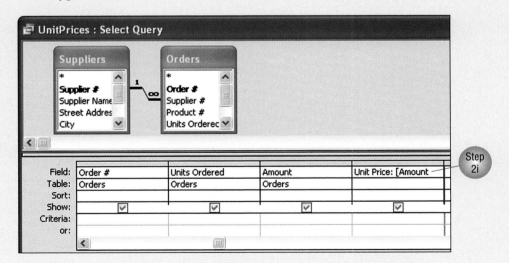

Step 2i

j. Click the Run button on the Query Design toolbar. (All records will display with the unit price calculated for each order.)

k. Save, print, and then close the query.

3. Close the **OutdoorOptions** database file.

Designing Queries with Aggregate Functions

QUICK STEPS

Design Query with Aggregate Function
1. At select query window, click the Totals button.
2. Click the down-pointing arrow in *Group By* list box.
3. Click desired aggregate function.

An aggregate function such as Sum, Avg, Min, Max, or Count can be included in a query to calculate statistics from numeric field values of all the records in the table. When an aggregate function is used, Access displays one row in the query results datasheet with the formula result for the function used. For example, in a table with a numeric field containing the annual salary amounts, you could use the Sum function to calculate the total of all salary amount values.

To display the aggregate function list, click the Totals button on the Query Design toolbar. Access adds a Total row to the design grid with a drop-down list from which you select the desired function. Access also inserts the words *Group By* in the list box. Click the down-pointing arrow and then click the desired aggregate function from the drop-down list. In Exercise 8, you will create a query in Design view and use aggregate functions to find the total of all order amounts, the average order amount, the maximum and the minimum order amount, and the total number of orders. The completed query will display as shown in Figure 4.6. Access automatically chooses the column heading names.

FIGURE

4.6   *Query Results for Exercise 8*

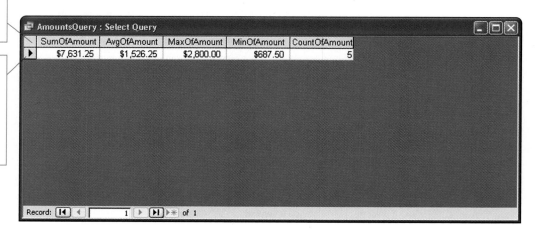

Access automatically chose the column heading names.

The aggregate functions calculated the order amounts in the *Amount* column in the Orders table.

1. Open the **OutdoorOptions** database file.
2. Determine the total, average, minimum, and maximum order amounts as well as the total number of orders. To begin, click the Queries button on the Objects bar.
3. Double-click *Create query in Design view*.
4. At the Show Table dialog box, click *Orders* in the list box, click the Add button, and then click the Close button.
5. Drag the *Amount* field from the Orders table list box (you will need to scroll down the list box to display this field) to the first *Field* text box.
6. Drag the *Amount* field to the second, third, fourth, and fifth *Field* text boxes.

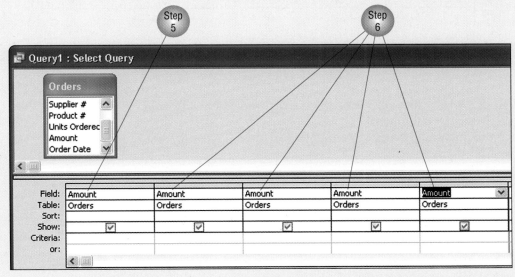

Step 5

Step 6

7. Click the Totals button on the Query Design toolbar. (This adds a *Total* row to the design grid between *Table* and *Sort* with the default option of *Group By*.)
8. Specify a Sum function for the first *Group By* list box by completing the following steps:
   a. Click in the first *Group By* option box in the *Total* row.
   b. Click the down-pointing arrow that displays at the right side of the list box.
   c. Click *Sum* at the drop-down list.

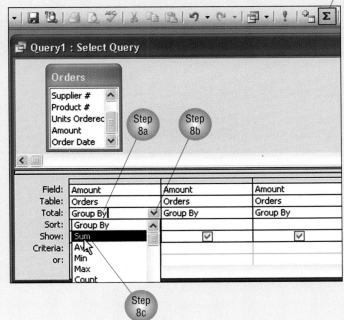

Step 7

Step 8a

Step 8b

Step 8c

9. Complete steps similar to those in Step 8 to insert *Avg* in the second *Group By* list box in the *Total* row.
10. Complete steps similar to those in Step 8 to insert *Max* in the third *Group By* list box in the *Total* row.
11. Complete steps similar to those in Step 8 to insert *Min* in the fourth *Group By* list box in the *Total* row.
12. Complete steps similar to those in Step 8 to insert *Count* in the fifth *Group By* list box in the *Total* row.

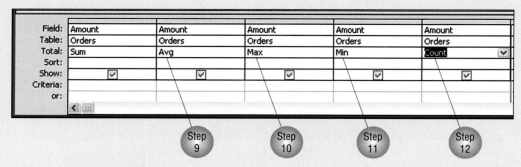

13. Click the Run button on the Query Design toolbar. (Notice the headings that Access chooses for the columns.)
14. Save the query and name it AmountsQuery.
15. Print and then close the query.

Using the *Group By* option in the Total drop-down list you can add a field to the query upon which you want Access to group records for statistical calculations. For example, to calculate the total of all orders for a specific supplier, add the *Supplier #* field to the design grid with the Total set to *Group By*. In Exercise 9, you will create a query in Design view and use aggregate functions to find the total of all order amounts and the average order amounts grouped by the supplier number.

exercise 9

USING AGGREGATE FUNCTIONS AND GROUPING RECORDS

1. Determine the total and average order amounts for each supplier. To begin, make sure the **OutdoorOptions** database file is open, and then click the Queries button on the Objects bar.
2. Double-click *Create query in Design view*.
3. At the Show Table dialog box, click *Orders* in the list box, and then click the Add button.
4. Click *Suppliers* in the list box, click the Add button, and then click the Close button.

ACCESS

5. Drag the *Amount* field from the Orders table list box to the first *Field* text box.
6. Drag the *Amount* field from the Orders table list box to the second *Field* text box.
7. Drag the *Supplier #* field from the Orders table list box to the third *Field* text box.
8. Drag the *Supplier Name* field from the Suppliers table to the fourth *Field* text box.
9. Click the Totals button on the Query Design toolbar.

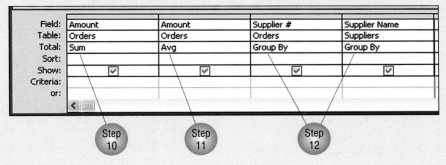

10. Click in the first *Group By* option box in the *Total* row, click the down-pointing arrow, and then click *Sum* at the drop-down list.
11. Click in the second *Group By* option box in the *Total* row, click the down-pointing arrow, and then click *Avg* at the drop-down list.
12. Make sure *Group By* displays in the third and fourth *Group By* option boxes.

13. Click the Run button on the Query Design toolbar.
14. Save the query and name it SupplierAmountsQuery.
15. Print and then close the query.

Changing Query Column Headings

When you ran the queries in Exercises 8 and 9, Access chose the query column heading names for the columns containing aggregate functions. You can create your own headings. To do this, click in the *Field* text box, and then click the Properties button on the Query Design toolbar. This displays the Field Properties dialog box with the General tab selected as shown in Figure 4.7. At this dialog box, click in the *Caption* text box, and then type the desired column heading name.

4.7 *Field Properties Dialog Box with General Tab Selected*

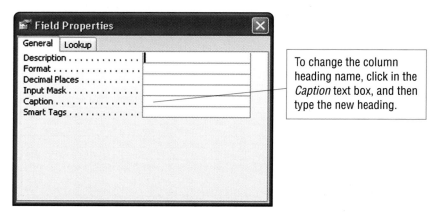

To change the column heading name, click in the *Caption* text box, and then type the new heading.

exercise 10

1. Change two of the query column heading names in SupplierAmountsQuery. To begin, make sure the **OutdoorOptions** database file is open, and then click the Queries button on the Objects bar.
2. Double-click *SupplierAmountsQuery*. (This opens the query in Datasheet view.)
3. Click the View button on the Query Datasheet toolbar to display the query in Design view.
4. Change the name of the first column heading by completing the following steps:
   a. With *Amount* selected in the first *Field* text box, click the Properties button on the Query Design toolbar.
   b. At the Field Properties dialog box with the General tab selected, click in the *Caption* text box, and then type Total Amount.
   c. Click the Close button (located in the upper right corner of the dialog box).
5. Change the name of the second column heading by completing the following steps:
   a. Click in the second *Field* text box.
   b. Click the Properties button on the Query Design toolbar.
   c. At the Field Properties dialog box with the General tab selected, click in the *Caption* text box, type Average Order, and then click the Close button.
6. Click the View button on the Query Design toolbar to change to the Datasheet view and then notice the column headings you created.
7. Save, print, and then close the query.
8. Close the **OutdoorOptions** database file.

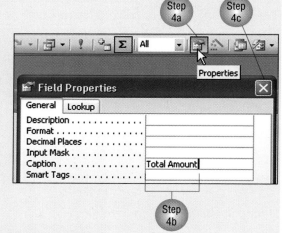

Step 4a Step 4c

Properties

Step 4b

Step 6

	Total Amount	Average Order	Supplier #	Supplier Name
▶	$1,787.50	$893.75	68	Freedom Corporation
	$2,800.00	$2,800.00	70	Rosewood, Inc.
	$3,043.75	$1,521.88	99	KL Distributions

Creating a Crosstab Query

A crosstab query calculates aggregate functions such as Sum and Avg in which field values are grouped by two fields. A wizard is included that guides you through the steps to create the query. The first field selected causes one row to display in the query results datasheet for each group. The second field selected displays one column in the query results datasheet for each group. A third field is specified which is the numeric field to be summarized. The intersection of each row and column holds a value which is the result of the specified aggregate function for the designated row and column group.

Create a crosstab query from fields in one table. If you want to include fields from more than one table, you must first create a query containing the desired fields, and then create the crosstab query. For example, in Exercise 11, you will create a new query that contains fields from each of the three tables in the Outdoor Options database file. Using this query, you will use the Crosstab Query Wizard to create a query that summarizes the order amounts by supplier name and by product ordered. Figure 4.8 displays the results of that crosstab query. The first column displays the supplier names, the second column displays the total of amounts for each supplier, and the remaining columns display the amounts by suppliers for specific items.

QUICK STEPS

Create a Crosstab Query
1. Open database file.
2. Click Queries button.
3. Click New button.
4. Double-click *Crosstab Query Wizard*.
5. Complete wizard steps.

HINT

You can also create your own crosstab query in query Design view.

FIGURE

4.8 *Crosstab Query Results for Exercise 11*

In this query, the order amounts are grouped by supplier name and by individual product.

Supplier Name	Total Of Amount	Backpack	Ski goggles	Snowboard	Two-person tent	Wool ski hats
Freedom Corporation	$1,787.50		$1,100.00			$687.50
KL Distributions	$3,043.75	$1,906.25			$1,137.50	
Rosewood, Inc.	$2,800.00			$2,800.00		

Record: 1 of 3

exercise 11

CREATING A CROSSTAB QUERY

1. Open the **OutdoorOptions** database file.
2. Create a query containing fields from the three tables by completing the following steps:
   a. Click the Queries button on the Objects bar.
   b. Double-click *Create query in Design view*.
   c. At the Show Table dialog box, click *Orders* in the list box and then click the Add button.
   d. Click *Products* in the list box and then click the Add button.

e. Click *Suppliers* in the list box, click the Add button, and then click the Close button.
f. Drag the following fields to the specified *Field* text boxes:
   1) From the Orders table, drag the *Product #* field to the first *Field* text box.
   2) From the Products table, drag the *Product* field to the second *Field* text box.
   3) From the Orders table, drag the *Units Ordered* field to the third *Field* text box.
   4) From the Orders table, drag the *Amount* field to the fourth *Field* text box.
   5) From the Suppliers table, drag the *Supplier Name* field to the fifth *Field* text box.
   6) From the Orders table, drag the *Order Date* field to the sixth *Field* text box.

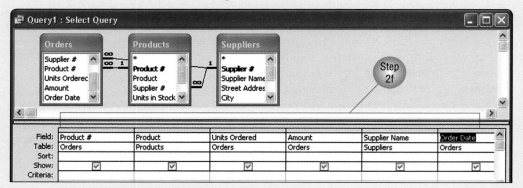

g. Click the Run button to run the query.
h. Save the query and name it Items Ordered.
i. Close the query.
3. Create a crosstab query that summarizes the orders by supplier name and by product ordered by completing the following steps:
   a. At the OutdoorOptions : Database window, make sure the Queries button is selected on the Objects bar, and then click the New button on the window toolbar.
   b. At the New Query dialog box, double-click *Crosstab Query Wizard* in the list box.
   c. At the first Crosstab Query Wizard dialog box, click the *Queries* option in the *View* section, and then click *Query: Items Ordered* in the list box.

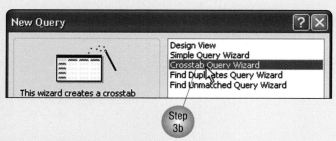

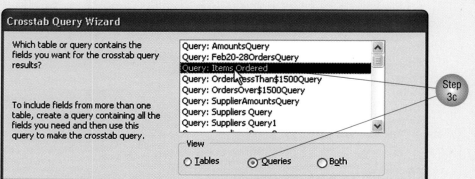

   d. Click the Next button.

ACCESS

e. At the second Crosstab Query Wizard dialog box, click *Supplier Name* in the *Available Fields* list box, and then click the button containing the greater than (>) symbol. (This inserts *Supplier Name* in the *Selected Fields* list box and specifies that you want *Supplier Name* for the row headings.)

f. Click the Next button.

g. At the third Crosstab Query Wizard dialog box, click *Product* in the list box. (This specifies that you want *Product* for the column headings.)

h. Click the Next button.

i. At the fourth Crosstab Query Wizard dialog box, click *Amount* in the *Fields* list box, and click *Sum* in the *Functions* list box.

j. Click the Next button.

k. At the fifth Crosstab Query Wizard dialog box, type **Orders by Supplier by Product** in the *What do you want to name your query?* text box.

l. Click the Finish button.

4. At the Orders by Supplier by Product query window, change the page orientation to landscape and then print the query by clicking the Print button on the Query Datasheet toolbar.

5. Close the query, and then close the **OutdoorOptions** database file.

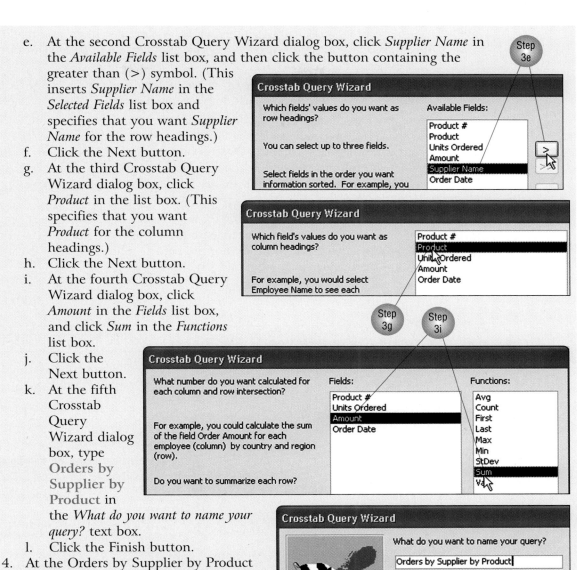

Creating a Find Duplicates Query

Use the find duplicates query to search a specified table or query for duplicate field values within a designated field or fields. Create this type of query, for example, if you suspect a record, such as a product record has inadvertently been entered twice under two different product numbers. A find duplicates query has many applications. A few other examples of how you can use a find duplicates query include:

• Find the records in an Orders table with the same customer number so that you can identify your loyal customers.

QUICK STEPS

Create a Find Duplicates Query
1. Open database file.
2. Click Queries button.
3. Click New button.
4. Double-click *Find Duplicates Query Wizard*.
5. Complete wizard steps.

- Find the records in a Customer table with the same last name and mailing address so that you send only one mailing to a household to save on printing and postage costs.

- Find the records in an Employee Expenses table with the same employee number so that you can see which employee is submitting the most claims.

Access provides the Find Duplicates Query Wizard that builds the select query based on the selections made in a series of dialog boxes. To use this wizard, open the desired database table, click the Queries button on the Objects bar, and then click the New button on the window toolbar. At the New Query dialog box, double-click *Find Duplicates Query Wizard* in the list box, and then complete the steps provided by the wizard.

In Exercise 12, you will assume that you have been asked to update the address for a supplier in the OutdoorOptions database file. Instead of updating the address, you create a new record. You will then use the Find Duplicates Query Wizard to find duplicate field values in the Suppliers table.

exercise 12

CREATING A FIND DUPLICATES QUERY

1. Open the **OutdoorOptions** database file.
2. Click the Tables button on the Objects bar and then open the Suppliers table.
3. Add the following record to the table:

Supplier #	=	29
Supplier Name	=	Langley Corporation
Street Address	=	805 First Avenue
City	=	Burnaby
Province	=	BC
Postal Code	=	V5V 9K2
E-mail Address	=	langley@emcp.net

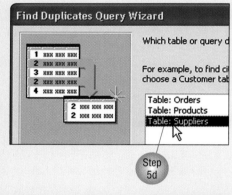

4. Close the Suppliers table.
5. Use the Find Duplicates Query Wizard to find any duplicate supplier names by completing the following steps:
   a. Click the Queries button on the Objects bar.
   b. Click the New button on the window toolbar.
   c. At the New Query dialog box, double-click *Find Duplicates Query Wizard*.
   d. At the first wizard dialog box, click *Table: Suppliers* in the list box.
   e. Click the Next button.
   f. At the second wizard dialog box, click *Supplier Name* in the *Available fields* list box, and then click the button containing the greater than (>) symbol. (This moves the *Supplier Name* field to the *Duplicate-value fields* list box.)
   g. Click the Next button.

Step 5d

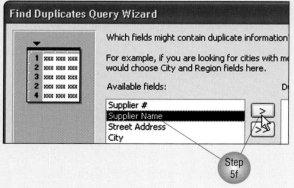

Step 5f

h. At the third wizard dialog box, click the button containing the two greater than (>>) symbols. (This moves all the fields to the *Additional query fields* list box. You are doing this because if you find a duplicate supplier name, you want to view all the fields to determine which record is accurate.)

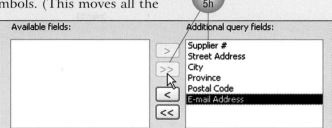

Step 5h

i. Click the Next button.
j. At the fourth (and last) wizard dialog box, type **DuplicateSuppliers** in the *What do you want to name your query?* text box.

Step 5j

k. Click the Finish button.
l. Change the orientation to landscape and then print the DuplicateSuppliers query.

6. As you look at the query results, you realize that an inaccurate record was entered for Langley so you decide to delete one of the records. To do this, complete the following steps:
a. With the DuplicateSuppliers query open, position the mouse pointer in the record selector bar next to the first record (the one with a supplier number of *29*) until the pointer changes to a right-pointing black arrow, and then click the left mouse button. (This selects the entire row.)
b. Click the Delete Record button on the Query Datasheet toolbar.

Step 6b

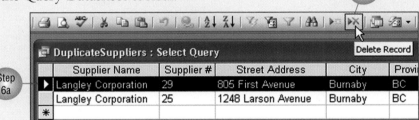

Step 6a

c. At the message asking you to confirm, click the Yes button.
d. Close the DuplicateSuppliers query.

7. Change the street address for Langley Corporation by completing the following steps:
a. Click the Tables button on the Objects bar.
b. Double-click the *Suppliers* table.
c. With the Suppliers table open in Datasheet view, change the address for Langley Corporation from *1248 Larson Avenue* to *805 First Avenue*. Leave the other fields as displayed.
d. Close the Suppliers table.

8. Close the **OutdoorOptions** database file.

In Exercise 12, you used the Find Duplicates Query Wizard to find records containing the same field. In Exercise 13, you will use the Find Duplicates Query Wizard to find information on the suppliers you order from the most. You could use this information to negotiate for better prices or to ask for discounts.

exercise 13

1. Open the **OutdoorOptions** database file.
2. Create a query with the following fields (in the order shown) from the specified tables:

Order #	=	Orders table
Supplier #	=	Orders table
Supplier Name	=	Suppliers table
Product #	=	Orders table
Units Ordered	=	Orders table
Amount	=	Orders table
Order Date	=	Orders table

3. Run the query.
4. Save the query with the name SupplierOrders and then close the query.
5. Use the Find Duplicates Query Wizard to find the suppliers you order from the most by completing the following steps:
    a. Click the Queries button on the Objects bar.
    b. Click the New button on the window toolbar.
    c. At the New Query dialog box, double-click *Find Duplicates Query Wizard*.
    d. At the first wizard dialog box, click *Queries* in the *View* section, and then double-click *Query: SupplierOrders*.
    e. Click the Next button.
    f. At the second wizard dialog box, click *Supplier #* in the *Available fields* list box and then click the button containing the greater than (>) symbol.

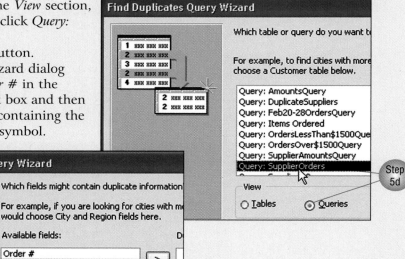

    g. Click the Next button.
    h. At the third wizard dialog box, click the button containing the two greater than (>>) symbols. (This moves all the fields to the *Duplicate-value fields* list box.)
    i. Click the Next button.

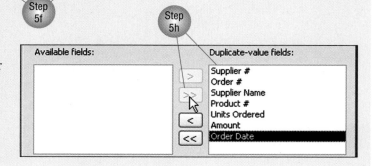

ACCESS

j. At the fourth (and last) wizard dialog box, type **DuplicateSupplierOrders** in the *What do you want to name your query?* text box.

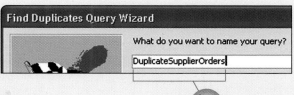

k. Click the Finish button.
l. Print the DuplicateSupplierOrders query.
6. Close the query, and then close the **OutdoorOptions** database file.

Creating an Unmatched Query

Create a find unmatched query to compare two tables and produce a list of the records in one table that have no matching record in the other related table. This type of query is useful to produce lists such as customers who have never placed an order or an invoice with no payment record. Access provides the Find Unmatched Query Wizard that builds the select query by guiding you through a series of dialog boxes.

In Exercise 14, you will use the Find Unmatched Query Wizard to find all products that have no units on order. This information is helpful because it indicates which products are not selling and might need to be discontinued or returned. To use the Find Unmatched Query Wizard, open the database file, and then click the Queries button on the Objects bar. At the New Query dialog box, click the New button on the window toolbar, and then double-click *Find Unmatched Query Wizard* in the list box.

QUICK STEPS

Create an Unmatched Query
1. Open database file.
2. Click Queries button.
3. Click New button.
4. Double-click *Find Unmatched Query Wizard.*
5. Complete wizard steps.

exercise 14

CREATING A FIND UNMATCHED QUERY

1. Open the **OutdoorOptions** database file.
2. Use the Find Unmatched Query Wizard to find all products that do not have any units on order by completing the following steps:
    a. Click the Queries button on the Objects bar.
    b. Click the New button on the window toolbar.
    c. At the New Query dialog box, double-click *Find Unmatched Query Wizard.*
    d. At the first wizard dialog box, click *Table: Products* in the list box. (This is the table containing the fields you want to see in the query results.)
    e. Click the Next button.
    f. At the second wizard dialog box, make sure *Table: Orders* is selected in the list box. (This is the table containing the related records.)
    g. Click the Next button.

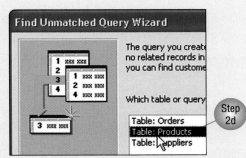

h. At the third wizard dialog box, make sure *Product #* is selected in the *Fields in 'Products'* list box and in the *Fields in 'Orders'* list box.

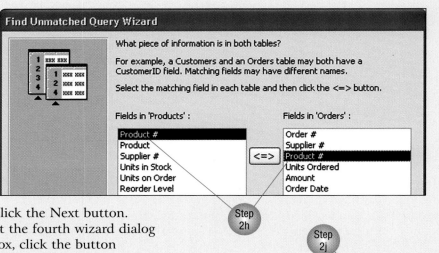

i. Click the Next button.
j. At the fourth wizard dialog box, click the button containing the two greater than symbols (>>) to move all fields from the *Available fields* list box to the *Selected fields* list box.
k. Click the Next button.
l. At the fifth wizard dialog box, click the Finish button. (Let the wizard determine the query name: *Products Without Matching Orders*.)

3. Print and then close the Products Without Matching Orders query.

Filtering Data

You can place a set of restrictions, called a **filter**, on records in a database table or form to temporarily isolate specific records. A filter, like a query, lets you select specific field values in a database table or form. Data can be filtered by selection or by form.

Filter by Selection
1. Open database table.
2. Select specific data.
3. Click Filter By Selection button.

Filter By Selection

Apply Filter

Using Filter By Selection

With the Filter By Selection button that displays on the Table Datasheet toolbar, you can select specific data in a field and then tell Access to display only those records containing the selected data. For example, if you want to display only those records for a specific supplier number, select the supplier number in the appropriate database table, and then click the Filter By Selection button on the Table Datasheet toolbar. Only those records matching the selected data are displayed on the screen.

The Table Datasheet toolbar contains a button named Apply Filter. When a filter is applied by selection, this button changes to Remove Filter (and also displays with a blue border). If you want to remove the filter and display the original data in the database table, click the Remove Filter button on the Table Datasheet toolbar.

exercise 15

1. Open the **OutdoorOptions** database file.
2. At the OutdoorOptions : Database window, click the Tables button on the Objects bar.
3. Open the Products database table by double-clicking *Products* in the list box.
4. Use the Filter By Selection button to display only those records with no units on order by completing the following steps:
   a. Select a 0 (zero) in one of the fields in the *Units on Order* column.
   b. Click the Filter By Selection button on the Table Datasheet toolbar. (This displays only those records with no units on order.)
   c. Sort the records in ascending order by the supplier number by completing the following steps:
      1) Click in any field in the *Supplier #* column.
      2) Click the Sort Ascending button on the Table Datasheet toolbar.
   d. Print the database table.
   e. After printing the table, click the Remove Filter button on the Table Datasheet toolbar (this redisplays all records in the database table).
5. Close the Products database table without saving the changes to the design.
6. Open the Suppliers database table by double-clicking *Suppliers* in the list box.
7. Use the Filter By Selection button to display only those records of suppliers in Burnaby by completing the following steps:
   a. Select *Burnaby* in one of the fields in the *City* column.
   b. Click the Filter By Selection button on the Table Datasheet toolbar.
   c. Print the database table in landscape orientation.
   d. After printing the table, click the Remove Filter button on the Table Datasheet toolbar (this redisplays all records in the database table).
8. Close the Suppliers database table without saving changes to the design.
9. Close the **OutdoorOptions** database file.

Step 4b

Step 4a

Filter By Selection

#	Units in Stock	Units on Order	Reorder Level
	61	0	50
	58	0	50
	36	0	30
	12	0	10
	0	0	0

Step 4c

Sort Ascending

Supplier #	Units in Stock
54	61
31	58
68	36
99	12
	0

Step 4e

Remove Filter

Supplier #	Units in Stock	Units on Order
31	58	0
54	61	0
68	36	0
99	12	0
	0	0

Step 7b

Filter By Selection

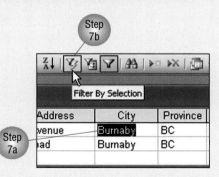

Address	City	Province
venue	Burnaby	BC
ad	Burnaby	BC

Step 7a

Filter By Form

QUICK STEPS

Filter by Form
1. Open database table.
2. Click Filter By Form button.
3. Click in desired field.
4. Click the down-pointing arrow in field.
5. Click desired option.
6. Click Apply Filter button.

Using Filter By Form

The Table Datasheet toolbar contains a Filter By Form button that, when clicked, displays the database table with a blank record. You set the values you want filtered records to contain at this blank record. Figure 4.9 shows a blank record for the Orders database table in the OutdoorOptions database file. At the Orders : Filter By Form window displayed in Figure 4.9, notice that two tabs display toward the bottom. The Look for tab is active by default and tells Access to look for whatever data you insert in a field. To display only those records for supplier number 68, you would click inside the *Supplier #* field. This causes a down-pointing arrow to display. Click this down-pointing arrow and then click *68* at the drop-down list. To filter the records, click the Filter By Form button on the Table Datasheet toolbar and only those records for supplier number 68 are displayed on the screen.

FIGURE

4.9 *Orders: Filter By Form Window*

Click in the desired field, click the down-pointing arrow, and then click the desired item.

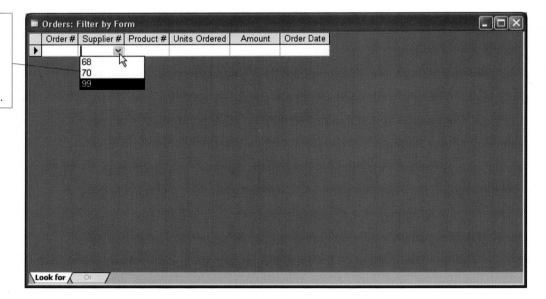

exercise 16

USING FILTER BY FORM TO DISPLAY SPECIFIC RECORDS

1. Open the **OutdoorOptions** database file.
2. At the OutdoorOptions : Database window, click the Tables button on the Objects bar, and then double-click *Orders* in the list box.
3. Use the Filter By Form button to display only those records containing supplier number 68 in the *Supplier #* field by completing the following steps:
   a. Click the Filter By Form button on the Table Datasheet toolbar.
   b. At the blank record, click in the *Supplier #* field.

c. Click the down-pointing arrow at the right side of the *Supplier #* field and then click *68* at the drop-down list.

d. Click the Apply Filter button on the Table Datasheet toolbar.

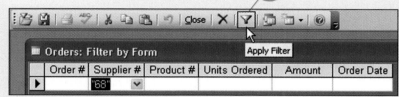

Step 3c

Step 3d

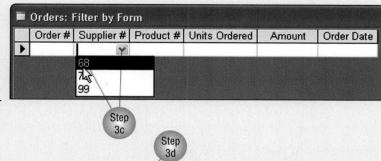

Apply Filter

e. Print the records.

4. Close the Orders : Table window without saving the changes to the design.

5. At the OutdoorOptions : Database window, double-click *Products* in the list box.

6. Use the Filter By Form button to display only those records containing supplier number 99 in the *Supplier #* field by completing the following steps:

a. Click the Filter By Form button on the Table Datasheet toolbar.

b. At the blank record, click in the *Supplier #* field.

c. Click the down-pointing arrow at the right side of the *Supplier #* field and then click *99* at the drop-down list.

d. Click the Apply Filter button on the Table Datasheet toolbar.

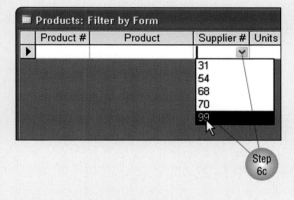

Step 6c

e. Print the records.

7. Close the Products : Table window without saving the changes to the design.

8. Close the **OutdoorOptions** database file.

A tab displays at the bottom of the Orders: Filter By Form window shown in Figure 4.6 with the word *Or*. Click this tab if you want to filter on two field values. When you click the Or tab, another blank record displays below the first one. As an example of when you would use the Or tab, suppose you wanted to display only those records for supplier # 68 *or* supplier # 31. You would insert *68* in the *Supplier #* field of the first blank record, click the Or button, and then insert *31* in the *Supplier #* field in the second blank record. As another example, in a database table containing suppliers' addresses, you could display only those records for suppliers located in Vancouver *or* Port Moody.

HINT
Data can be filtered on two field values.

1. Open the **OutdoorOptions** database file.
2. At the OutdoorOptions : Database window, click the Tables button on the Objects bar, and then double-click *Suppliers* in the list box.
3. Use the Filter By Form button to display only those records for suppliers in Port Moody *or* Burnaby by completing the following steps:
   a. Click the Filter By Form button on the Table Datasheet toolbar.
   b. At the blank record, click in the *City* field.
   c. Click the down-pointing arrow at the right side of the *City* field, and then click *Port Moody* at the drop-down list.
   d. Click the Or tab located toward the bottom of the Suppliers : Filter by Form window.
   e. At the new blank record, click the down-pointing arrow at the right side of the *City* field, and then click *Burnaby* at the drop-down list.
   f. Click the Apply Filter button on the Table Datasheet toolbar.
   g. Print the records in landscape orientation.
4. Close the Suppliers : Table window without saving the changes to the design.
5. Close the **OutdoorOptions** database file.

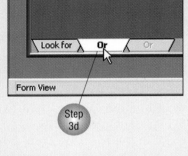

Step
3d

CHAPTER summary

➤ Being able to extract specific information is one of the most important functions of a database. Data can be extracted from an Access database file by performing a query, which can be done by designing a query or using the Simple Query Wizard.

➤ Designing a query consists of identifying the database table, the field or fields from which the data will be drawn, and the criteria for selecting the data.

➤ During the designing of a query, write the criterion (or criteria) for extracting the specific data. Access inserts any necessary symbols in the criterion when the Enter key is pressed.

➤ In a criterion, quotation marks surround field values and pound symbols (#) surround dates. The asterisk (*) can be used as a wildcard symbol.

➤ A query can be performed on fields within one database table or on fields from related database tables.

➤ When designing a query, you can specify the sort order of a field or fields.

➤ The Simple Query Wizard guides you through the steps for preparing a query. A query designed by the Simple Query Wizard can be modified.

➤ A calculated field can be inserted in a *Field* text box when designing a query.

➤ Include an aggregate function such as Sum, Avg, Min, Max, or Count to calculate statistics from numeric field values. Click the Totals button on the Query Design toolbar to display the aggregate function list.

➤ Use the *Group By* option in the Total drop-down list to add a field to a query upon which you want Access to group records for statistical calculations.

➤ Create a crosstab query to calculate aggregate functions such as Sum and Avg in which fields are grouped by two fields. Create a crosstab query from fields in one table. If you want to include fields from more than one table, create a query first, and then create the crosstab query.

➤ Use the find duplicates query to search a specified table or query for duplicate field values within a designated field or fields.

➤ Create a find unmatched query to compare two tables and produce a list of the records in one table that have no matching record in the other related table.

➤ A set of restrictions, called a filter, can be set on records in a database table or form. A filter lets you select specific field values.

➤ Filter specific data in a field with the Filter By Selection button that displays on the Table Datasheet toolbar.

➤ Click the Filter By Form button on the Table Datasheet toolbar and a blank record is displayed. Set the values you want filtered records to contain at this blank record.

➤ When a filter is done by selection or by form, the Apply Filter button on the Table Datasheet toolbar changes to Remove Filter.

FEATURES summary

FEATURE	BUTTON	MENU
New Query dialog box	New	Insert, Query
Simple Query Wizard		Insert, Query, Simple Query Wizard
Run a query	!	Query, Run
Add Total row to Design grid	Σ	View, Totals
Crosstab Query Wizard		Insert, Query, Crosstab Wizard
Find Duplicates Query Wizard		Insert, Query, Find Duplicates Query Wizard
Find Unmatched Query Wizard		Insert, Query, Find Unmatched Query Wizard
Filter by selection		Records, Filter, Filter By Selection
Filter by form		Records, Filter, Filter By Form

CONCEPTS check

Completion: On a blank sheet of paper, indicate the correct term, symbol, or command for each description.

1. A query can be performed by designing your own query or using this wizard.
2. This is the term used for the results of the query.
3. This is the symbol Access will automatically insert around a field value when establishing criteria for a query.
4. This is the symbol Access will automatically insert around a date when establishing criteria for a query.
5. Use this symbol when establishing criteria to indicate a wildcard character.
6. This is the criterion you would type to return field values greater than $500.
7. This is the criterion you would type to return field values that begin with the letter *L*.
8. This is the criterion you would type to return field values that are not in Oregon.
9. This type of function, such as Sum, Avg, Min, Max, or Count can be included in a query to calculate statistics from numeric field values of all the records in the table.
10. With this option from the Total drop-down list, you can add a field to the query upon which you want Access to group records for statistical calculations.
11. This type of query calculates aggregate functions in which field values are grouped by two fields.
12. Use this type of query to compare two tables and produce a list of the records in one table that have no matching record in the other related table.
13. A set of restrictions placed on records in a database table or form is referred to as this.
14. Click this button on the Table Datasheet toolbar to display only those records containing the selected data.
15. Click this tab, located at the bottom of the Filter By Form dialog box, to filter on two field values.
16. List the steps you would complete to display only those records with order dates between February 15, 2005, and February 20, 2005, in the Orders database table located in the OutdoorOptions database file.

SKILLS check

Assessment 1

1. Copy the **LegalServices** database file from the CD that accompanies this textbook to your disk. Remove the read-only attribute from the **LegalServices** database file.
2. Open the **LegalServices** database file.
3. Design the following queries on data in the **LegalServices** database file:
   a. Extract records from the Billing database table with the following specifications:
      1) Include the fields *Billing #*, *Client ID*, and *Category* in the query.
      2) Extract those records with the SE category.
      3) Save the query and name it SECategoryBillingQuery.
      4) Print and then close the query.
   b. Extract records from the Billing database table with the following specifications:
      1) Include the fields *Billing #*, *Client ID*, and *Date*.

2) Extract those records in the *Date* field with dates between 6/7/2005 and 6/9/2005.
3) Save the query and name it June7-9BillingQuery.
4) Print and then close the query.

c. Extract records from the Clients database table with the following specifications:
1) Include the fields *First Name*, *Last Name*, and *City*.
2) Extract those records with any city other than Kent in the *City* field.
3) Save the query and name it KentClientsQuery.
4) Print and then close the query.

Assessment 2

1. With the **LegalServices** database file open, perform a query by extracting information from two tables with the following specifications:
   a. Include the fields *Billing #*, *Client ID*, *Date*, and *Rate #* from the Billing database table.
   b. Include the field *Rate* from the Rates database table.
   c. Extract those records with a rate number greater than 2.
   d. Save the query and name it RateGreaterThan2Query.
   e. Print and then close the query.
2. Extract information from three tables with the following specifications:
   a. Include the field *Attorney* from the Attorneys database table.
   b. Include the fields *First Name* and *Last Name* from the Clients database table.
   c. Include the fields *Attorney ID*, *Date,* and *Hours* from the Billing database.
   d. Extract those records with an Attorney ID of 12.
   e. Save the query and name it AttorneyQuery.
   f. Print and then close the query.

Assessment 3

1. With the **LegalServices** database file open, use the Simple Query Wizard to extract specific information from three tables with the following specifications:
   a. At the first Simple Query Wizard dialog box, include the following fields:

   From the Attorneys table: *Attorney ID* and *Attorney*
   From Categories table: *Category Name*
   From Billing table: *Hours*

   b. At the second Simply Query Wizard dialog box, click Next.
   c. At the third Simple Query Wizard dialog box, click the *Modify the query design* option, and then click the Finish button.
   d. At the query window, insert *14* in the *Criteria* text box in the *Attorney ID* column.
   e. Run the query.
2. Save the query with the default name.
3. Print and then close the query.

Assessment 4

1. With the **LegalServices** database file open, create a query in Design view with the Billing table. Drag the *Hours* field from the Billing table to the first, second, third, fourth, and fifth *Field* text boxes.
2. Click the Totals button on the Query Design toolbar.
3. Insert *Sum* in the first *Group By* list box in the *Total* row.
4. Insert *Avg* in the second *Group By* list box in the *Total* row.

5. Insert *Min* in the third *Group By* list box in the *Total* row.
6. Insert *Max* in the fourth *Group By* list box in the *Total* row.
7. Insert *Count* in the fifth *Group By* list box in the *Total* row.
8. Run the query.
9. Save the query and name it HoursAmountQuery.
10. Print and then close the query.

Assessment 5

1. With the **LegalServices** database file open, create a query in Design view with the following specifications:
   a. Add the Attorneys table and the Billing table to the query window.
   b. Drag the *Attorney* field from the Attorneys table to the first *Field* text box.
   c. Drag the *Attorney ID* field from the Billing table to the second *Field* text box.
   d. Drag the *Hours* field from the Billing table to the third *Field* text box.
2. Click the Totals button on the Query Design toolbar.
3. Insert *Sum* in the third *Group By* list box in the *Hours* column (in the *Total* row).
4. Run the query.
5. Save the query and name it AttorneyHours.
6. Print and then close the query.

Assessment 6

1. With the **LegalServices** database file open, create a query in Design view with the following specifications:
   a. Add the Attorneys, Clients, Categories, and Billing tables to the query window.
   b. Drag the *Attorney* field from the Attorneys table to the first *Field* text box.
   c. Drag the *Client ID* field from the Clients table to the second *Field* text box.
   d. Drag the *Category Name* field from the Categories table to the third *Field* text box.
   e. Drag the *Hours* field from the Billing table to the fourth *Field* text box.
   f. Run the query.
   g. Save the query and name it AttorneyClientHours.
   h. Print and then close the query.
2. Create a crosstab query that summarizes the hours by attorney by category with the following specifications:
   a. At the first Crosstab Query Wizard dialog box, click the *Queries* option in the *View* section, and then click *Query: AttorneyClientHours* in the list box.
   b. At the second Crosstab Query Wizard dialog box, click *Attorney* in the *Available Fields* list box, and then click the button containing the greater than (>) symbol.
   c. At the third Crosstab Query Wizard dialog box, click *Category Name* in the list box.
   d. At the fourth Crosstab Query Wizard dialog box, click *Hours* in the *Fields* list box, and click *Sum* in the *Functions* list box.
   e. At the fifth Crosstab Query Wizard dialog box, type Hours by Attorney by Category in the *What do you want to name your query?* text box.
3. Change the page orientation to landscape and then print and then close the Hours by Attorney by Category query.

Assessment 7

1. With the **LegalServices** database file open, use the Find Duplicates Query Wizard to find those clients with the same last name with the following specifications:
   a. At the first wizard dialog box, click *Table: Clients* in the list box.
   b. At the second wizard dialog box, click *Last Name* in the *Available fields* list box, and then click the button containing the greater than (>) symbol.

    c. At the third wizard dialog box, click the button containing the two greater than (>>) symbols.

    d. At the fourth wizard dialog box, name the query DuplicateLastNames.

2. Change the page orientation to landscape and then print and then close the query.

Assessment 8

1. With the **LegalServices** database file open, use the Find Unmatched Query Wizard to find all clients who do not have any billing hours with the following specifications:

    a. At the first wizard dialog box, click *Table: Clients* in the list box.

    b. At the second wizard dialog box, click *Table: Billing* in the list box.

    c. At the third wizard dialog box, make sure *Client ID* is selected in the *Fields in 'Clients'* list box and in the *Fields in 'Billing'* list box.

    d. At the fourth wizard dialog box, click the button containing the two greater than symbols (>>) to move all fields from the *Available fields* list box to the *Selected fields* list box.

    e. At the fifth wizard dialog box, click the Finish button. (Let the wizard determine the query name: *Clients Without Matching Billing*.)

2. Change the page orientation to landscape and then print and then close the Clients Without Matching Billing query.

Assessment 9

1. With the **LegalServices** database file open, open the Clients database table and then use the Filter By Selection button on the Table Datasheet toolbar to display the following records:

    a. Display only those records of clients who live in Renton. When the records of clients in Renton display, change the page orientation to landscape, print the results, and then click the Remove Filter button.

    b. Display only those records of clients with the Zip Code of 98033. When the records of clients with the Zip Code 98033 display, change the page orientation to landscape, print the results, and then click the Remove Filter button.

2. Close the Clients database table without saving the changes.

3. Open the Billing database table, and then use the Filter By Selection button on the Table Datasheet toolbar to display the following records:

    a. Display only those records with a Category of CC. Print the CC records and then click the Remove Filter button.

    b. Display only those records with an Attorney ID of 12. Print the records, and then click the Remove Filter button.

4. Close the Billing database table without saving the changes.

Assessment 10

1. With the **LegalServices** database file open, open the Clients database table, and then use the Filter By Form button to display clients in Auburn or Renton. (Be sure to use the Or tab at the very bottom of the table.) Change the page orientation to landscape, print the table, and then click the Remove Filter button.

2. Close the Clients database table without saving the changes.

3. Open the Billing database table, and then use the Filter By Form button to display categories G or P. Print the table and then click the Remove Filter button.

4. Close the Billing database table without saving the changes.

5. Close the **LegalServices** database file.

Assessment 11

1. Use the Access Help feature to learn how to hide fields in a query's result.
2. After reading the information on hiding fields, complete the following steps:
   a. Open the **LegalServices** database file.
   b. Design the following query:
      1) At the Show Table dialog box, add the Billing table, the Clients table, and the Rates table.
      2) At the Query1 : Select Query window, drag the following fields to *Field* text boxes:

         Clients table:
         > *First Name*
         > *Last Name*
         Billing table:
         > *Hours*
         Rates table:
         > *Rate*

      3) Insert in the fifth *Field* text box the calculated field *Total:[Hours]*[Rate]*.
      4) Hide the *Hours* and the *Rate* fields.
   c. Run the query.
   d. Print the query and then close it without saving it.
3. Close the **LegalServices** database file.

CHAPTER challenge

You are a sales associate for a small boutique named Gigi's Gifts and Things. A shipment of items has just arrived. Prices need to be determined for each of the items. You have been asked by the manager to use the store's database, named **Gigi'sGifts**, to help with this process. You decide to create a query, based on the Inventory table. Include the *Item* and *Cost* fields in the query. In addition, create a calculated field that determines the selling price of each item. Assume a 65% markup for each item. Be sure the *Cost* field doesn't show when the query is run. Save the query as Selling Price.

When a calculated field is created in a query, no formatting is applied to the new field. Use the Help feature to learn about formatting fields in a query. Then use the Selling Price query created in the first part of the Chapter Challenge and format the Selling Price field to currency. Save the query again.

The prices of the new items will be posted to Gigi's Gifts and Things Web site. Prepare the query created and used in the first two parts of the Chapter Challenge for the Web site by exporting it as an HTML file. Save the HTML file as **Gigi'sInventory**.

WORK IN Progress

Creating Database Tables, Queries, and Filters

ASSESSING proficiencies

In this unit, you have learned to design and create database files, modify data in tables, and create a one-to-many relationship between database tables. You also learned how to create a database table using the Table Wizard, perform queries on data in tables, and filter records in a table.

Assessment 1

1. Use Access to create database tables for Cornerstone Catering. Name the database file **Cornerstone**. Create a database table named Employees that includes the following fields (you determine the data type, field size, and description):

   Employee # (primary key)
   First Name
   Last Name
   Cell Phone Number (Consider using the Input Mask Wizard for this field.)

2. After creating the database table, save the table. Switch to Datasheet view and then enter the following data in the appropriate fields:

Employee #: 10	*Employee #:* 14
First Name: Erin	*First Name:* Mikio
Last Name: Jergens	*Last Name:* Ogami
Cell Phone Number: (505) 555-3193	*Cell Phone Number:* (505) 555-1087
Employee #: 19	*Employee #:* 21
First Name: Martin	*First Name:* Isabelle
Last Name: Vaughn	*Last Name:* Baptista
Cell Phone Number: (505) 555-4461	*Cell Phone Number:* (505) 555-4425
Employee #: 24	*Employee #:* 26
First Name: Shawn	*First Name:* Madison
Last Name: Kettering	*Last Name:* Harris
Cell Phone Number: (505) 555-3885	*Cell Phone Number:* (505) 555-2256

3. Automatically adjust the column widths.
4. Save, print, and then close the Employees database table.
5. Create a database table named Plans that includes the following fields (you determine the data type, field size, and description):

   Plan Code (primary key)
   Plan

6. After creating the database table, save it and name it Plans. Switch to Datasheet view and then enter the following data in the appropriate fields:

Plan Code: A
Plan: Sandwich Buffet

Plan Code: B
Plan: Cold Luncheon Buffet

Plan Code: C
Plan: Hot Luncheon Buffet

Plan Code: D
Plan: Combination Dinner

7. Automatically adjust the column widths.
8. Save, print, and then close the Plans database table.
9. Create a database table named Prices that includes the following fields (you determine the data type, field size, and description [except as shown]):

Price Code (primary key)
Price Per Person (identify this data type as Currency)

10. After creating the database table, save the table. Switch to Datasheet view and then enter the following data in the appropriate fields:

Price Code: 1
Price Per Person: $11.50

Price Code: 2
Price Per Person: $12.75

Price Code: 3
Price Per Person: $14.50

Price Code: 4
Price Per Person: $16.00

Price Code: 5
Price Per Person: $18.50

11. Automatically adjust the column widths.
12. Save, print, and then close the Prices database table.
13. Create a database table named Clients that includes the following fields (you determine the data type, field size, and description):

Client # (primary key)
Client Name
Street Address
City
State
ZIP Code
Telephone (Consider using the Input Mask Wizard for this field.)

14. After creating the database table, save the table. Switch to Datasheet view and then enter the following data in the appropriate fields:

Client #: 104
Client Name: Sarco Corporation
Street Address: 340 Cordova Road
City: Santa Fe
State: NM
ZIP Code: 87510
Telephone: (505) 555-3880

Client #: 155
Client Name: Creative Concepts
Street Address: 1046 Market Street
City: Los Alamos
State: NM
ZIP Code: 87547
Telephone: (505) 555-1200

Client #: 218
Client Name: Allenmore Systems
Street Address: 7866 Second Street

Client #: 286
Client Name: Sol Enterprises
Street Address: 120 Cerrillos Road

City: Espanola   *City:* Santa Fe
State: NM   *State:* NM
ZIP Code: 87535   *ZIP Code:* 87560
Telephone: (505) 555-3455   *Telephone:* (505) 555-7700

15. Automatically adjust the column widths.
16. Save, print, and then close the Clients database table.
17. Create a database table named Events that includes the following fields (you determine the data type, field size, and description [except as shown]):

> *Event #* (primary key; identify this data type as AutoNumber)
> *Client #*
> *Employee #*
> *Date* (identify this data type as Date/Time)
> *Plan Code*
> *Price Code*
> *Number of People* (identify this data type as Number)

18. After creating the database table, save the table. Switch to Datasheet view and then enter the following data in the appropriate fields:

Event #: (AutoNumber)   *Event #:* (AutoNumber)
Client #: 218   *Client #:* 104
Employee #: 14   *Employee #:* 19
Date: 7/1/2005   *Date:* 7/2/2005
Plan Code: B   *Plan Code:* D
Price Code: 3   *Price Code:* 5
Number of People: 250   *Number of People:* 120

Event #: (AutoNumber)   *Event #:* (AutoNumber)
Client #: 155   *Client #:* 286
Employee #: 24   *Employee #:* 10
Date: 7/8/2005   *Date:* 7/9/2005
Plan Code: A   *Plan Code:* C
Price Code: 1   *Price Code:* 4
Number of People: 300   *Number of People:* 75

Event #: (AutoNumber)   *Event #:* (AutoNumber)
Client #: 218   *Client #:* 104
Employee #: 14   *Employee #:* 10
Date: 7/10/2005   *Date:* 7/12/2005
Plan Code: C   *Plan Code:* B
Price Code: 4   *Price Code:* 3
Number of People: 50   *Number of People:* 30

19. Automatically adjust the column widths.
20. Save, print, and then close the Events database table.

Assessment 2

1. With the **Cornerstone** database file open, create the following one-to-many relationships enforcing referential integrity and cascading fields and records:
   a. *Client #* in the Clients table is the "one" and *Client #* in the Events table is the "many."

    b. *Employee #* in the Employees table is the "one" and *Employee #* in the Events table is the "many."

    c. *Plan Code* in the Plans table is the "one" and *Plan Code* in the Events table is the "many."

    d. *Price Code* in the Prices table is the "one" and *Price Code* in the Events table is the "many."

2. Save and then print the relationships.
3. Close the report and the Relationships window.

Assessment 3

1. With the **Cornerstone** database file open, open the Plans database table in Datasheet view and then add the following record at the end of the table:

> *Plan Code:* E
> *Plan:* Hawaiian Luau Buffet

2. Save, print, and then close the Plans database table.
3. Open the Events database table in Datasheet view and then add the following record at the end of the table:

> *Event #:* (AutoNumber)
> *Client #:* 104
> *Employee #:* 21
> *Date:* 7/16/2005
> *Plan Code:* E
> *Price Code:* 5
> *Number of People:* 125

4. Save, print, and then close the Events database table.

Assessment 4

1. With the **Cornerstone** database file open, perform a query by extracting records from the Events database table with the following specifications:
    a. Include the fields *Client #*, *Date*, and *Plan Code*.
    b. Extract those records with a Plan Code of C.
    c. Save the query and name it PlanCodeC.
    d. Print and then close the query.
2. Extract records from the Clients database table with the following specifications:
    a. Include the fields *Client Name*, *City*, and *Telephone*.
    b. Extract those records with a city of Santa Fe.
    c. Save the query and name it SantaFeClients.
    d. Print and then close the query.
3. Extract information from two tables with the following specifications:
    a. From the Clients table, include the fields *Client Name* and *Telephone*.
    b. From the Events table, include the field *Date*, *Plan Code*, and *Number of People*.
    c. Extract those records with a date between July 10 and July 25, 2005.
    d. Save the query and name it July10-25Events.
    e. Print and then close the query.

Assessment 5

1. With the **Cornerstone** database file open, create a query in Design view with the Events table and the Prices table, and drag the following fields to the specified locations:
   a. Drag *Event #* from the *Events* table to the first *Field* text box.
   b. Drag *Date* from the *Events* table to the second *Field* text box.
   c. Drag *Number of People* from the *Events* table to the third *Field* text box.
   d. Drag *Price Per Person* from the *Prices* table to the fourth *Field* text box.
2. Insert the following calculated field entry in the fifth *Field* text box: Amount:[Number of People]*[Price Per Person].
3. Run the query.
4. Save the query and name it EventAmounts.
5. Print and then close the query.

Assessment 6

1. With the **Cornerstone** database file open, create a query in Design view using the EventAmounts query with the following specifications:
   a. At the Cornerstone : Database window with Queries selected in the Objects bar, double-click *Create query in Design view*.
   b. At the Show Tables dialog box, click the Queries tab.
   c. Double-click *EventAmounts* in the list box, and then click the Close button.
   d. Drag the *Amount* field to the first, second, third, and fourth *Field* text boxes.
   e. Click the Totals button on the Query Design toolbar.
   f. Insert *Sum* in the first *Group By* list box in the *Total* row.
   g. Insert *Avg* in the second *Group By* list box in the *Total* row.
   h. Insert *Min* in the third *Group By* list box in the *Total* row.
   i. Insert *Max* in the fourth *Group By* list box in the *Total* row.
2. Run the query.
3. Save the query and name it AmountTotals.
4. Print and then close the query.

Assessment 7

1. With the **Cornerstone** database file open, create a query in Design view using the Employees table, the Clients table, the Events table, and the EventAmounts query with the following specifications:
   a. At the Cornerstone : Database window with Queries selected in the Objects bar, double-click *Create query in Design view*.
   b. At the Show Tables dialog box, click *Employees* and then click the Add button.
   c. Click *Clients* and then click the Add button.
   d. Click *Events* and then click the Add button.
   e. Click the Queries tab, click *EventAmounts* in the list box, click the Add button, and then click the Close button.
   f. Drag the *Last Name* field from the Employees table to the first *Field* text box.
   g. Drag the *Client Name* field from the Clients table to the second *Field* text box.
   h. Drag the *Amount* field from the EventAmounts query to the third *Field* text box.

     i.   Drag the *Date* field from the Events table to the fourth *Field* text box.
2. Run the query.
3. Save the query and name it EmployeeEvents.
4. Close the query.
5. Using the Crosstab Query Wizard, create a query that summarizes the total amount of events by employee by client using the following specifications:
    a.   At the first Crosstab Query Wizard dialog box, click the *Queries* option in the *View* section, and then click *Query: EmployeeEvents* in the list box.
    b.   At the second Crosstab Query Wizard dialog box, click *Last Name* in the *Available Fields* list box, and then click the button containing the greater than (>) symbol.
    c.   At the third Crosstab Query Wizard dialog box, make sure *Client Name* is selected in the list box.
    d.   At the fourth Crosstab Query Wizard dialog box, make sure *Amount* is selected in the *Fields* list box, and then click *Sum* in the *Functions* list box.
    e.   At the fifth Crosstab Query Wizard dialog box, type Amounts by Employee by Client in the *What do you want to name your query?* text box.
6. Print and then close the Amounts by Employee by Client query.

Assessment 8

1. With the **Cornerstone** database file open, use the Find Duplicates Query Wizard to find employees who are responsible for at least two events with the following specifications:
    a.   At the first wizard dialog box, click *Table: Events* in the list box.
    b.   At the second wizard dialog box, click *Employee #* in the *Available fields* list box, and then click the button containing the greater than (>) symbol.
    c.   At the third wizard dialog box, move the *Date* field and the *Number of People* field from the *Available fields* list box to the *Additional query fields* list box.
    d.   At the fourth wizard dialog box, name the query *DuplicateEvents*.
2. Print and then close the DuplicateEvents query.

Assessment 9

1. With the **Cornerstone** database file open, use the Find Unmatched Query Wizard to find any employees who do not have an upcoming event scheduled with the following specifications:
    a.   At the first wizard dialog box, click *Table: Employees* in the list box.
    b.   At the second wizard dialog box, click *Table: Events* in the list box.
    c.   At the third wizard dialog box, make sure *Employee #* is selected in the *Fields in 'Employees'* list box and in the *Fields in 'Events'* list box.
    d.   At the fourth wizard dialog box, click the button containing the two greater than symbols (>>) to move all fields from the *Available fields* list box to the *Selected fields* list box.
    e.   At the fifth wizard dialog box, click the Finish button. (Let the wizard determine the query name: *Employees Without Matching Events*.)
2. Print and then close the Employees Without Matching Events query.

Assessment 10

1. With the **Cornerstone** database file open, open the Events database table, and then use the Filter By Selection button on the Table Datasheet toolbar to display the following records:
   a. Display only those records with an Employee # of 14. When the records display, print the results, and then click the Remove Filter button.
   b. Display only those records with a Price Code of 4. When the records display, print the results, and then click the Remove Filter button.
2. Close the Events database table without saving the changes.
3. Open the Clients database table and then use the Filter By Form button to display clients in Espanola or Los Alamos. (Be sure to use the Or tab at the very bottom of the table.) Print the results and then click the Remove Filter button.
4. Close the Clients database table without saving the changes.
5. Open the Events database table and then use the Filter By Form button to display Plan Code A or C. Print the results and then click the Remove Filter button.
6. Close the Events database table without saving the changes.
7. Close the **Cornerstone** database file.

WRITING activities

The following activities give you the opportunity to practice your writing skills along with demonstrating an understanding of some of the important Access features you have mastered in this unit. Use correct grammar, appropriate word choices, and clear sentence constructions.

Activity 1

The manager of Cornerstone Catering has asked you to add information to the **Cornerstone** database file on employee payroll. You need to create another database table that will contain information on payroll. The manager wants the database table to include the following (you determine the appropriate data type, field size, and description):

Employee #: 10
Status: Full-time
Monthly Salary: $2,850

Employee #: 14
Status: Part-time
Monthly Salary: $1,500

Employee #: 19
Status: Part-time
Monthly Salary: $1,400

Employee #: 21
Status: Full-time
Monthly Salary: $2,500

Employee #: 24
Status: Part-time
Monthly Salary: $1,250

Employee #: 26
Status: Part-time
Monthly Salary: $1,000

Print and then close the payroll database table. Open Word and then write a report to the manager detailing how you created the database table. Include a title for the report, steps on how the database table was created, and any other pertinent information. Save the completed report and name it **sau1act01**. Print and then close **sau1act01**.

INTERNET project

Vehicle Search

In this activity you will search the Internet for information on different vehicles before doing actual test drives. Learning about a major product, such as a vehicle, can increase your chances of finding a good buy, can potentially guide you away from a poor purchase, and can help speed up the process of narrowing the search to the type of vehicle that will meet your needs. Before you begin, list the top five criteria you would look for in a vehicle. For example, it must be a 4-door vehicle, needs to be 4-wheel drive, and so on.

Using key search words, find at least two Web sites that list vehicle reviews. Use the search engines provided within the different review sites to find vehicles that fulfill the criteria you listed to meet your particular needs. Create a database file in Access and create a table in that file that will contain the results from your vehicle search. Design the table keeping in mind what type of data you need to record for each vehicle that meets your requirements. Include at least the make, model, year, price, description, and special problems in the table. Also, include the ability to rate the vehicle as poor, fair, good, or excellent. You will decide on the rating of each vehicle depending on your findings.

JOB study

Mobile Home Park Project

In this activity you are working in the office of a large mobile home park. The manager of the part has asked you to find a way to document information about the people living in the park so that she can better meet their needs. For example, when road work has to be done, she would like to know which patrons would have difficulty parking their cars a long distance from their homes. When utility workers are scheduled to be in the park, she would like to notify the children's parents of any potentially dangerous situations.

The mobile home lots are numbered 1 through 200 and each is rated by size and location for rent as either standard or premium. The manager has asked you to record for each lot number, the names and phone numbers of the residents, whether or not it is a premium lot, whether or not any disabled individuals live in the home, the number of children living in the home, and the date the individuals occupied the lot. Create a database file and a table within the file to store the information. Enter 10 records to test the table. (Make up the data for the table.) Create a query for all lots where children live and another query for all lots with disabled individuals. For each query, provide the residents' names and phone numbers, and then print the results. The queries should be saved with appropriate names for later use.

SPECIALIST

MICROSOFT®

ACCESS

Unit 2: Creating Forms and Reports

➤ Creating Forms

➤ Creating Reports, Mailing Labels, and Charts

➤ Importing and Exporting Data

➤ Creating Web Pages and Using Database Wizards

MICROSOFT ACCESS 2003

MICROSOFT OFFICE ACCESS 2003
SPECIALIST SKILLS – UNIT 2

Reference No.	Skill	Pages
AC03S-1-1	**Create database using a Database Wizard**	**S243-S251**
AC03S-1-8	Create forms	
	Create a form using AutoForm	S142-S145
	Create a form using the Form Wizard	S145-S151
	Create a form with related database tables	S150-S151
	Create a form in Design view	S151-S164
AC03S-1-9	Add and modify form controls and properties	
	Add, move, resize, format, and align control objects	S152-S164
	Add a calculated control	S161-S164
AC03S-1-10	Create reports	
	Create a report using AutoReport	S172
	Create a report using the Report Wizard	S172-S178
	Create a report with related database tables	S178-S179
	Create a report in Design view	S179-S194
AC03S-1-11	Add and modify report control properties	S181-S185
AC03S-1-12	Create a data access page	S237-S243
AC03S-2	**Entering Data**	
AC03S-2-2	Find and move among records	
	Navigating to specific records	S142-S143
AC03S-2-3	Import data to Access	
	Import data to a new table	S221-S222
	Link data to a new table	S223-S224
AC03S-3	**Organizing Data**	
AC03S-3-2	Modify form layout	
	Move, resize, format, and align form control objects	S151-S158
	Add a form header and form footer	S159-S161
AC03S-3-3	Modify report layout and page setup	
	Move, resize, and add customize control objects	S181-S185
	Add a report header and report footer	S181-S185
AC03S-4	**Managing Databases**	
AC03S-4-1	Identify and modify object dependencies	S226-S230
AC03S-4-2	View objects and object data in other views	
	View objects and object dependencies	S226-S230
	Use PivotTable view	S194-S199
	Use PivotChart view	S199-S202
AC03S-4-3	Print database objects and data	
	Print a form	S142-S143
AC03S-4-4	Export data from Access	
	Export data to Excel	S209-S212
	Export data to Word	S212-S221

CREATING FORMS

PERFORMANCE OBJECTIVES

Upon successful completion of Chapter 5, you will be able to:

➤ **Create a form using AutoForm**
➤ **Create a form using the Form Wizard**
➤ **Create a form with fields from related database tables**
➤ **Create a form in Design view**
➤ **Move, resize, format, and align control objects**
➤ **Use fields to add controls**
➤ **Add controls using buttons on the Toolbox**
➤ **Add a Form Header and Form Footer to a form**
➤ **Add a calculated control to a form**

In this chapter, you will learn to create a form from database tables, improving the data display and making data entry easier. Access offers several methods for presenting data on the screen for easier data entry. You can create a form using the AutoForm and the Form Wizard. You can also create a form in Design view and then edit control objects in the form.

Creating a Form

> **HINT**
> Use a form to easily enter, edit, and/or view data.

> **HINT**
> A form allows you to focus on a single record at a time.

Access offers a variety of options for presenting data in a more easily read and attractive format. When entering data in a database table at the Datasheet view, multiple records are displayed at the same time. If a record contains several fields, you may not be able to view all fields within a record at the same time. If you create a form, generally all fields for a record are visible at one time.

Several methods are available for creating a form. In this section, you will learn how to use AutoForm to insert existing data into a form, use the Form Wizard to create a form, and use the Form Wizard to create a form with fields from related database tables.

New Object

Creating a Form Using AutoForm

Data in a database table can be viewed, added, or edited in the Datasheet view. You can perform these functions on data inserted in a form. The advantage to a form is that the functions are generally easier to perform because the data is easier to read. Access offers the AutoForm feature, which automatically copies data in a database table and creates a form. To use the AutoForm feature, click the down-pointing arrow at the right side of the New Object button on the Database toolbar, and then click AutoForm at the drop-down list. The AutoForm automatically creates a form and inserts it on the screen.

In Exercise 1, you will be using AutoForm to create a form for data contained in the Orders table, which is part of the OutdoorOptions database file. When AutoForm creates the form, the first record will display as shown in Figure 5.1.

FIGURE

5.1 *Form Created from Data in Orders Table*

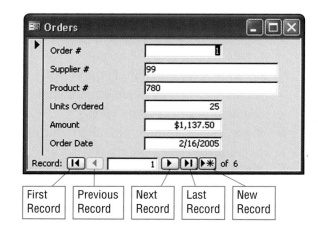

Navigation buttons display along the bottom of the first Orders record. The function each button performs is shown in Figure 5.1. Using these navigation buttons, you can display the first record in the database table, the previous record, the next record, the last record, and a new record.

Sorting Records

In Chapter 1, you learned about the Sort Ascending and Sort Descending buttons on the Table Datasheet toolbar. These buttons are also available on the Formatting (Form/Report) toolbar. Display a form in Form view and then click in the field on which you want to sort. Click the Sort Ascending button to sort the records in ascending alphabetic or numeric order (A-Z or lowest number to highest number). Click the Sort Descending button to sort the records in descending alphabetic or numeric order (Z-A or highest number to lowest number).

Printing a Form

Print a form in the same manner as a database table. If desired, changes can be made to the page margins and/or page orientation at the Page Setup dialog box. To display this dialog box, click File and then Page Setup. Print all records in the form by clicking the Print button on the Database toolbar. If you want to print a specific record, display the desired record, and then display the Print dialog box by clicking File and then Print. At the Print dialog box, click the *Selected Record(s)* option, and then click OK.

exercise 1

(Note: Delete any database files from your disk.)

1. Copy the **OutdoorOptions** database file from the CD that accompanies this textbook to your disk. Remove the read-only attribute from the **OutdoorOptions** database file.
2. Open the **OutdoorOptions** database file.
3. Use the AutoForm feature to create a form with the data in the Orders table by completing the following steps:
   a. At the OutdoorOptions : Database window, click *Orders* in the list box.
   b. Click the down-pointing arrow at the right of the New Object button on the Database toolbar.
   c. At the drop-down list that displays, click the AutoForm option.
   d. When the first record displays in Form view, click in the *Product #* field and then click the Sort Ascending button on the Form View toolbar.
   e. Display the next record by clicking the button toward the bottom of the Orders dialog box (see Figure 5.1) that contains a right-pointing arrow.
   f. Practice displaying different records using the navigation buttons along the bottom of the Orders dialog box.

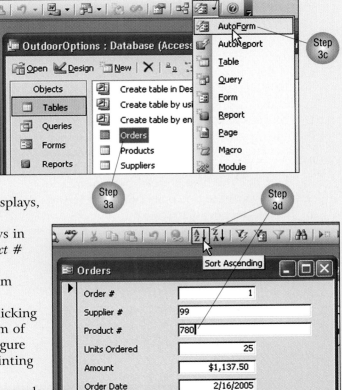

4. Save the form by completing the following steps:
   a. Click the Save button on the Form View toolbar.
   b. At the Save As dialog box, with *Orders* inserted in the *Form Name* text box, click OK.
5. Print all records in the form by clicking the Print button on the Form View toolbar.
6. Close the Orders form.
7. Close the **OutdoorOptions** database file.

Adding/Deleting Records

New Record

Delete Record

Navigate through records in a form using the navigation buttons that display along the bottom of the form, as shown in Figure 5.1. Add a new record to the form by clicking the New Record button that displays along the bottom of the form and contains a right-pointing arrow followed by an asterisk. You can also add a new record to a form by clicking the New Record button on the Form View toolbar that displays toward the top of the screen.

To delete a record, display the record, and then click the Delete Record button on the Form View toolbar. At the message telling you that the record will be deleted permanently, click Yes.

exercise 2

ADDING AND DELETING RECORDS IN A FORM

1. Open the **OutdoorOptions** database file.
2. At the OutdoorOptions : Database window, click the Forms button on the Objects bar located at the left side of the window.
3. Double-click *Orders* in the list box.
4. With the Orders form open and the first record showing, add new records and delete an existing record by completing the following steps:
   a. Click the New Record button located toward the bottom of the first record.
   b. At the new blank record, type the following information in the specified fields (move to the next field by pressing Tab or Enter; move to the previous field by pressing Shift + Tab):

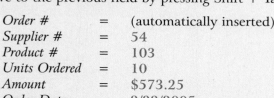

Step 2

Step 3

Order #	=	(automatically inserted)
Supplier #	=	54
Product #	=	103
Units Ordered	=	10
Amount	=	$573.25
Order Date	=	2/22/2005

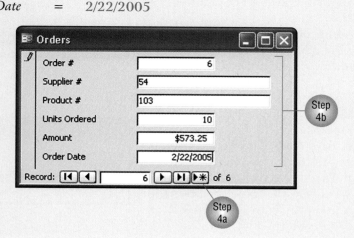

Step 4b

Step 4a

c. After typing the information for the new record, press the Tab key to display the next new record (you can also click the New Record button), and then type the following information in the specified fields:

Order #	=	(automatically inserted)
Supplier #	=	99
Product #	=	647
Units Ordered	=	5
Amount	=	$325.00
Order Date	=	2/22/2005

d. Delete the second record by completing the following steps:

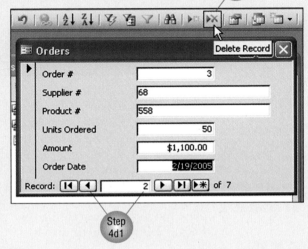

Step 4d2

1) Click the button toward the bottom of the record that displays with a left-pointing arrow until Record 2 displays.
2) With Record 2 displayed, click the Delete Record button on the Form View toolbar.
3) At the message telling you that you will not be able to undo the delete operation, click Yes.

Step 4d1

e. Click the Save button on the Form View toolbar.
f. Print all records in the form by clicking the Print button on the Form View toolbar.
g. Close the Orders form.

5. Close the **OutdoorOptions** database file.

Creating a Form Using the Form Wizard

Access offers a Form Wizard that will guide you through the creation of a form. The Form Wizard offers more formatting choices than the AutoForm feature. To create a form using the Form Wizard, open the database file containing the table for which you want to create a form. At the database window, click the Forms button on the Objects bar, and then click the New button on the window toolbar. At the New Form dialog box shown in Figure 5.2, double-click *Form Wizard* in the list box and the first Form Wizard dialog box displays as shown in Figure 5.3.

HINT

The Form Wizard is a general-purpose wizard that provides more flexibility than the AutoForm choices.

QUICK STEPS

Create a Form Using Form Wizard

1. Open database file.
2. Click Forms button on Objects bar.
3. Click New button.
4. Double-click *Form Wizard.*
5. Choose desired options at each of the Form Wizard dialog boxes.

FIGURE

5.2 **New Form Dialog Box**

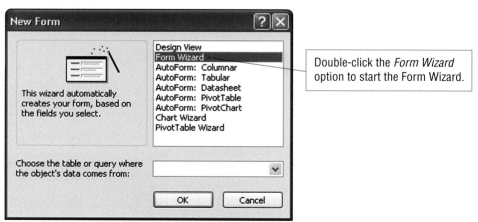

Double-click the *Form Wizard* option to start the Form Wizard.

The Form Wizard automates the creating of a form and lets you specify some or all of the fields to be used in the form.

At the first Form Wizard dialog box, specify the table and then the fields you want included in the form. To select the table, click the down-pointing arrow at the right side of the *Tables/Queries* text box, and then click the desired table. Select the desired field in the *Available Fields* list box, click the button containing the greater than symbol (>), and the field is inserted in the *Selected Fields* list box. Continue in this manner until all desired fields are inserted in the *Selected Fields* list box. If you want to insert all fields into the *Selected Fields* list box at one time, click the button containing the two greater than symbols (>>). After specifying fields, click the Next button.

FIGURE

5.3 **First Form Wizard Dialog Box**

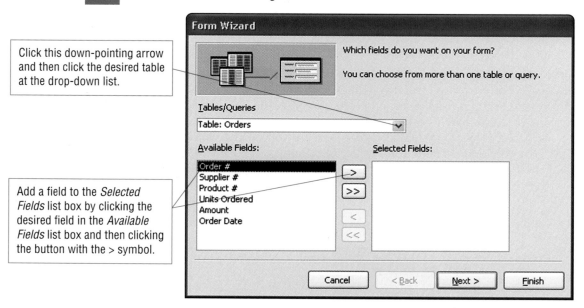

Click this down-pointing arrow and then click the desired table at the drop-down list.

Add a field to the *Selected Fields* list box by clicking the desired field in the *Available Fields* list box and then clicking the button with the > symbol.

At the second Form Wizard dialog box, shown in Figure 5.4, specify the layout for the records. You can choose from *Columnar*, *Tabular*, *Datasheet*, and *Justified* (with *Columnar* the default). After choosing the layout, click the Next button.

5.4 *Second Form Wizard Dialog Box*

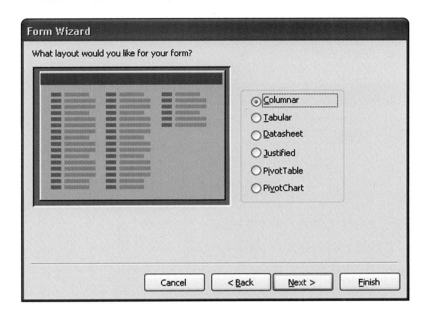

One of the advantages offered by the Form Wizard is the ability to choose from a variety of formats. At the third Form Wizard dialog box, shown in Figure 5.5, you choose a format style, such as *Blends, Blueprint, Expedition, Industrial,* and so forth. Click a format style and the results of the style are shown in the preview box. After selecting the desired format style, click the Next button.

FIGURE

5.5 *Third Form Wizard Dialog Box*

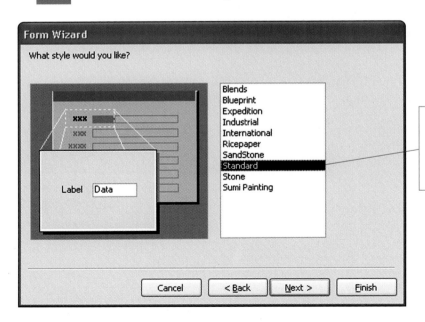

Click the desired format with options in the list box and then preview the format in the preview box at the left side of the dialog box.

At the last Form Wizard dialog box, shown in Figure 5.6, the Form Wizard offers a title for the form and also provides the option *Open the form to view or enter information*. Make any necessary changes in this dialog box and then click the Finish button.

FIGURE

5.6 *Fourth Form Wizard Dialog Box*

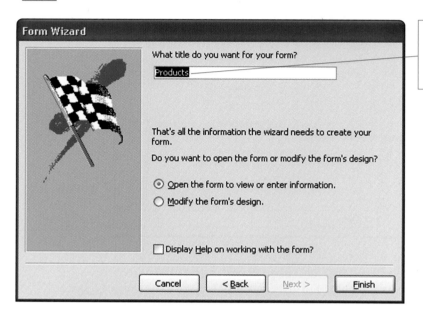

Type a title for the form in this text box or accept the default name provided by the wizard.

exercise 3

CREATING A FORM USING THE FORM WIZARD

1. Open the **OutdoorOptions** database file.
2. At the OutdoorOptions : Database window, click the Forms button on the Objects bar located at the left side of the window.
3. Delete the Orders form you created in Exercise 1 by completing the following steps:
   a. Position the arrow pointer on *Orders* in the list box and then click the *right* mouse button.
   b. At the shortcut menu that displays, click Delete using the left mouse button.
   c. At the question asking if you want to permanently delete the form, click Yes.
4. At the OutdoorOptions : Database window with the Forms button selected, create a form with the Form Wizard by completing the following steps:
   a. Click the New button on the window toolbar.
   b. At the New Form dialog box, double-click the *Form Wizard* option in the list box.
   c. At the first Form Wizard dialog box, click the down-pointing arrow at the right side of the *Tables/Queries* text box, and then click *Table: Products* at the drop-down list.

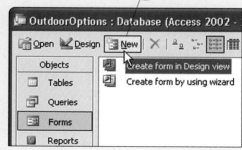

Step 4a

d. Specify that you want all fields included in the form by clicking the button containing the two greater than symbols (>>).

e. Click the Next button.

f. At the second Form Wizard dialog box, click the Next button. (This leaves the layout at the default of *Columnar*.)

g. At the third Form Wizard dialog box, click the *International* option in the list box.

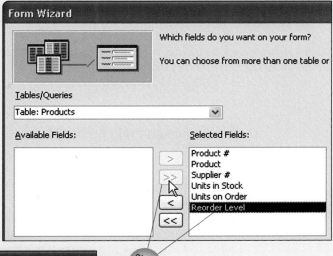

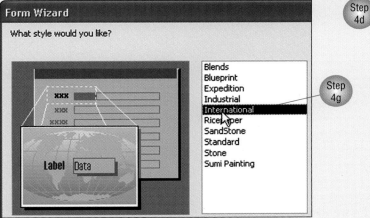

h. Click the Next button.

i. At the fourth Form Wizard dialog box, leave the options at the default, and then finish the form by clicking the Finish button.

5. When the first record is shown in the form, click the New Record button, and then add the following records:

Product #	=	448
Product	=	Canteen kit
Supplier #	=	54
Units in Stock	=	41
Units on Order	=	50
Reorder Level	=	50
Product #	=	302
Product	=	Pocket warmer
Supplier #	=	31
Units in Stock	=	13
Units on Order	=	15
Reorder Level	=	15

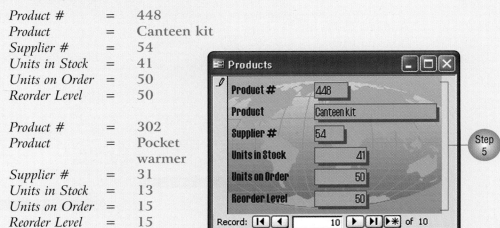

6. Delete the record containing information on ski goggles. (At the warning message, click Yes.)
7. Click the Save button on the Form View toolbar.
8. Click the Print button to print all records in the form.
9. Close the form by clicking the Close button in the upper right corner of the record.
10. Close the **OutdoorOptions** database file.

Creating a Form with Related Database Tables

The forms you have created so far in this chapter have included all of the fields from one database table. Forms can also be created with fields from tables that are connected by a one-to-many relationship. You can use the Form Wizard to create a form with fields from related database tables. At the first Form Wizard dialog box (see Figure 5.3), choose fields from the selected database table and then choose fields from a related database table. To change to the related database table, click the down-pointing arrow at the right of the *Tables/Queries* text box, and then click the name of the desired database table.

exercise 4

CREATING A FORM WITH RELATED DATABASE TABLES

1. Create a form that includes fields from the Products database table and fields from the Suppliers database table by completing the following steps:
   a. Open the **OutdoorOptions** database file.
   b. At the OutdoorOptions : Database window, click the Forms button on the Objects bar.
   c. Click the New button on the window toolbar.
   d. At the New Form dialog box, double-click *Form Wizard* in the list box.
   e. At the first Form Wizard dialog box, click the down-pointing arrow at the right of the *Tables/Queries* text box, and then click *Table: Products*.
   f. Complete the following steps to insert fields in the *Selected Fields* list box:
      1) With *Product #* selected in the *Available Fields* list box, click the button containing the greater than symbol (>).
      2) With *Product* selected in the *Available Fields* list box, click the button containing the greater than symbol (>).
      3) Click *Units in Stock* in the *Available Fields* list box and then click the button containing the greater than symbol (>).
      4) Click the down-pointing arrow at the right of the *Table/Queries* text box and then click *Table: Suppliers*.

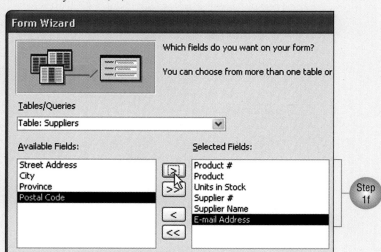

5) With *Supplier #* selected in the *Available Fields* list box, click the button containing the greater than symbol (>).
6) With *Supplier Name* selected in the *Available Fields* list box, click the button containing the greater than symbol (>).
7) Click *E-mail Address* in the *Available Fields* list box and then click the button containing the greater than symbol (>).
8) Click the Next button.

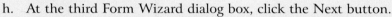

g. At the second Form Wizard dialog box, make sure *by Products* is selected in the list box that displays in the upper left corner of the dialog box, and then click the Next button.
h. At the third Form Wizard dialog box, click the Next button.
i. At the fourth Form Wizard dialog box, click *Blends* in the format style list box, and then click the Next button.
j. At the fifth Form Wizard dialog box, type the name **Units in Stock**, and then click the Finish button.

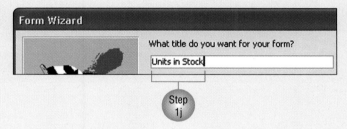

2. When the first record displays, print the record by displaying the Print dialog box, clicking *Selected Record(s)* in the *Print Range* section, and then clicking OK.
3. Close the form by clicking the Close button.
4. Close the **OutdoorOptions** database file.

Creating a Form in Design View

A form is comprised of a series of controls, which are objects that display titles or descriptions, accept data, or perform actions. In the forms you created in this chapter, the AutoForm feature or the Form Wizard created the controls for the form using fields from the tables. Another method for creating a form is to use the Design view. To display the Design view, as shown in Figure 5.7, click the Forms button on the Objects bar, and then double-click the *Create form in Design view* option in the list box. In the Design view, you can use fields from a table to create controls in the Design grid and you can also add controls with buttons on the Toolbox palette. The Toolbox palette, shown in Figure 5.7, appears automatically in the Design view.

Create a Form in Design View
1. Open database file.
2. Click Forms button.
3. Double-click *Create form in Design view*.
4. Click Properties button.
5. Click Form properties sheet All tab.
6. Click in *Record Source* text box.
7. Click down-pointing arrow and then click desired table.
8. Drag desired fields from field list box to Design grid.

5.7 Form in Design View

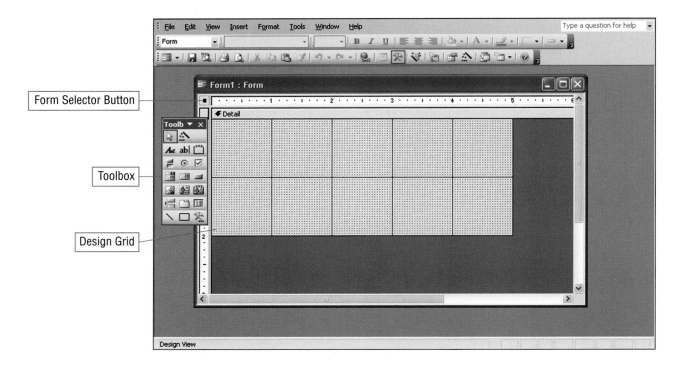

Form Selector Button

Toolbox

Design Grid

Form Selector

A form in Design view contains three sections—Form Header, Detail, and Form Footer. The Detail section is the only section that displays by default. (You will learn more about the Form Header and Form Footer sections later in this chapter.) The Detail section of the form in Design view is set up as a grid. Use the rulers along the top and left side of the section and the lines and dots that make up the grid to precisely position fields and controls.

Using Fields to Add Controls

Associate a table with the form to use fields to create controls. To associate a table, click the Properties button on the Form Design toolbar. This displays the Form properties sheet. At the Form properties sheet, click the All tab, and then click in the Record Source text box. Click the down-pointing arrow that displays at the right side of the text box and then click the desired table. This displays the table fields in a field list box. (If the field list box does not display, click the Field List button on the Form Design toolbar.) Using the mouse, drag the desired field from the field list box to the Design grid.

Moving Control Objects

When a field is moved to the Design grid, a label control containing the field name and a text box control used to accept data are placed adjacent to each other on the grid. The label control containing the field name is included for descriptive purposes so that the user knows which data to type into the corresponding text box.

The label control and its corresponding text box control for a field can be moved individually or together to another location on the form. To move the two control objects together, click one of the objects. This inserts eight sizing handles around the object you clicked with a large black handle displaying in the upper left corner as shown in Figure 5.8. The adjacent object displays with one large black sizing handle in the upper left corner. Position the arrow pointer on the border of the control object containing the eight sizing handles (on the border, not on a sizing handle) until the pointer turns into a hand. Hold down the left mouse button and then drag the objects to the desired position. Move multiple control objects at the same time by holding down the Shift key while clicking each object. You can also select multiple control objects by drawing a border around the desired control objects.

F I G U R E

5.8 *Selected Control Object*

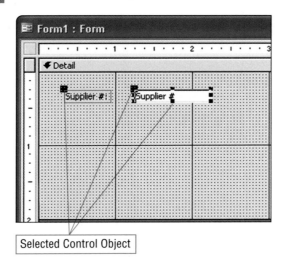

Selected Control Object

To move a control object separately from the adjacent object, position the mouse pointer on the large black handle that displays in the upper left corner of the object, hold down the left mouse button, and then drag the object to the desired position.

Resizing Control Objects

Increase or decrease the size of a selected control object using the sizing handles that display around the object. Drag the middle sizing handles at the left or right edge to make the control wider or narrower; drag the middle sizing handles at the top or bottom to make the control taller or shorter; and use the corner sizing handles to resize the object both horizontally and vertically at the same time.

Formatting Control Objects

Customize the formatting of selected control objects with options at the properties sheet. (The name of the properties sheet will vary depending on what is selected.) With the All tab selected, all formatting options are available. Click the Format tab to display only formatting options such as options to change the font size, font style, font color, foreground color, background color, and caption. Click in a text box for some options and a button containing three black dots displays at the right side. Click this button to display additional formatting choices.

Aligning Control Objects

Control objects inserted in the Design grid align with horizontal and vertical lines in the grid. This is because the Snap to Grid effect is on by default. Even with the Snap to Grid effect on, you may want to control the alignment of control objects. To align control objects, select the desired objects, and then click the Format option on the Menu bar. At the drop-down menu that displays, point to the Align option, and then click the desired alignment at the side menu.

exercise 5

1. Open the **OutdoorOptions** database file.
2. At the OutdoorOptions : Database window, click the Forms button on the Objects bar.
3. Create a form in Design view by completing the following steps:
   a. Double-click the *Create form in Design view* option in the list box.

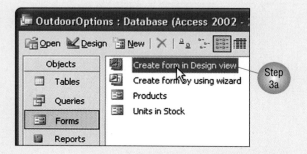

   b. At the Design window, click the Properties button on the Form Design toolbar.
   c. At the Form properties sheet, click the All tab.
   d. At the Form properties sheet with the All tab selected, click in the *Record Source* text box, and then click the down-pointing arrow that displays at the right side of the text box.
   e. At the drop-down list that displays, click *Suppliers*.

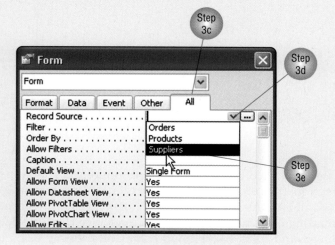

f. Drag the *Supplier #* field from the field list box to the Design grid to the approximate location shown below. (You will be aligning the control objects later in this exercise.)

g. Drag the remaining fields from the field list box to the Design grid to the approximate locations shown below. (You will be formatting the control objects later in this exercise.)

h. Align the control objects by completing the following steps:

1) With the mouse, draw a border around all control objects located in the first column. (This selects the control objects.)

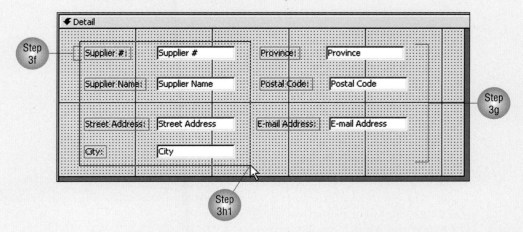

2) With the control objects selected, click Format on the Menu bar, point to Align, and then click Right at the side menu.

3) With the mouse, draw a border around all control objects located in the second column.

4) Click Format on the Menu bar, point to Align, and then click Right at the side menu.

5) If the control objects are not positioned in the locations shown in Figure 5.9, select and then drag the object to the desired position.

i. Change the *Supplier #:* caption by completing the following steps:

1) Click the *Supplier #:* label control object (displays with a gray background).

2) Click in the *Caption* text box in the Label properties sheet. (The Form properties sheet became the Label properties sheet when the label control object was selected.) (You may need to scroll up the list to display the *Caption* text box.)

3) Edit the text in the *Caption* text box so it displays as *Supplier Number:*.

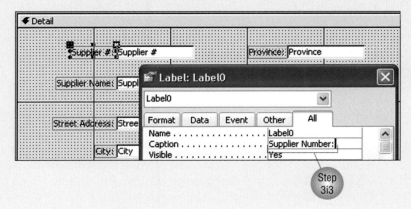

4) Click anywhere in the Design grid outside a control object to deselect the object.
j. Format the label control objects by completing the following steps:
   1) Click the *Supplier Number* label control object (displays with a gray background).
   2) Hold down the Shift key, and then click each of the remaining label control objects (objects that display with a gray background).

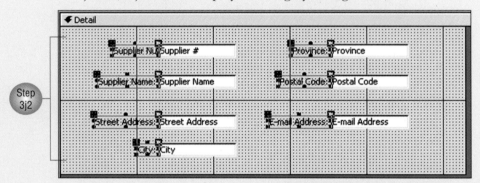

Step 3j2

3) Click in the *Fore Color* text box in the Multiple selection properties sheet. (The Label properties sheet became the Multiple selection properties sheet when you selected the labels.) (You will need to scroll down the list to display the *Fore Color* text box.)
4) Click the button containing three black dots that displays at the right side of the text box.

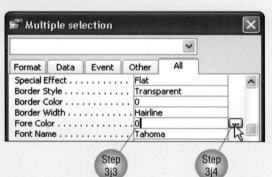

Step 3j3   Step 3j4

5) At the color palette that displays, click the Turquoise color (fifth color from the left in the top row), and then click OK to close the palette. (The color will not be visible in the Design grid until you choose another option.)
6) Click in the *Back Color* text box, and then click the button containing three black dots.
7) At the color palette that displays, click the Blue color (sixth color from the left in the fourth row from the top), and then click OK to close the palette.
8) Click in the *Font Name* text box in the properties sheet, and then click the down-pointing arrow that displays at the right side of the text box.
9) At the drop-down list that displays, scroll up the list to display *Arial* and then click *Arial*.
10) Click in the *Font Size* text box, click the down-pointing arrow that displays at the right, and then click *10*.
11) Click in the *Font Weight* text box, click the down-pointing arrow that displays at the right, and then click *Bold*.
k. Click in the Design grid outside a control object to deselect the objects.
l. Resize each of the label control objects so the complete label name displays. (To do this, select the label control object and then use the middle sizing handle at the left side of the object to increase the width.)

m. Format the text control objects by completing the following steps:
   1) Click the *Supplier Number* text control object (contains a white background).
   2) Hold down the Shift key and then click each of the remaining text control objects (objects that display with a white background).

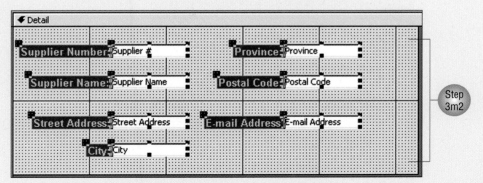

   3) Click in the *Fore Color* text box in the Multiple selection properties sheet, click the button containing three black dots, click the Blue color (sixth color from the left in the fourth row), and then click OK.
   4) Click in the *Back Color* text box, click the button containing three black dots, click the Turquoise color (fifth color from the left in the top row), and then click OK.
   5) Click in the *Font Name* text box, click the down-pointing arrow that displays at the right, and then click *Arial* at the drop-down list. (You will need to scroll up the list to display *Arial*.)
   6) Click in the *Font Size* text box, click the down-pointing arrow that displays at the right, and then click *10*.
   7) Click in the *Font Weight* text box, click the down-pointing arrow that displays at the right, and then click *Bold*.

n. Click in the Design grid outside a control object to deselect the objects.

4. Close the properties sheet. (To do this, click the Close button that displays in the upper right corner of the sheet [contains an *X*].)
5. View the form in Form view by clicking the View button on the Form Design toolbar.
6. Save the form and name it Suppliers Form.
7. Print the currently displayed form by completing the following steps:
   a. Click File and then Print.
   b. At the Print dialog box, click the *Selected Record(s)* option in the *Print Range* section.
   c. Click OK.
8. Close the Suppliers Form form.
9. Close the **OutdoorOptions** database file.

5.9 *Exercise 5*

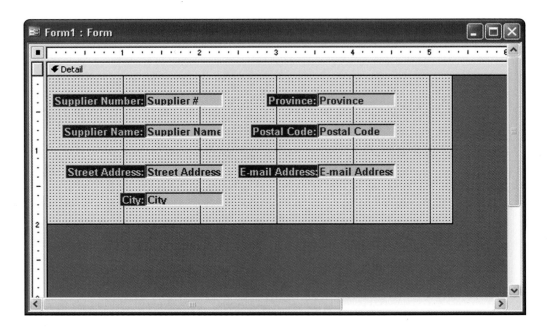

Adding Controls Using the Toolbox

The Toolbox is a palette of control object buttons that automatically appears when a form is displayed in Design view. With the buttons on this Toolbox, shown in Figure 5.10, you can add and modify controls in the form. (Figure 5.10 identifies a few of the buttons on the toolbar.) To add a control in Design view, click the desired button on the Toolbox. This causes the mouse pointer to change to a crosshair pointer with an icon attached. The icon that displays will vary depending on the control object button selected. Move the pointer to the position on the form where you want to place the object and then drag to create the object. Use the sizing handles that display around the control to increase or decrease the size.

FIGURE

5.10 *Toolbox Buttons*

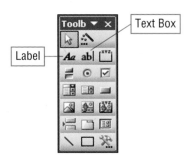

Adding a Form Header and Form Footer

A form in Design view can contain up to three sections—Detail, Form Header, and Form Footer. The Detail section is the only section that displays by default. You created a form in Exercise 5 in the Detail section of the form. A Form Header displays at the top of the form in Form view and at the beginning of a printout started from the Form view screen. A Form Footer appears at the bottom of the form in Form view and at the end of a printout started from the Form view screen.

Display a Form Header and Form Footer by clicking View on the Menu bar and then clicking Form Header/Footer. Another method is to right-click on the Form 1 : Form title bar and then click Form Header/Footer at the shortcut menu. Use the same methods for turning off the display of a Form Header and Form Footer.

To insert text in a Form Header or Form Footer use the Label button on the Toolbox. Click the Label button and then draw the label in the Form Header or Form Footer. Type text inside the label control object and apply the desired formatting.

Apply formatting to a Form Header with options at the FormHeader properties sheet. Display this sheet by right-clicking the Form Header gray border bar and then clicking Properties at the shortcut menu. Complete similar steps to display the FormFooter properties sheet.

QUICK STEPS

Add Form Header and Form Footer to Form
1. Open form in Design view.
2. Click View, Form Header/Footer.

Label

exercise 6

ADDING A FORM HEADER AND FORM FOOTER TO A FORM

1. Open the **OutdoorOptions** database file.
2. If necessary, click the Forms button on the Objects bar.
3. Double-click *Suppliers Form* in the list box.
4. Add and modify a Form Header and Form Footer in Design view by completing the following steps:
   a. Change to the Design view by clicking the View button on the Form View toolbar.
   b. Add and modify a Form Header by completing the following steps:
      1) Right-click on the Suppliers Form : Form title bar and then click Form Header/Footer at the shortcut menu.
      2) Increase the height of the Form Header section by positioning the pointer at the top of the gray Detail border line until the pointer changes to a black vertical line with an up- and down-pointing arrow, and then drag the mouse down to the approximate height shown at the right.
      3) Click the Label button on the Toolbox. (If the Toolbox is not displayed, click the Toolbox button on the Form Design toolbar.)

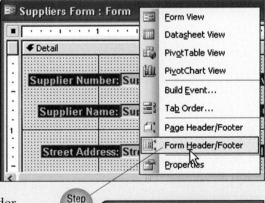

Step 4b1

Step 4b2

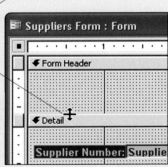

Step 4b3

4) Position the crosshair pointer with the label icon attached to it at the top left edge of the first black gridline in the Form Header section, drag the mouse down to the approximate height and width shown below, and then release the mouse button.

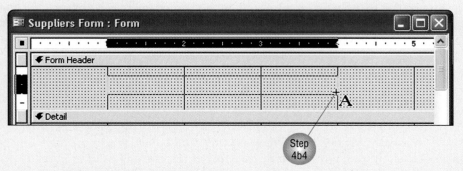

Step
4b4

5) A label box will appear with the insertion point automatically positioned in the top left edge of the box. Type OutdoorOptions Suppliers Form and then click outside the box.
6) Click once on the label control object to select it.
7) Click the Properties button on the Form Design toolbar.
8) Click the Format tab at the Label properties sheet.
9) Click in the *Font Name* text box (you will need to scroll down the Format list box to display this text box), click the down-pointing arrow at the right, and then click *Arial* at the drop-down menu. (You will need to scroll up the drop-down menu to display *Arial*.)
10) Click in the *Font Size* text box, click the down-pointing arrow at the right, and then click *14* at the drop-down menu.
11) Click in the *Font Weight* text box, click the down-pointing arrow at the right, and then click *Bold* at the drop-down menu.
12) Click outside the label control box. (Increase the height and width of the label control box so the entire title displays.)

c. Add and modify a Form Footer by completing the following steps:
1) Drag down the bottom border of the form to display the Form Footer section.
2) Click the Label button on the Toolbox.
3) Position the crosshair pointer with the label icon attached to it at the top left edge of the first black gridline in the Form Footer section, drag the mouse down and to the right to the approximate height and width shown at the right, and then release the mouse button.

Step
4c1

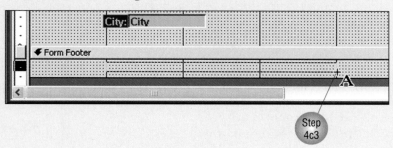

Step
4c3

4) A label box will appear with the insertion point automatically positioned in the box. Type **Suppliers Form designed by Student Name** (type your name instead of *Student Name*), and then click outside the box.

5) Click once on the label control object to select it. (The Label properties sheet should be visible. If it is not visible, click the Properties button on the Form Design toolbar.)

6) If necessary, click the Format tab at the Label properties sheet.

7) Make the following changes:
   a) Change the font name to Arial.
   b) Change the font size to 10.
   c) Change the font weight to bold.

8) Click outside the label control box.

9) If necessary, increase the height and width of the label control box so the entire footer displays.

5. Close the properties sheet. (To do this, click the Close button that displays in the upper right corner of the sheet [contains an *X*].)

6. View the form in Form view by clicking the View button on the Form Design toolbar.

7. Click the Save button to save the form.

8. Click the New Record button that displays along the bottom of the form.

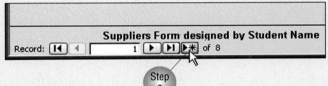

Step 8

9. Add the following record:

Supplier Number	=	44
Supplier Name	=	Everwear Supplies
Street Address	=	4500 Second Avenue
City	=	Vancouver
Province	=	BC
Postal Code	=	V2V 6K2
E-mail Address	=	everwear@emcp.net

10. Print the currently displayed record.

11. Close the Suppliers Form form.

12. Close the **OutdoorOptions** database file.

Adding a Calculated Control

A calculated control uses a mathematical equation to determine the contents that are displayed in the control object. Insert a calculated control field in Design view by creating a text box control object and then entering the mathematical equation in the text box. A calculated field is used to perform mathematical operations on existing fields, but it does not exist in the table associated with the form. In Exercise 7, you will create a calculated control in a form that divides the order amount by the number of units.

> **HINT**
> Press Ctrl + Enter to begin a new line in a text box.

Type a mathematical expression in a calculated control box. Begin the expression with the equals sign (=) and insert square brackets around field names. Use mathematical operators such as +, -, *, and / to perform calculations.

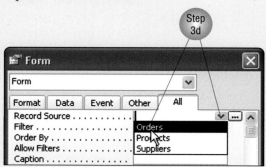

exercise 7

CREATING A FORM IN DESIGN VIEW AND ADDING A CALCULATED CONTROL

1. Open the **OutdoorOptions** database file.
2. At the OutdoorOptions : Database window, if necessary, click the Forms button on the Objects bar.
3. Create a form in Design view by completing the following steps:
   a. Double-click the *Create form in Design view* option in the list box.
   b. At the Design grid, click the Properties button on the Form Design toolbar.
   c. At the Form properties sheet, click the All tab.
   d. Click in the *Record Source* text box, click the down-pointing arrow at the right, and then click *Orders* at the drop-down list.
   e. Drag the fields in the field list box to the Design grid to the approximate locations shown below.

Step 3d

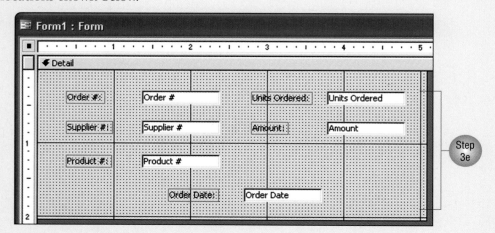

Step 3e

   f. Select the three label and text box control objects at the left side of the Design grid and then align them at the right.
   g. Select the two label and text box control objects at the right side of the Design grid and then align them at the right.
   h. Select the label and text box control objects located at the bottom of the design grid and align them at the right. (This moves the label control object next to the text box control object.)
   i. Add a calculated control field by completing the following steps:
      1) Click the Text Box button on the Toolbox. (If the Toolbox is not visible, click the Toolbox button on the Form Design toolbar.)

Step 3i1

2) Position the crosshair pointer with the text box icon attached below the *Amount* text box control and then drag the outline of a box approximately the same size as the text box control above it.

3) Click in the text box control (which currently displays *Unbound*), type =[Amount]/[Units Ordered], and then click outside the control to deselect it.

4) Click the label control object adjacent to the text box control (which currently displays *Text6:* [your number may vary]) to select it.

5) Click the label control object again to position the insertion point inside the label box.

6) Delete the current entry, type **Unit Price:**, and then click outside the label control to deselect it.

7) Move and/or size the calculated control and the label control to align them with the fields displayed above.

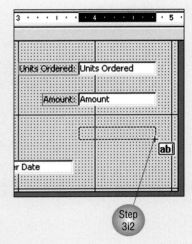

Step
3i2

j. Click the View button on the Form Design toolbar to display the form in Form view. Notice the Unit Price amount displays aligned at the left edge of the control. Change the format properties for the calculated control by completing the following steps:

1) Click the View button on the Form View toolbar.

2) Click the text box calculated control to select it.

3) At the Text Box properties sheet, click the Format tab.

4) Click in the *Format* text box (you may need to scroll up to display this text box), click the down-pointing arrow at the right, and then click *Currency* at the drop-down list.

5) Click in the *Text Align* text box (you will need to scroll down the list to display this text box), click the down-pointing arrow at the right, and then click *Right* at the drop-down list.

6) Close the Text Box properties sheet.

Step
3j4

Text Box: Text6

Text6

| Format | Data | Event | Other | All |

Format . . . .
Decimal Places . . . . Medium Time 5
Visible . . . . Short Time 1
Display When . . . . General Number 3
Scroll Bars . . . . Currency $
Can Grow . . . . Euro €
Can Shrink . . . . Fixed 3

4. View the form in Form view by clicking View button on the Form Design toolbar. Your form should look similar to what you see in Figure 5.11.

5. Save the form and name it Orders Form.

6. Print the first record.

7. Close the Orders Form form.

8. Close the **OutdoorOptions** database file.

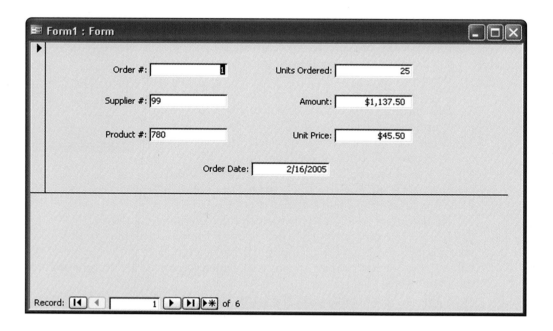

CHAPTER summary

➤ A form generally improves the ease with which data is entered into a database table. A form can be created with the AutoForm feature and also with the Form Wizard.

➤ A record in a form displays with navigation buttons that are used to display various records in the form.

➤ Print a form in the same manner as a database table. Changes can be made to the page margins and/or page orientation at the Page Setup dialog box.

➤ Add a new record to a form by clicking the New Record button on the Form View toolbar or by clicking the button at the bottom of the record that displays with a right-pointing arrow followed by an asterisk.

➤ Delete a record by displaying the record and then clicking the Delete Record button on the Form View toolbar.

➤ The Form Wizard walks you through the steps for creating a form and lets you specify the fields you want included in the form, a layout for the records, the desired formatting, and a name for the form.

➤ A form can be created with fields from tables that are connected by a one-to-many relationship.

- A form is comprised of a series of controls, which are objects that display titles or descriptions, accept data, or perform actions.
- In Design view, you can use fields from a table to create controls in the Design grid and also add controls with buttons on the Toolbox palette.
- Associate a table with the form to use fields to create controls.
- Move control objects in the Design grid. A label control and its corresponding text box control for a field can be moved individually or together.
- Use the sizing handles around a selected control object to change the size of the object.
- Customize control objects with options at the properties sheet.
- To align control objects in the Design grid, select the objects, click Format, point to Align, and then click the desired alignment at the side menu.
- To add a control using a button on the Toolbox, click the button, move the pointer to the position on the form where you want to place the object, and then drag to create the object.
- Turn on the display of the Form Header and the Form Footer by clicking View and then Form Header/Footer.
- A Form Header displays at the top of the form in Form view and at the beginning of a printout started from the Form view screen.
- A Form Footer displays at the bottom of the form in Form view and at the end of a printout started from the Form view screen.
- A calculated control uses a mathematical equation to determine the contents that are displayed in the control object. A calculated field is used to perform mathematical operations on existing fields, but it does not exist in the table associated with the form.

FEATURES summary

FEATURE	BUTTON	MENU	KEYBOARD
New Form dialog box	New	Insert, Form	
Begin Form Wizard		Insert, Form, Form Wizard	
Properties sheet		View, Properties	Alt + Enter
Toolbox		View, Toolbox	

CONCEPTS check

Completion: On a blank sheet of paper, indicate the correct term, symbol, or command for each description.

1. To create a form with the AutoForm feature, open the database file, click the database table in the list box, and then click this button on the Database toolbar.
2. Use these buttons, which appear along the bottom of a record in a form, to display the first record in the form, the previous record, the next record, or the last record.
3. Click this button on the Form View toolbar to add a new record to the form.
4. Click this button on the Form View toolbar to delete a record from the form.
5. In the form Design view, add controls with buttons on this palette.
6. This section of the form in Design view is set up as a grid.
7. This appears at the bottom of the form in Form view and at the end of a printout started from the Form view screen.
8. This type of control uses a mathematical equation to determine the contents that are displayed in the control object.

SKILLS check

Assessment 1

1. Open the **OutdoorOptions** database file.
2. Use the AutoForm feature to create a form with the data in the Suppliers database table.
3. After creating the form, add the following records to the Suppliers form:

Supplier #	=	12
Supplier Name	=	Seaside Suppliers
Street Address	=	4120 Shoreline Drive
City	=	Vancouver
Province	=	BC
Postal Code	=	V2V 8K4
E-mail Address	=	seaside@emcp.net

Supplier #	=	34
Supplier Name	=	Carson Company
Street Address	=	120 Plaza Center
City	=	Vancouver
Province	=	BC
Postal Code	=	V2V 1K6
E-mail Address	=	carson@emcp.net

4. Delete the record containing information on Manning, Inc.
5. Save the form with the name offered by Access (Suppliers).
6. Print and then close the Suppliers form.
7. Close the **OutdoorOptions** database file.

Assessment 2

1. Open the **OutdoorOptions** database file.
2. At the OutdoorOptions : Database window, click the Forms button on the Objects bar.
3. Delete the Suppliers form that displays in the list box. (For assistance, refer to Exercise 3, Step 3.)
4. Create a form for the Suppliers database table using the Form Wizard. Use all of the fields in the Suppliers database table to create the form. You determine the format style. Name the form *Suppliers*.
5. When the Form Wizard is finished, add the following record:

Supplier # = 50
Supplier Name = Binder Corporation
Street Address = 9033 East 32nd
City = Vancouver
Province = BC
Postal Code = V2V 3K2
E-mail Address = binder@emcp.net

6. Delete the record containing information on Langley Corporation.
7. Save the Suppliers form.
8. Print the Suppliers form and then close the form.
9. Close the **OutdoorOptions** database file.

Assessment 3

1. Open the **OutdoorOptions** database file.
2. Create a form from two related database tables using the Form Wizard with the following specifications:
   a. At the first Form Wizard dialog box, insert the following fields in the *Selected Fields* list box:

   From the Products database table:
   Product #
   Product
   Units on Order

   From the Suppliers database table:
   Supplier #
   Supplier Name
   Street Address
   City
   Province
   Postal Code

   b. Do not make any changes at the second Form Wizard dialog box.
   c. Do not make any changes at the third Form Wizard dialog box.
   d. You determine the format style at the fourth Form Wizard dialog box.
   e. At the fifth Form Wizard dialog box, type the name Units on Order.
   f. When the first record displays, print the form.
   g. Close the record that displays.
3. Close the **OutdoorOptions** database file.

Assessment 4

1. Open the **OutdoorOptions** database file.
2. Open the Orders table and then make the following changes:
   a. Display the table in Design view.
   b. Insert a row above *Order Date*.
   c. Specify the following for the new row:

Field Name	=	*Unit Price*
Data Type	=	*Currency*
Description	=	*Unit price*

   d. Save the table.
   e. Change to the Datasheet view and then enter the following unit price in the specified order number record:

Order #4	=	72.25
Order #5	=	112.00

   f. Save and then close the table.
3. Create a form by design with the following specifications:
   a. Create a form by design with all of the fields in the Orders table *except* the *Amount* field. (You determine the location of the fields in the Design grid.)
   b. Add a calculated control that contains *[Unit Price]*[Units Ordered]* in the text box control (the box that contains the word *Unbound*) and *Amount* in the label control (the box that contains the word *Text* followed by a number). Change the format of the text box calculated control to *Currency*.
   c. Apply formatting of your choosing to the label and text box control objects. (Change at least the font name, fore color, and back color.)
   d. Add the Form Header *OutdoorOptions – Orders Form*. Change the font name, font size, and font weight of the Form Header. (You determine the font, size, and weight.)
   e. Add the Form Footer *Order Totals*. Change the font name, font size, and font weight of the Form Footer. (You determine the font, size, and weight.)
   f. Save the form and name it Order Totals.
   g. Change to the Form view.
   h. Print the currently displayed record.
4. Close the Order Totals form.
5. Close the **OutdoorOptions** database file.

Assessment 5

1. The New Form dialog box contains a number of options for creating a form. In this chapter, you have used the Form Wizard to prepare forms. Experiment with two other options available at the New Form dialog box—*AutoForm: Columnar* and *AutoForm: Tabular*.
2. After experimenting with these two wizards, open the **OutdoorOptions** database file and then complete the following:
   a. Use the AutoForm: Columnar option to create a form with all of the fields in the Suppliers database table. Print the first record that displays and then close the form.
   b. Use the AutoForm: Tabular option to create a form with all of the fields in the Products database table. Print the first record that displays and then close the form.
3. Close the **OutdoorOptions** database file.

CHAPTER challenge

You are the office manager at Tri-State Vision Care Center. The Center houses several optometrists and ophthalmologists. To maintain patients' billing records, you decide to create a database named **Tri-StateVisionCare** to automate this process. Create two tables in the database. One table named Patients will be created for patient information, such as *Patient ID*, *Name*, *Address*, *Phone Number*, etc. Another table named Patient Billing will be created for patient billing and should include fields such as *Patient ID*, *Date of Visit*, *Doctor's Name*, *Method of Payment*, and *Fees Rendered*. Create and format a form (with a title) for each of the tables so others working in the office can easily and quickly add records. Add an additional calculated control to the Patient Billing form called Total Due that displays the total due when a 5% tax has added to fees rendered. Once the forms are complete, add at least five records to each of them.

You are looking for ways to improve the efficiency of entering records in the forms created in the first part of the Chapter Challenge. One method is through the use of combo boxes. Use the Help feature to learn more about combo boxes. Then create combo boxes for the *Doctor's Name* field and *Method of Payment* field in the Patient Billing form created in the first part of the Chapter Challenge. Save the form again.

All billing information from the Tri-State Vision Care Center is sent to headquarters every month. The billing department at headquarters is using Excel and wants all information sent in an Excel format. Export the Patient Billing table created in the first part of the Chapter Challenge to Excel so that it will be ready to send to headquarters. Save the Excel file with the same name as the table.

CREATING REPORTS, MAILING LABELS, AND CHARTS

PERFORMANCE OBJECTIVES

Upon successful completion of Chapter 6, you will be able to:
- ➤ **Create a report using AutoReport**
- ➤ **Create a report using the Report Wizard**
- ➤ **Create a report in Design view**
- ➤ **Add a Report Header and Report Footer**
- ➤ **Create mailing labels using the Label Wizard**
- ➤ **Create a chart using the Chart Wizard**
- ➤ **Summarize data using PivotTable View and PivotChart View**

ACCESS

In this chapter, you will learn how to prepare reports from data in a database table using the AutoReport feature and also the Report Wizard. A report lets you specify how data will appear when printed. You will also learn how to create mailing labels using the Label Wizard, how to create a chart with the Chart Wizard, and how to summarize data using the PivotTable View and PivotChart View.

Creating Reports

> **HINT**
>
> Create a report to control what data appears on the page when printed.

The primary purpose for inserting data in a form is to improve the display of the data and to make data entry easier. Data can also be inserted in a report. The purpose for this is to control what data appears on the page when printed. Reports generally answer specific questions (queries). For example, a report could answer the question *What customers have submitted claims?* or *What products do we currently have on order?* Access includes the AutoReport feature that automatically creates a report based on data in a table and also the Report Wizard that walks you through the process of creating a report. Like the Form Wizard, you specify fields, format style, and the report name when creating a report.

Creating a Report Using AutoReport

The AutoReport feature automatically creates a plainly formatted report in a columnar arrangement. To use the AutoReport feature, select the desired table, click the down-pointing arrow at the right side of the New Object button on the Database toolbar, and then click AutoReport at the drop-down list.

exercise 1

CREATING A REPORT USING AUTOREPORT

(Note: Delete any database files from your disk.)

1. Copy the **OutdoorOptions** database file from the CD that accompanies this textbook to your disk. Remove the read-only attribute from the **OutdoorOptions** database file.
2. Open the **OutdoorOptions** database file.
3. At the OutdoorOptions : Database window, click the Tables button on the Objects bar.
4. Create and print a report using AutoReport by completing the following steps:
   a. Click *Suppliers* in the list box to select the Suppliers table.
   b. Click the down-pointing arrow at the right side of the New Object button on the Database toolbar.
   c. At the drop-down list that displays, click *AutoReport*.
   d. When the report displays in Print Preview, view the report, and then click the Print button on the Print Preview toolbar.
   e. Click the Close button at the right side of the Suppliers title bar.
   f. At the message asking if you want to save the changes to the design of the report, click the No button.
5. Close the **OutdoorOptions** database file.

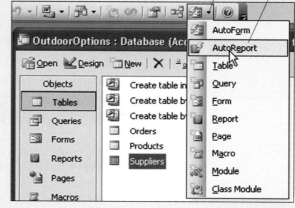

Creating a Report Using the Report Wizard

To create a report using the Report Wizard, open the database file, click the Reports button on the Objects bar, and then click the New button. At the New Report dialog box, double-click *Report Wizard* in the list box. The first Report Wizard dialog box is similar to the first Form Wizard dialog box. Choose the desired table with options from the *Tables/Queries* text box. Specify the fields you want included in the report by inserting them in the *Selected Fields* list box and then clicking the Next button.

ACCESS

At the second Report Wizard dialog box, shown in Figure 6.1, you can increase or decrease the priority level of fields in the report. To increase the priority level, click the desired field name in the list box at the left side of the dialog box, and then click the button containing the greater than symbol (>). To decrease the priority level, click the desired field, and then click the button containing the less than symbol (<). This changes the sample information displayed at the right side of the dialog box. After specifying the field levels, click the Next button.

Create a Report Using Report Wizard
1. Open database file.
2. Click Reports button on Objects bar.
3. Click New button.
4. Double-click *Report Wizard.*
5. Choose desired options at each of the Report Wizard dialog boxes.

FIGURE

6.1 *Second Report Wizard Dialog Box*

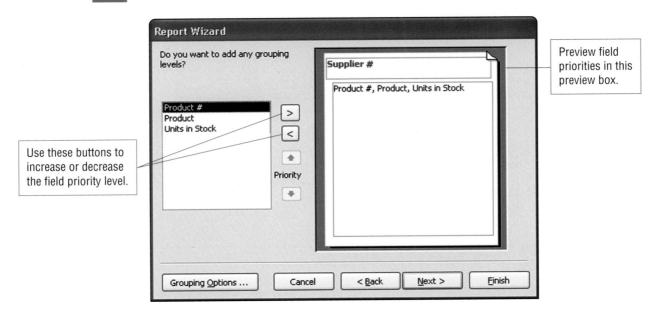

You can specify the order in which records are displayed in the report at the third Report Wizard dialog box shown in Figure 6.2. To specify a sort order, click the down-pointing arrow at the right of the text box preceded by a number 1, and then click the field name. The default sort is done in ascending order. This can be changed to descending by clicking the button that displays at the right side of the text box. After identifying the sort order, click the Next button.

6.2 *Third Report Wizard Dialog Box*

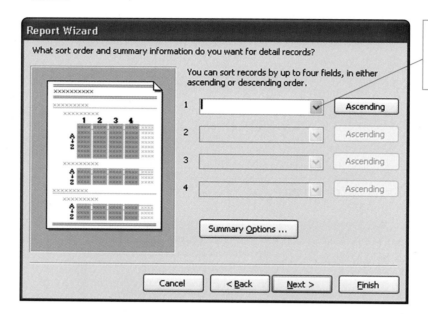

The layout of the report is determined in the fourth Report Wizard dialog box shown in Figure 6.3. You can choose from a variety of layouts such as *Stepped*, *Block*, *Outline 1*, *Outline 2*, *Align Left 1*, and *Align Left 2*. Click a layout option and a sample of the layout is displayed on the sample page at the left side of the dialog box. The page orientation can also be selected at this dialog box. After choosing a layout and/or orientation, click the Next button.

6.3 *Fourth Report Wizard Dialog Box*

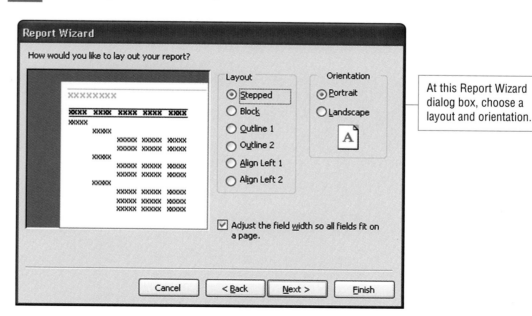

The Report Wizard offers several report styles at the fifth Report Wizard dialog box shown in Figure 6.4. Click a report style and the wizard will display a sample at the left side of the dialog box. Click the Next button to display the sixth Report Wizard dialog box.

FIGURE

6.4   *Fifth Report Wizard Dialog Box*

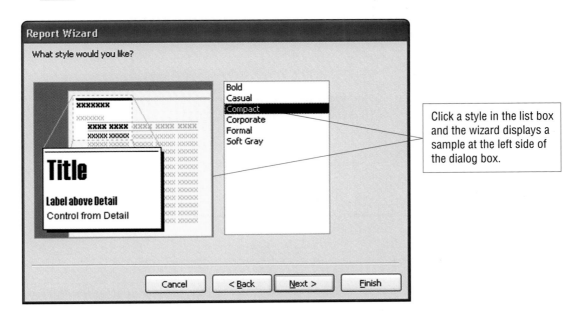

Click a style in the list box and the wizard displays a sample at the left side of the dialog box.

At the sixth Report Wizard dialog box, shown in Figure 6.5, type a name for the report, and then click Finish. Creating the report may take a few moments. When the report is finished, it displays on the screen in Print Preview. In Print Preview, you can change the percentage of display of data and also send the report to the printer. To print the report, click the Print button on the Print Preview toolbar. After viewing and/or printing the report, close Print Preview by clicking the Close button.

HINT
Switch to the Design view to make changes to the report design.

6.5   **Sixth Report Wizard Dialog Box**

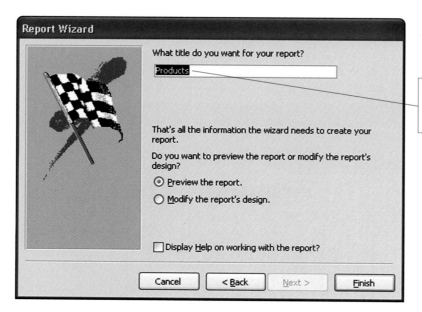

Use the report title offered by the wizard or type your own name.

exercise 2

USING THE REPORT WIZARD TO PREPARE A REPORT

1. Open the **OutdoorOptions** database file.
2. At the OutdoorOptions : Database window, click the Reports button on the Objects bar.
3. Create a report with the Report Wizard by completing the following steps:
   a. Click the New button on the window toolbar.
   b. At the New Report dialog box, double-click the *Report Wizard* option in the list box.
   c. At the first Report Wizard dialog box, click the down-pointing arrow at the right side of the *Tables/Queries* text box, and then click *Table: Products* at the drop-down list.
   d. Insert the following fields in the *Selected Fields* list box:

   Product #
   Product
   Supplier #
   Units in Stock

   e. After inserting the fields, click the Next button.

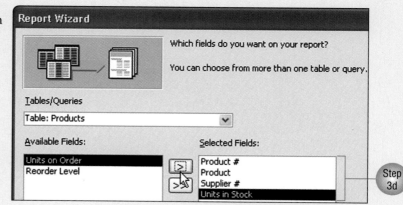

f. At the second Report Wizard dialog box, decrease and increase priority levels by completing the following steps:

   1) Click the button to the right of the list box that displays with a less than symbol (<). (This decreases the priority level of the *Supplier #* field.)

   2) Click *Product* in the list box that displays at the left side of the dialog box, and then click the button to the right of the list box that displays with a greater than symbol (>). (This increases the priority level of the *Product* field.)

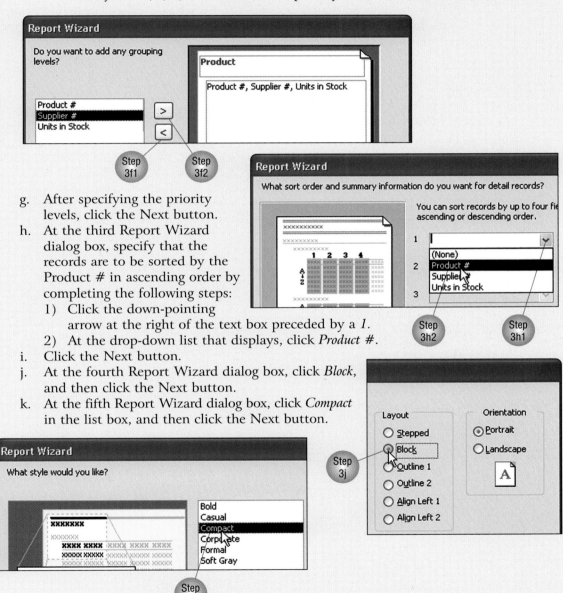

g. After specifying the priority levels, click the Next button.

h. At the third Report Wizard dialog box, specify that the records are to be sorted by the Product # in ascending order by completing the following steps:

   1) Click the down-pointing arrow at the right of the text box preceded by a *1*.

   2) At the drop-down list that displays, click *Product #*.

i. Click the Next button.

j. At the fourth Report Wizard dialog box, click *Block*, and then click the Next button.

k. At the fifth Report Wizard dialog box, click *Compact* in the list box, and then click the Next button.

l. At the sixth Report Wizard dialog box, click the Finish button.

m. When the report displays in Print Preview, view the report, and then click the Print button that displays on the Print Preview toolbar.

n. Click the Close button at the right side of the Products title bar.

4. Close the **OutdoorOptions** database file.

Preparing a Report Based on Two Database Tables

In the previous chapter on creating forms, you learned to create a form with fields from related database tables. Fields from related database tables can also be used to create a report. The steps to prepare a report with fields from two database tables are basically the same as those you completed in Exercise 2. The only difference is that an additional Report Wizard dialog box displays during the steps asking you to specify whether the fields should be grouped by the fields from the primary table or fields from the related table. In Exercise 3, you will prepare a report with fields from the Products database table and also the Suppliers table. These tables are joined by a one-to-many relationship.

exercise 3

PREPARING A REPORT WITH FIELDS FROM TWO DATABASE TABLES

1. Open the **OutdoorOptions** database file.
2. At the OutdoorOptions : Database window, click the Reports button on the Objects bar.
3. Create a report with the Report Wizard by completing the following steps:
   a. Click the New button on the window toolbar.
   b. At the New Report dialog box, double-click *Report Wizard* in the list box.
   c. At the first Report Wizard dialog box, insert the following fields in the *Selected Fields* list box:

   From the Suppliers database table:

   > *Supplier Name*
   > *Street Address*
   > *City*
   > *Province*
   > *Postal Code*

   From the Products database table:

   > *Product*
   > *Product #*

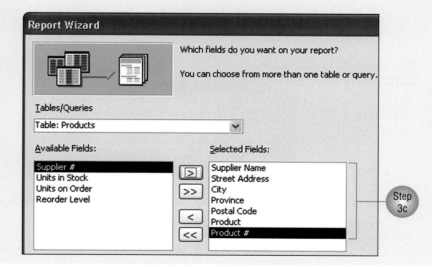

d. After inserting the fields, click the Next button.
e. At the second Report Wizard dialog box, make sure *by Suppliers* is selected in the list box in the upper left corner, and then click the Next button.
f. At the third Report Wizard dialog box, increase the priority level of the *Supplier Name* field. To do this, make sure *Supplier Name* is selected in the list box, and then click the button containing the greater than symbol (>).

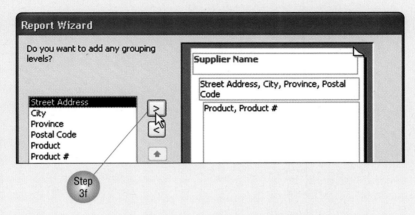

g. Click the Next button.
h. At the fourth Report Wizard dialog box, click the Next button. (Do not specify a sort order.)
i. At the fifth Report Wizard dialog box, click *Align Left 1*, and then click the Next button.
j. At the sixth Report Wizard dialog box, click *Corporate* in the list box, and then click the Next button.
k. At the seventh Report Wizard dialog box, click the Finish button.
l. When the report displays in Print Preview, view the report, and then click the Print button that displays on the Print Preview toolbar.
m. Click the Close button (displays with an *X*) that displays at the right side of the Suppliers title bar.
4. Close the **OutdoorOptions** database file.

Creating a Report in Design View

A report, like a form, is comprised of a series of controls, which are objects that display titles or descriptions, accept data, or perform actions. In the reports you created in this chapter, the Report Wizard created the controls for the report using fields from the tables. A report, like a form, can be created in Design view. To display the report Design view, click the Reports button on the Objects bar, and then double-click *Create report in Design view*.

A report can include up to five sections including Report Header, Page Header, Detail, Page Footer, and Report Footer. These five sections are identified in the sample report shown in Figure 6.6.

Report Header ─── **OUTDOOR OPTIONS ORDERS**

Page Header ─── ORDER   AMOUNT

Order #:	6	$573.25
Supplier #:	54	
Product #:	103	
Units Ordered:	10	
Unit Price:	$57.33	
Order #:	1	$1,137.50
Supplier #:	99	
Product #:	780	
Units Ordered:	25	
Unit Price:	$45.50	
Order #:	4	$1,906.25
Supplier #:	99	
Product #:	673	
Units Ordered:	25	
Unit Price:	$76.25	
Order #:	5	$2,800.00
Supplier #:	70	
Product #:	897	
Units Ordered:	25	
Unit Price:	฿112.00	
Order #:	7	$325.00
Supplier #:	99	
Product #:	647	
Units Ordered:	5	
Unit Price:	$65.00	

Detail ─── (points to Detail section)

Report Footer ─── Report designed by Student Name

Page Footer ─── Page 1 of 1

The Report Header generally includes the title of the report and/or the company logo. The Page Header appears at the top of each page and generally includes column headings identifying the data in the report. The Detail section of the report contains the data from the table. The Page Footer appears at the bottom of each page and might include information such as the page number. The Report Footer appears on the last page of the report and might include information such as the person designing the report.

Using Fields to Add Controls

To add fields to a report in Design view, associate the report with the desired table. To do this, click the Properties button on the Report Design toolbar. This displays the Report properties sheet. At the Report properties sheet, click the All tab, and then click in the *Record Source* text box. Click the down-pointing arrow that displays at the right side of the text box, and then click the desired table. This displays the table fields in a field list box. Using the mouse, drag the desired field from the field list box to the Design grid.

HINT
Other methods for displaying the property sheet include pressing Alt + Enter or double-clicking the control.

Moving, Resizing, and Customizing Control Objects

The steps to move, resize, and/or customize control objects in report Design view are the same as the steps to remove, resize, and/or customize control objects in form Design view. Select an object and then either move the individual object or move the label control object and the text box control object together. Customize control objects with options at the properties sheet. (The name of the properties sheet will vary depending on what is selected.)

HINT
Display Help on a property by clicking in the property and then pressing F1.

When a field is added to the report in Design view, a label control containing the field name and a text box control used to accept data are placed adjacent to each other. The label control containing the field name is included for descriptive purposes so that the user knows which data to type into the corresponding text box. In a report, a column heading is generally included in the Page Header describing the data and, therefore, some label control objects may not be needed.

Adding Controls Using the Toolbox

Add controls to the report using buttons on the Toolbox. To add a control in Design view, click the desired button on the Toolbox. This causes the mouse pointer to change to a crosshair pointer with an icon attached. The icon that displays will vary depending on the control object button selected. Move the pointer to the position on the form where you want to place the object and then drag to create the object. Use the sizing handles that display around the control to increase or decrease the size.

Adding a Report Header and Report Footer

The Design view, by default, displays the Detail section and the Page Header and Page Footer. To add a Report Header and/or Report Footer to a report, click View on the Menu bar and then click Report Header/Footer. Another method is to right-click on the Report 1 : Report title bar, and then click Report Header/Footer at the shortcut menu. Use the same methods to turn off the display of a Report Header and Report Footer.

To insert text in a Page Header, Report Header, Page Footer, or Report Footer, use the Label button on the Toolbox. Click the Label button and then draw the label in the desired section. Type text inside the label control object and apply the desired formatting.

QUICK STEPS

Add Report Header and Report Footer
1. Open report in Design view.
2. Click View, Report Header/Footer.

exercise 4

1. Open the **OutdoorOptions** database file.
2. At the OutdoorOptions : Database window, click the Reports button on the Objects bar.
3. Create the report shown in Figure 6.7 in Design view by completing the following steps:
   a. Double-click the *Create report in Design view* option in the list box.
   b. At the Design grid, click the Properties button on the Report Design toolbar.
   c. At the Report properties sheet, click the All tab.
   d. At the Report properties sheet with the All tab selected, click in the *Record Source* text box, and then click the down-pointing arrow that displays at the right side of the text box.
   e. At the drop-down list that displays, click *Orders*.
   f. Drag the *Order #* field from the field list box to the Design grid to the approximate location shown below.
   g. Drag the other fields (*Supplier #*, *Product #*, *Units Ordered*, and *Amount*) from the field list box to the Design grid in the approximate locations shown below.

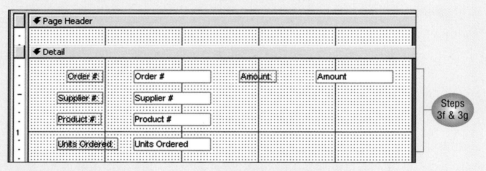

   h. Delete the label control object for the Amount. (The label control object contains *Amount* with a transparent background [gray dots from the grid show through].)
   i. Insert a calculated control field by completing the following steps:
      1) Click the Text Box button on the Toolbox. (If the Toolbox is not visible, click the Toolbox button on the Report Design toolbar.)
      2) Position the crosshair pointer with the text box icon attached below the Units Ordered text box control and then drag the outline of a box approximately the same size as the text box control above.
      3) Click in the text box control (which currently displays *Unbound*) and type =[Amount]/[Units Ordered].
      4) Click outside the box, and then click the text box control to select it.

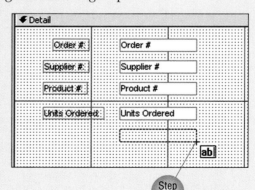

ACCESS

5) With the text box control selected, click in the *Format* text box in the Text Box properties sheet (you may need to scroll up to display the *Format* text box), click the down-pointing arrow, and then click *Currency* at the drop-down list.

6) Click outside the text box control to deselect it.

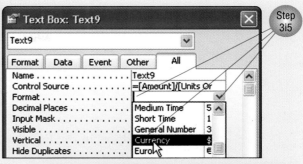

Step 3i5

j. Change the caption in the new label control box by completing the following steps:

1) Click the label control box to select it (contains *Text #* [where a number displays in place of the # symbol]).

2) Click in the *Caption* text box located in the Label properties sheet. (You may need to scroll up to display the *Caption* text box.)

3) Delete the text currently displayed in the *Caption* text box and then type **Unit Price:**.

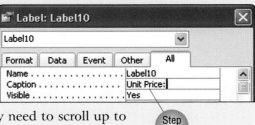

Step 3j3

k. Decrease the size of the text box controls as shown at the right.

l. Select the label control objects at the left side of the Design grid (just the label control objects—not the text box control objects) and then align them at the right.

m. With the label object control boxes still selected, change the font weight to bold.

n. With the label object control boxes still selected, change the text alignment to right. To do this, click in the *Text Align* text box in the Multiple selection properties sheet (you may need to scroll down the list to display this text box), click the down-pointing arrow, and then click *Right* at the drop-down list.

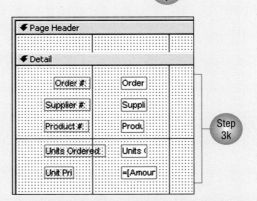

Step 3k

o. With the label object control boxes still selected, position the mouse pointer on one of the selected boxes and then click the right mouse button. At the shortcut menu that displays, point to Size, and then click To Fit at the side menu.

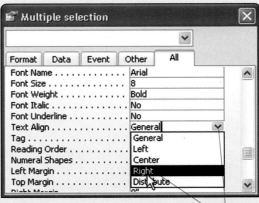

Step 3n

p. Select all of the text box control objects (contain a white background) and then click in the *Text Align* text box in the Multiple selection properties sheet. Click the down-pointing arrow at the right side of the text box and then click *Right* at the drop-down list.

q. Decrease the height of the Detail section by completing the following steps:

1) Position the mouse pointer on the top of the gray bar containing the text *Page Footer* until the pointer turns into an up- and down-pointing arrow with a line between.

2) Hold down the left mouse button, drag up until the border displays just below the bottom label and text box control objects, and then release the mouse button.

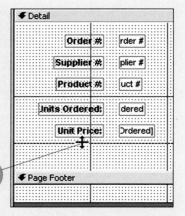

Step 3q2

r. Add column headings in the Page Header by completing the following steps:

1) Click the Label button on the Toolbox.

2) Position the crosshair pointer with the label icon attached to it at the top left edge of the first black gridline in the Page Header section, drag the mouse down to the approximate height and width shown at the right (and in Figure 6.7), and then release the mouse button.

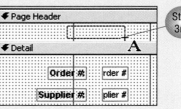

Step 3r2

3) Type ORDER in the label control box, and then click outside the box.

4) Use the Label button on the Toolbox to create the AMOUNT label shown in Figure 6.7.

5) Select the two labels and then apply the following formatting:
   a) Change the font name to Times New Roman.
   b) Change the font size to 12.
   c) Change the font weight to bold.
   d) Change the fore color to Dark Teal (fourth color from the left in the third row from the top).

6) Increase the size of the label control boxes so the entire text displays in each label.

Step 3s2c

Step 3s2a

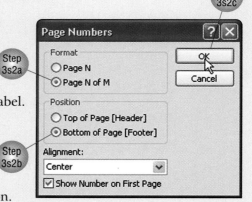

s. Insert page numbering in the Page Footer by completing the following steps:

1) Click Insert and then Page Numbers.

2) At the Page Numbers dialog box, make the following changes:

Step 3s2b

   a) Click *Page N of M* in the *Format* section.
   b) Click *Bottom of Page [Footer]* in the *Position* section.
   c) Click OK to close the dialog box.

t. Add a Report Header by completing the following steps:

1) Display the Report Header and Report Footer by clicking View on the Menu bar and then clicking Report Header/Footer.

2) Increase the Report Header section by about .5 inch by dragging down the top of the gray bar (contains the words *Page Header*).

3) Click the Label button on the Toolbox.

4) Drag to create a label box inside the Report Header that is large enough to hold the title shown in Figure 6.7.

5) Type the text OUTDOOR OPTIONS ORDERS inside the label, and then click outside the box.

6) Click the label control box and then apply the following formatting:
   a) Change the font name to Times New Roman.
   b) Change the font size to 14.

c) Change the font weight to bold.
   d) Change the fore color to Dark Teal (the fourth color from the left in the third row from the top).
   7) Click outside the label box to deselect it.
u. Add a Report Footer by completing the following steps:
   1) Increase the height of the Report Footer section by about .5 inch. (To do this, drag down the bottom edge of the Report Footer section.)
   2) Click the Label button on the Toolbox and then draw a label box inside the Report Footer large enough to hold the text shown in Figure 6.7.
   3) Type the text Report designed by Student Name (insert your name instead of *Student Name*).
4. Close the properties sheet. (To do this, click the Close button that displays in the upper right corner of the sheet.)
5. View the report in Print Preview by clicking the View button on the Report Design toolbar.
6. Check the headings *ORDERS* and *AMOUNT* and make sure the headings display approximately centered over the information in columns. (If they do not, change to Design view, move the heading or headings to the desired location, and then change back to Print Preview.)
7. Print the report by clicking the Print button on the Print Preview toolbar.
8. Click the View button to return to the Design view.
9. In Design view, save the report and name it Orders Report.
10. Close Orders Report.
11. Close the **OutdoorOptions** database file.

FIGURE

6.7 **Exercise 4**

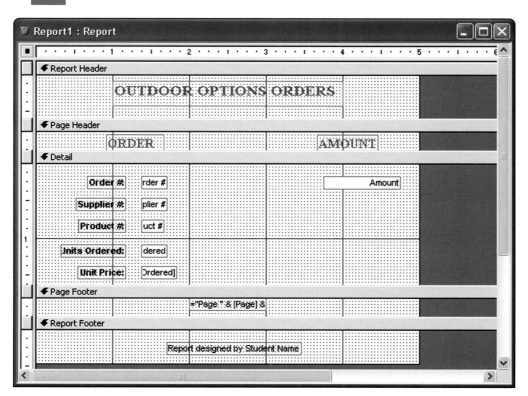

Preparing Mailing Labels

HINT

Use the Label Wizard to create mailing labels easily.

Access includes a Mailing Label Wizard that walks you through the steps for creating mailing labels with fields in a database table. To create mailing labels, open the database file, click the Reports button on the Objects bar, and then click the New button. This displays the New Report dialog box. At this dialog box, specify the database table where the information for creating the mailing labels is located, and then double-click *Label Wizard* in the list box. At the first Label Wizard dialog box shown in Figure 6.8, specify the label size, units of measure, and the label type, and then click the Next button.

FIGURE

6.8 *First Label Wizard Dialog Box*

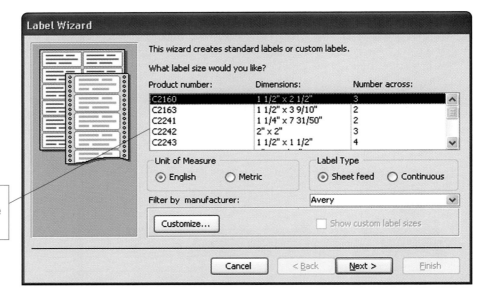

Scroll through this list box and choose the desired label.

QUICK STEPS

Create Mailing Labels Using Label Wizard
1. Open database file.
2. Click Reports button on Objects bar.
3. Click New button.
4. Specify desired table.
5. Double-click *Label Wizard*.
6. Choose desired options at each of the Label Wizard dialog boxes.

At the second Label Wizard dialog box shown in Figure 6.9, specify the font name, size, weight, and color, and then click the Next button.

6.9 **Second Label Wizard Dialog Box**

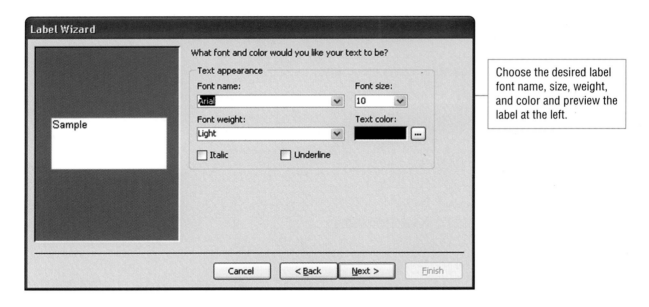

Choose the desired label font name, size, weight, and color and preview the label at the left.

Specify the fields you want included in the mailing labels at the third Label Wizard dialog box shown in Figure 6.10. To do this, select the field in the *Available fields* list box, and then click the button containing the greater than symbol (>). This moves the field to the Prototype label. Insert the fields in the Prototype label as you want the text to display on the label. After inserting the fields in the Prototype label, click the Next button.

6.10 **Third Label Wizard Dialog Box**

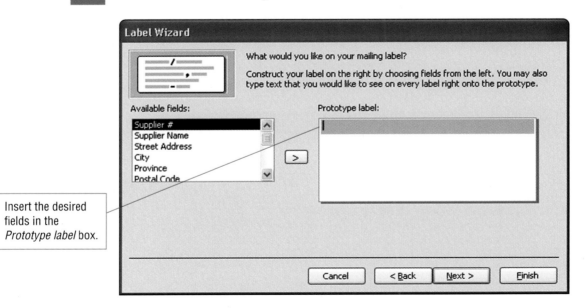

Insert the desired fields in the *Prototype label* box.

At the fourth Label Wizard dialog box, shown in Figure 6.11, you can specify a field from the database file by which the labels are sorted. If you want the labels sorted (for example, by last name, postal code, and so on.), insert the field by which you want the fields sorted in the *Sort by* list box, and then click the Next button.

FIGURE

6.11 *Fourth Label Wizard Dialog Box*

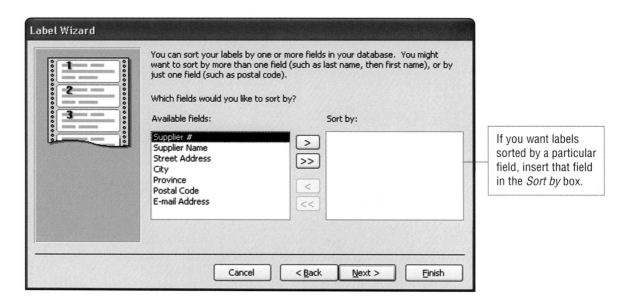

If you want labels sorted by a particular field, insert that field in the *Sort by* box.

At the last Label Wizard dialog box, type a name for the label file, and then click the Finish button. After a few moments, the labels display on the screen in Print Preview. Print the labels and/or close Print Preview.

exercise 5

PREPARING MAILING LABELS

1. Open the **OutdoorOptions** database file.
2. At the OutdoorOptions : Database window, prepare mailing labels with supplier names and addresses by completing the following steps:
   a. Click the Reports button on the Objects bar.
   b. Click the New button on the window toolbar.
   c. At the New Report dialog box, click the down-pointing arrow at the right of the *Choose the table or query where the object's data comes from* option box, and then click *Suppliers* at the drop-down list.
   d. Double-click *Label Wizard* in the list box.
   e. At the first Label Wizard dialog box, make the following changes:

ACCESS

1) Click *English* in the *Unit of Measure* section. (Skip this step if *English* is already selected.)
2) Click the down-pointing arrow at the right side of the *Filter by manufacturer* option, and then click *Avery* at the drop-down list. (Skip this step if *Avery* is already selected.)
3) Make sure *C2160* is selected in the *Product number* list box.
4) Click the Next button.

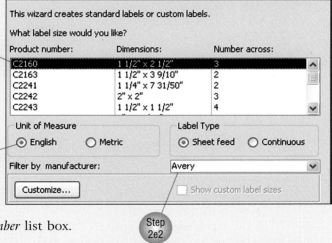

f. At the second Label Wizard dialog box (see Figure 6.9), change the font size to 10, and then click the Next button.

g. At the third Label Wizard dialog box, complete the following steps to insert the fields in the Prototype label:

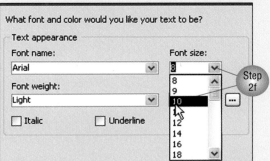

1) Click *Supplier Name* in the *Available fields* list box, and then click the button containing the greater than symbol (>).
2) Press the Enter key (this moves the insertion point down to the next line in the Prototype label).
3) With *Street Address* selected in the *Available fields* list box, click the button containing the greater than symbol (>).
4) Press the Enter key.
5) With *City* selected in the *Available fields* list box, click the button containing the greater than symbol (>).
6) Type a comma (,) and then press the spacebar.
7) With *Province* selected in the *Available fields* list box, click the button containing the greater than symbol (>).
8) Press the Enter key.
9) With *Postal Code* selected in the *Available fields* list box, click the button containing the greater than symbol (>).

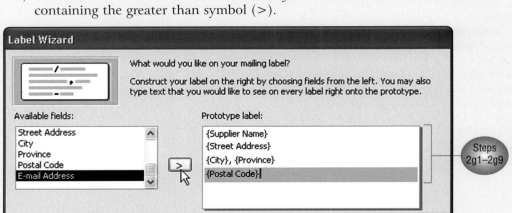

10) Click the Next button.
   h. At the fourth Label Wizard dialog box, sort by postal code. To do this, click *Postal Code* in the *Available fields* list box and then click the button containing the greater than symbol (>).
   i. Click the Next button.
   j. At the last Label Wizard dialog box, click the Finish button. (The Label Wizard automatically names the label file Labels Suppliers.)

3. Print the labels by clicking the Print button on the Print Preview toolbar.
4. Close the labels file. (To do this, click the Close button that displays at the right side of the Labels Suppliers : Report title bar.)
5. Close the **OutdoorOptions** database file.

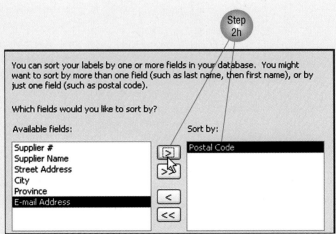

Step 2h

You can sort your labels by one or more fields in your database. You might want to sort by more than one field (such as last name, then first name), or by just one field (such as postal code).

Which fields would you like to sort by?

Available fields: Sort by:

Supplier #   Postal Code
Supplier Name
Street Address
City
Province
E-mail Address

HINT
Create a chart with data from a database table to provide a visual display of data.

HINT
The Chart Wizard is shared by Microsoft Office applications.

QUICK STEPS

Create Chart Using Chart Wizard
1. Open database file.
2. Click Reports button on Objects bar.
3. Click New button.
4. Specify desired table.
5. Double-click *Chart Wizard*.
6. Choose desired options at each of the Chart Wizard dialog boxes.

Creating a Chart

Access includes a Chart Wizard you can use to display data more visually than a table, form, or report. Use the Chart Wizard to create a chart with data from a database table. To create a chart with the Chart Wizard, open the database file, and then click either the Forms button or the Reports button on the Objects bar. Specify the database table containing the fields to be included in the chart and then double-click the *Chart Wizard* option in the list box. This displays the first Chart Wizard dialog box, shown in Figure 6.12.

6.12 *First Chart Wizard Dialog Box*

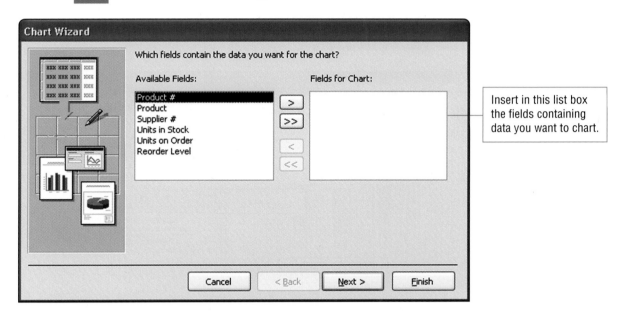

Insert in this list box the fields containing data you want to chart.

At the first Chart Wizard dialog box, insert the fields you want included in the chart in the *Fields for Chart* list box. The first field inserted in the *Fields for Chart* list box will be used by the Chart Wizard as the x-axis in the chart. After inserting the fields, click the Next button. This displays the second Chart Wizard dialog box, shown in Figure 6.13.

6.13 *Second Chart Wizard Dialog Box*

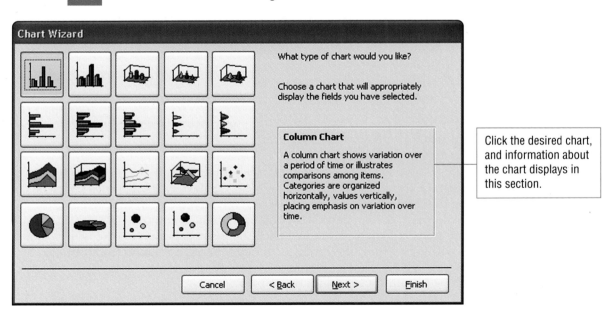

Click the desired chart, and information about the chart displays in this section.

Choose the chart type at the second Chart Wizard dialog box. To do this, click the icon representing the desired chart, and then click the Next button. This displays the third Chart Wizard dialog box, shown in Figure 6.14.

FIGURE

6.14 *Third Chart Wizard Dialog Box*

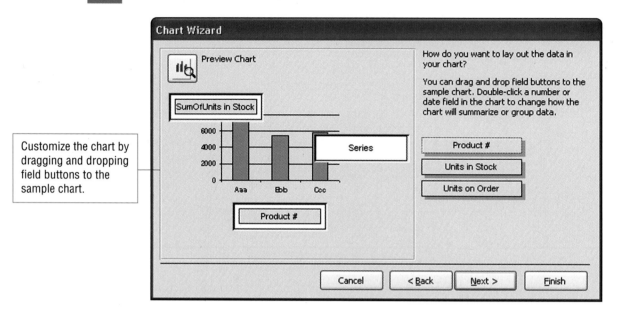

Customize the chart by dragging and dropping field buttons to the sample chart.

At the third Chart Wizard dialog box, specify how you want labels to appear in the chart. To do this, double-click a label in the preview chart. At the drop-down list that displays, click the desired label option. At this dialog box, you can also add another field to the chart. For example, in Exercise 6, you will be charting Units on Order as well as Units in Stock. To do this, you will drag the desired field from the right side of the dialog box to the appropriate location in the preview chart. When all changes have been made, click the Next button. At the fourth, and last, Chart Wizard dialog box, type a name for the chart, and then click the Finish button.

exercise 6

CREATING A CHART

1. Open the **OutdoorOptions** database file.
2. Click the Tables button on the Objects bar.
3. Open the Products table by double-clicking *Products* in the list box.
4. Delete the records of those products where zero *(0)* displays in the *Units on Order* field (at the warning message, click Yes). After deleting the records, click the Save button on the Table Datasheet toolbar, and then close the Products database table.
5. At the OutdoorOptions : Database window, click the Reports button on the Objects bar.
6. Create a chart with fields from the Products database table by completing the following steps:
   a. Click the New button on the window toolbar.

b. At the New Report dialog box, click the down-pointing arrow at the right of the *Choose the table or query where the object's data comes from* option, and then click *Products*.
c. Double-click *Chart Wizard* in the list box.
d. At the first Chart Wizard dialog box, complete the following steps:
    1) With *Product #* selected in the *Available Fields* list box, click the button containing the greater than symbol (>).
    2) Click *Units in Stock* in the *Available Fields* list box and then click the button containing the greater than symbol (>).
    3) With *Units on Order* selected in the *Available Fields* list box, click the button containing the greater than symbol (>).
    4) Click the Next button.

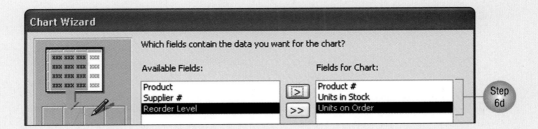

e. At the second Chart Wizard dialog box, click the Next button.
f. At the third Chart Wizard dialog box, complete the following steps:
    1) Position the arrow pointer on the Units on Order button at the right side of the dialog box, hold down the left mouse button, drag the outline of the button to the bottom of the *SumOfUnits in Stock* field that displays in the preview chart, and then release the left mouse button.

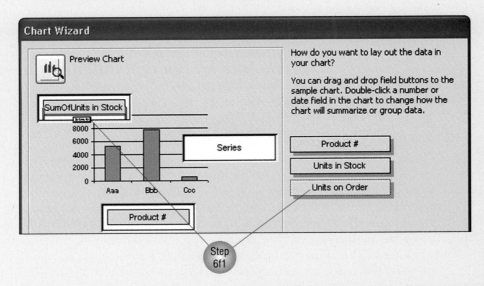

    2) Double-click the *SumOfUnits in Stock* field that displays in the preview chart.

3) At the Summarize dialog box, double-click *None* in the list box. (This changes *SumOfUnits in Stock* to *Units in Stock*. By default, the Chart Wizard will sum the number of units in stock. Changing the field to *Units in Stock* tells the Chart Wizard to simply display the number of units in stock and not the sum.)

Step 6f3

4) Double-click the *SumOfUnits on Order* field that displays in the preview chart.
5) At the Summarize dialog box, double-click *None* in the list box. (This changes *SumOfUnits on Order* to *Units on Order*.)
6) Click the Next button.

g. At the fourth Chart Wizard dialog box, type **Product Units**, and then click the Finish button.

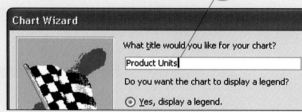

Step 6g

7. With the chart displayed in Print Preview, print the chart by clicking the Print button on the Print Preview toolbar.
8. After the chart is printed, click the Close button that displays at the right side of the Report1 : Report title bar. At the message asking if you want to save the changes to the design of the report, click No.
9. Close the **OutdoorOptions** database table.

Summarizing Data By Changing Views

Access provides additional views in a table and query that you can use to summarize data. Change to the PivotTable view to create a PivotTable that is an interactive table that organizes and summarizes data. Use the PivotChart view to create a PivotChart that summarizes data in a graph.

Summarizing Data Using PivotTable View

A PivotTable is an interactive table that organizes and summarizes data based on the fields you designate for row headings, column headings, and source record filtering. Aggregate functions such as Sum, Avg, and Count are easily added to the table using the AutoCalc button on the PivotTable toolbar. A PivotTable provides more options for viewing data than a crosstab query because you can easily change the results by filtering data by an item in a row, a column, or for all source records. This interactivity allows you to analyze the data for numerous scenarios. PivotTables are easily created using a drag-and-drop technique in PivotTable View.

To create a PivotTable, open a table or query in Datasheet view, click View, and then click PivotTable View. (You can also click the down-pointing arrow at the right of the View button on the table or query toolbar, and then click PivotTable View.) This changes the datasheet to PivotTable layout with four sections and a PivotTable Field List box. Dimmed text in each section describes the types of fields that should be dragged and dropped. Figure 6.15 displays the PivotTable layout you will be using in Exercise 7.

6.15 *PivotTable Layout*

Drag the desired item from this list box and drop it in the appropriate location.

Dimmed text in each section describes the types of fields that should be dragged and dropped.

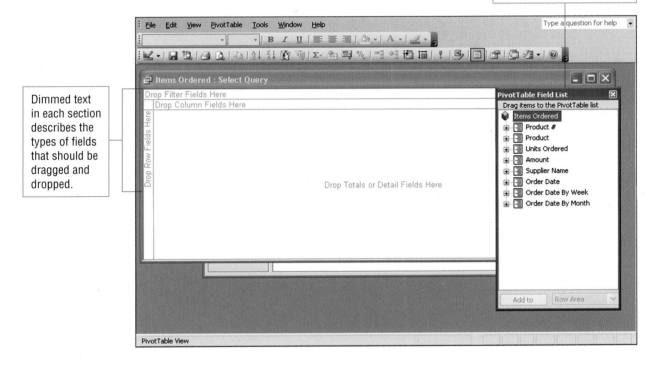

Drag the fields from the PivotTable Field List box to the desired locations in the PivotTable layout. The dimmed text in the PivotTable layout identifies the field that should be dropped in the location. In Exercise 7, you will drag the *Supplier Name* field to the Row field section, the *Product* field to the Column field section, the *Amount* field to the Totals or Details field section, and the *Order Date* to the Filter section. The PivotTable will then display as shown in Figure 6.16.

6.16 *PivotTable for Exercise 7*

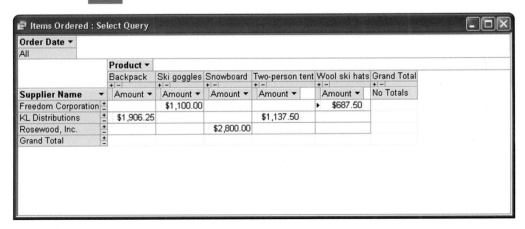

exercise 7

1. Open the **OutdoorOptions** database table.
2. Click the Queries button on the Objects bar and then create a new query in Design view with the following specifications:
   a. Add the Orders, Products, and Suppliers tables to the design grid.
   b. Add the following fields from the specified tables:

Product #	=	Orders table
Product	=	Products table
Units Ordered	=	Orders table
Amount	=	Orders table
Supplier Name	=	Suppliers table
Order Date	=	Orders table

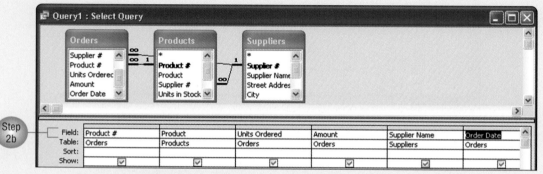

Step 2b

   c. Save the query and name it Items Ordered.
   d. Run the query.
3. Click View and then PivotTable View.
4. At the PivotTable layout, drag and drop the *Supplier Name* field to the Row field section by completing the following steps:
   a. Position the mouse pointer on the *Supplier Name* field in the PivotTable Field List box.
   b. Hold down the left mouse button, drag to the dimmed text *Drop Row Fields Here* located at the left side of the query window, and then release the mouse button.

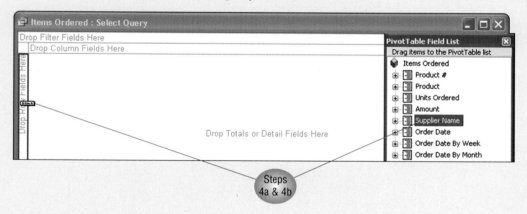

Steps 4a & 4b

5. Complete steps similar to those in Step 4 to drag and drop the following fields:
   a. Drag the *Product* field from the PivotTable Field List box and drop it on the dimmed text *Drop Columns Fields Here*.

    b. Drag the *Amount* field from the PivotTable Field List box and drop it on the dimmed text *Drop Totals or Detail Fields Here*.

    c. Drag the *Order Date* field from the PivotTable Field List box and drop it on the dimmed text *Drop Filter Fields Here*.

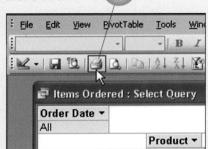

6. Remove the PivotTable Field List box from the screen by clicking the Field List button on the PivotTable toolbar. (Your PivotTable should look like the PivotTable shown in Figure 6.16.)

7. Click the Print button to print the query in PivotTable view.

8. Click View and then Datasheet View to return the query to the Datasheet view.

9. Close the query. At the message asking if you want to save the changes, click Yes.

10. Close the **OutdoorOptions** database table.

When you create a PivotTable in a query or table, it becomes a part of and is saved with the table or query. The next time you open the table or query, display the PivotTable by clicking View and then PivotTable. If you make changes to data in fields that are part of the table or query (and PivotTable), the data is automatically updated in the table or query.

The power of a PivotTable is the ability to analyze data for numerous scenarios. For example, in the PivotTable you created in Exercise 7, you can display orders for a specific date or isolate a specific supplier. Use the plus and minus symbols that display in a row or column heading to show (plus symbol) or hide (minus symbol) data. Use the down-pointing arrow (called the *filter* arrow) that displays in a field to display specific data in the field. You can also use buttons on the PivotTable toolbar to perform actions such as filtering data and performing calculations on data.

exercise 8

ANALYZING DATA IN PIVOTTABLE VIEW

1. Open the **OutdoorOptions** database table.

2. Click the Tables button on the Objects bar, open the Orders table, and then add the following records:

Order #	=	(AutoNumber)
Supplier #	=	68
Product #	=	558
Units Ordered	=	25
Amount	=	$550
Order Date	=	2/28/2005
Order #	=	(AutoNumber)
Supplier #	=	70
Product #	=	897
Units Ordered	=	10
Amount	=	$1,120
Order Date	=	2/28/2005

3. Close the Orders table.
4. Click the Queries button on the Objects bar and then double-click the *Items Ordered* query in the list box.
5. With the query open, click View and then PivotTable View. (Notice the PivotTable reflects the two new order records you inserted in the Orders table.)
6. Display only items ordered on February 28 by completing the following steps:
   a. Click the filter arrow (down-pointing arrow) at the right of the *Order Date* field (located in the upper left corner of the query window).
   b. At the drop-down list that displays, click the *(All)* check box to remove the check mark before each date.
   c. Click the check box to the left of *2/28/2005*.
   d. Click the OK button.
   e. Click the Print button on the PivotTable toolbar.
   f. Redisplay all items by clicking the filter arrow at the right of the *Order Date* field, clicking the check box to the left of *(All)*, and then clicking OK.

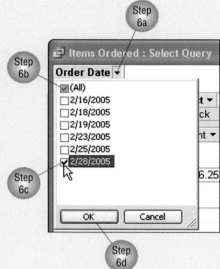

7. Display only those order amounts for Freedom Corporation by completing the following steps:
   a. Click the filter arrow at the right of the *Supplier Name* field.
   b. At the drop-down list, click the *(All)* check box to remove the check mark before each supplier name.
   c. Click the check box to the left of *Freedom Corporation*.
   d. Click the OK button.
   e. Click the Print button on the PivotTable toolbar.
   f. Redisplay all supplier names by clicking the filter arrow at the right of the *Supplier Name* field, clicking the check box to the left of *(All)*, and then clicking OK.
8. Display subtotals and totals of order amounts by completing the following steps:
   a. Position the mouse pointer on any *Amount* column heading until the pointer displays with a four-headed arrow attached and then click the left mouse button. (This displays all the *Amount* column headings and amounts with a light blue background.)

b. Click the AutoCalc button on the PivotTable toolbar, and then click *Sum* at the drop-down list. (This inserts subtotals and totals in the PivotTable.)

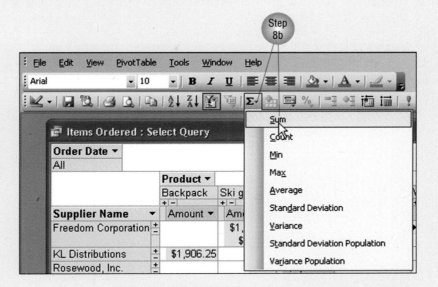

Step 8b

9. Change the page orientation to landscape and then print the PivotTable.
10. Close the PivotTable. (At the message asking if you want to save the changes, click Yes.)
11. Close the **OutdoorOptions** database table.

Summarizing Data Using PivotChart View

A PivotChart performs the same function as a PivotTable with the exception that the source data is displayed in a graph instead of a table. A chart is created by dragging fields from the Chart Field List box to the Filter, Data, Category, and Series sections of the chart. As with a PivotTable, the PivotChart can be easily altered using the filter arrows.

To create a PivotChart, open a table or query in Datasheet view, click View, and then click PivotChart View (or click the down-pointing arrow at the right of the View button, and then click PivotChart View). This changes the datasheet to PivotChart layout with four sections and a Chart Field List box. Dimmed text in each section describes the types of fields that should be dragged and dropped. Figure 6.17 displays the PivotChart layout you will be using in Exercise 9.

Display PivotChart View
1. Open table or query.
2. Click View, PivotChart View.

A PivotTable is dynamically linked to a PivotChart. Changes made to the filter settings in PivotChart view are also updated in PivotTable view.

PivotChart Layout

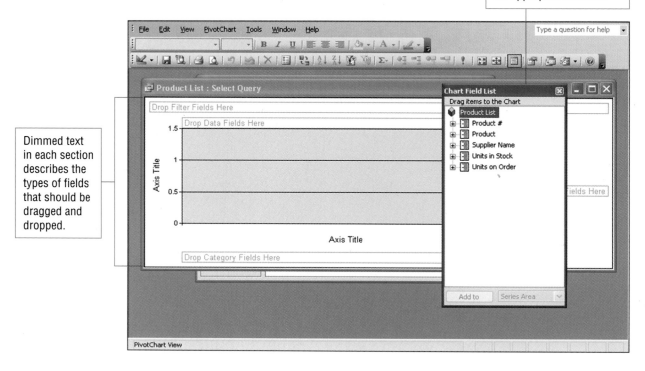

Drag the desired item from this list box and drop it in the appropriate location.

Dimmed text in each section describes the types of fields that should be dragged and dropped.

Drag the fields from the Chart Field List box to the desired locations in the PivotChart layout. The dimmed text in the PivotChart layout identifies the field that should be dropped in the location. In Exercise 9, you will drag the *Supplier Name* field to the Row field section, the *Product* field to the Column field section, the *Amount* field to the Totals or Details field section, and the *Order Date* to the Filter section. The PivotTable will then display as shown in Figure 6.18.

When you create a PivotChart, Access automatically creates a PivotTable. View a PivotTable based on a PivotChart by clicking View and then PivotTable.

FIGURE

6.18 **PivotChart for Exercise 9**

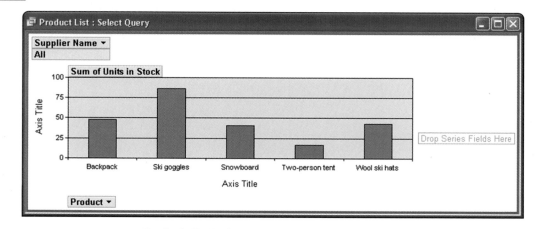

ACCESS

 exercise 9

1. Open the **OutdoorOptions** database table.
2. Click the Queries button on the Objects bar and then create a new query in Design view with the following specifications:
   a. Add the Products and Suppliers tables to the design grid.
   b. Add the following fields from the specified tables:

Product #	=	Products table
Product	=	Products table
Supplier Name	=	Suppliers table
Units in Stock	=	Products table
Units on Order	=	Products table

   c. Save the query and name it Product List.
   d. Run the query.
3. Click View and then PivotChart view.
4. At the PivotChart layout, drag and drop the following fields:
   a. Drag the *Supplier Name* field from the Chart Field List box and drop it on the dimmed text *Drop Filter Fields Here*.

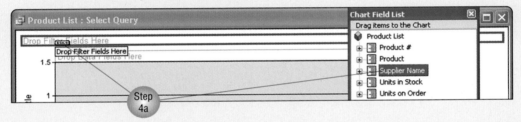

   b. Drag the *Product* field from the Chart Field List box and drop it on the dimmed text *Drop Category Fields Here*.
   c. Drag the *Units in Stock* field from the Chart Field List box and drop it on the dimmed text *Drop Data Fields Here*.
5. Remove the Chart Field List box from the screen by clicking the Field List button on the PivotTable toolbar. (Your PivotChart should look like the PivotChart shown in Figure 6.18.)
6. Click the Print button to print the query in PivotChart view.
7. Display specific items on order by completing the following steps:
   a. Click the filter arrow at the right of the *Product* field (located in the lower left corner of the query window).
   b. At the drop-down list that displays, click the *(All)* check box to remove the check mark before each date.
   c. Click the check box to the left of *Ski goggles*.
   d. Click the check box to the left of *Snowboard*.
   e. Click the check box to the left of *Wool ski hats*.
   f. Click the OK button.

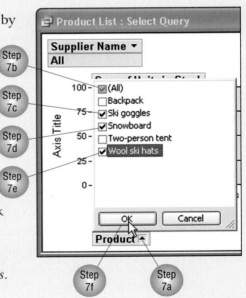

g. Click the Print button on the PivotChart toolbar.
h. Redisplay all items by clicking the filter arrow at the right of the *Product* field, clicking the check box to the left of *(All)*, and then clicking OK.

8. Display only those products ordered from KL Distributions by completing the following steps:
   a. Click the filter arrow at the right of the *Supplier Name* field.
   b. At the drop-down list, click the *(All)* check box to remove the check mark before each supplier name.
   c. Click the check box to the left of *KL Distributions*.
   d. Click the OK button.
   e. Click the Print button on the PivotChart toolbar.
   f. Redisplay all supplier names by clicking the filter arrow at the right of the *Supplier Name* field, clicking the check box to the left of *(All)*, and then clicking OK.

9. Click View and then PivotTable View to display the chart as a PivotTable.
10. Click the Print button on the PivotTable toolbar.
11. Click View and then Datasheet View to return the query to the Datasheet view.
12. Save and then close the query.
13. Close the **OutdoorOptions** database file.

Step 8a

Product List : Select Query

Step 8b

Supplier Name ▲

☑ (All)
☐ Freedom Corporation
☑ KL Distributions
☐ Rosewood, Inc.

ck

Step 8c

OK   Cancel   Ski goggles

Step 8d

CHAPTER summary

➤ Data in a database table can be inserted in a report, which lets you control how the data appears on the page when printed.

➤ Use the AutoReport feature automatically to create a plainly formatted report in a columnar arrangement.

➤ The Report Wizard walks you through the steps for creating a report and lets you specify the fields you want included in the report, the level of fields in the report, the order in which records display in the report, the layout of the report, the report style, and a name for the report.

➤ Like a form, a report can be created with fields from related database tables.

➤ A report, like a form, can be created in Design view. A report includes up to five sections including Report Header, Page Header, Detail, Page Footer, and Report Footer.

➤ To add fields to a report in Design view, associate the report with the desired table.

➤ Move, resize, and customize control objects in the report Design view in the same manner as control objects in the form Design view.

➤ Use buttons on the Toolbox to add controls to a report in Design view.

➤ Mailing labels can be created with data in a database table using the Label Wizard. The Label Wizard lets you specify the label type; the fields you want included in the labels; the font name, size, weight, and color; a sorting order; and a name for the mailing label file.

➤ A chart can be created with specific fields in a database table using the Chart Wizard. The Chart Wizard lets you specify the fields you want included in the chart, the chart type, how labels will appear in the chart, and the name for the chart file.

➤ Change to the PivotTable view to create a PivotTable that is an interactive table that organizes and summarizes data. Change to the PivotChart view to create a PivotChart that summarizes data in a graph.

➤ To create a PivotTable, open a table or query, click View, and then click PivotTable View. At the PivotTable layout, drag the fields to the desired locations.

➤ To create a PivotChart, open a table or query, click View, and then click PivotChart View. At the PivotChart layout, drag the fields to the desired locations.

FEATURES summary

FEATURE	BUTTON	MENU
Display New Report dialog box	New	
Begin Report Wizard		Insert, Report, Report Wizard
Begin Label Wizard		Insert, Report, specify table, double-click *Label Wizard*
Begin Chart Wizard		Insert, Report, specify table, double-click *Chart Wizard*
Display table or query in PivotTable view		View, PivotTable View
Display table or query in PivotChart view		View, PivotChart View

CONCEPTS check

Completion: On a blank sheet of paper, indicate the correct term, symbol, or command for each description.

1. Click the down-pointing arrow at the right side of this button to display the AutoReport option.
2. Use this to guide you through the steps for creating a report.
3. When all of the steps in the Report Wizard are completed, the report displays in this view.

4. This appears at the top of each page of a report and generally includes information such as column headings identifying the data in the report.
5. Use these to increase or decrease the size of a selected control object.
6. To create a chart with the Chart Wizard, open the database file, and then click either the Forms button or this button on the Objects bar.
7. When creating a chart with the Chart Wizard, the first field inserted in the *Fields for Chart* list box will be used as this axis in the chart.
8. Display a table or query in this view to summarize data based on the fields you designate for row headings, column headings, and source record filtering.
9. Suppose you are using the Report Wizard with the OutdoorOptions database file to show information on what products are currently on order, from what company, and the e-mail address of the companies. At the first Report Wizard step, what fields would you insert from the Products database table and what fields would you insert from the Suppliers database table?
10. When using the Chart Wizard, write the fields in the Products database table (in the OutdoorOptions database file) you would use to create a chart that shows the reorder level for products.

SKILLS check

(Note: Copy the Hilltop database file from the CD that accompanies this textbook to your disk and then remove the read-only attribute from the database file. Before completing the following assessments, consider deleting the OutdoorOptions database file from your disk.)

Assessment 1

1. Open the **Hilltop** database file.
2. Click the Tables button on the Objects bar.
3. Use AutoReport to create a report with the Inventory table.
4. When the report displays in Print Preview, print the report.
5. Close the report without saving it.

Assessment 2

1. With the **Hilltop** database file open, create a report using the Report Wizard with the following specifications:
   a. At the first Report Wizard dialog box, insert the following fields in the *Selected Fields* list box:

   From the Equipment database table:

   Equipment

   From the Inventory database table:

   Purchase Date
   Purchase Price
   Available Hours

   b. At the second Report Wizard dialog box, make sure *Equipment* is selected, and then click the button containing the greater than symbol (>).
   c. Do not make any changes at the third Report Wizard dialog box.

d. At the fourth Report Wizard dialog box, choose the *Align Left 1* option.
e. At the fifth Report Wizard dialog box, choose the *Soft Gray* option.
f. At the last Report Wizard dialog box, click the Finish button. (This accepts the default report name of Equipment.)
g. When the report displays in Print Preview, print the report.
2. Close the report.

Assessment 3

1. With the **Hilltop** database file open, create a report using the Report Wizard with the following specifications:
   a. At the first Report Wizard dialog box, insert the following fields in the *Selected Fields* list box:

   From the Customers database table:

   > *Customer*

   From the Invoices database table:

   > *Date*
   > *Hours*

   From the Equipment database table:

   > *Equipment*

   From the Rates database table:

   > *Rate*

   b. At the second Report Wizard dialog box, make sure *by Customers* is selected.
   c. Do not make any changes at the third Report Wizard dialog box.
   d. Do not make any changes at the fourth Report Wizard dialog box.
   e. At the fifth Report Wizard dialog box, choose the *Block* option.
   f. At the sixth Report Wizard dialog box, choose the *Casual* option.
   g. At the last Report Wizard dialog box, name the report Rentals.
   h. When the report displays in Print Preview, print the report.
2. Close the report.

Assessment 4

1. With the **Hilltop** database file open, use the Label Wizard to create mailing labels (you determine the label type) with the customer names and addresses and sorted by customer names. Name the mailing label report Customer Mailing Labels.
2. Print the mailing labels.
3. Close the mailing labels report.

Assessment 5

1. With the **Hilltop** database file open, create a query in Design view with the following specifications:
   a. Add the Invoices, Customers, Equipment, and Rates tables to the design grid.
   b. Add the following fields from the specified tables:

Date	=	Invoices table
Customer	=	Customers table
Equipment	=	Equipment table

Hours	=	Invoices table
Rate	=	Rates table

    c. Click in the sixth *Field* text and then insert a calculation to total the rental hour amounts by typing Total: [Hours]*[Rate]. (Press the Tab key to move to the next field.)

    d. Run the query.

    e. Save the query and name it RentalTotals.

2. Display the query in PivotTable view.

3. At the PivotTable layout, drag and drop the fields as follows:

    a. Drag the *Equipment* field to the *Drop Row Fields Here* section.

    b. Drag the *Customer* field to the *Drop Column Fields Here* section.

    c. Drag the *Total* field to the *Drop Totals or Detail Fields Here* section.

    d. Drag the *Date* field to the *Drop Filter Fields Here* section.

4. Remove the PivotTable Field List box from the screen.

5. Click the Print button to print the query in PivotTable view. (Numbers in the thousands will print as number symbols.)

6. In the *Date* field, display only equipment rentals for May 1, 2005.

7. Print the PivotTable and then redisplay all rental dates.

8. In the *Equipment* field, display records only for the Hydraulic Pump and Pressure Sprayer.

9. Print the PivotTable and then redisplay all equipment.

10. Switch to Datasheet view, save the query, and then close the query.

Assessment 6

1. With the **Hilltop** database file open, click the Queries button on the Objects bar and then create a query in Design view with the following specifications:

    a. Add the Equipment, Customers, and Invoices tables to the design grid.

    b. Add the following fields from the specified tables:

Equipment	=	Equipment table
Customer	=	Customers table
Hours	=	Invoices table

    c. Run the query.

    d. Save the query and name it CustomerHours.

2. Click View and then PivotChart View.

3. At the PivotChart layout, drag and drop the following fields:

    a. Drag the *Equipment* field to the *Drop Filter Fields Here* section.

    b. Drag the *Customer* field to the *Drop Category Fields Here* section.

    c. Drag the *Hours* field to the *Drop Data Fields Here* section.

4. Remove the Chart Field List box from the screen.

5. Click the Print button to print the query in PivotChart view.

6. In the *Equipment* field, display only *Backhoe*, print the PivotChart, and then redisplay all equipment.

7. In the *Customer* field, display only *Allied Builders* and *Cascade Enterprises*, print the PivotChart, and then redisplay all customers.

8. Click the Save button to save the PivotChart.

9. Switch to Datasheet view and then close the query.

10. Close the **Hilltop** database file.

Assessment 7

1. The New Report dialog box contains options for creating a form. In this chapter, you have used the Report Wizard to prepare forms. Experiment with two other options available at the New Report dialog box—AutoReport: Columnar and AutoReport: Tabular.
2. After experimenting with these two wizards, open the **Hilltop** database file and then complete the following:
   a. Use the AutoReport: Columnar option to create a report with all of the fields in the Inventory database table. Print the report that displays and then close the report.
   b. Use the AutoReport: Tabular option to create a report with all of the fields in the Customers database table. Print the report that displays and then close the report.
3. Close the **Hilltop** database file.

CHAPTER challenge

You are the office manager at Tri-State Vision Care Center. The Center houses several optometrists and ophthalmologists. Use the **Tri-StateVisionCare** database created in the Chapter 5 Chapter Challenge. (If you have not already created it, create the two tables described in the first part of the Chapter Challenge in Chapter 5 and add at least three records to each table. Creating the form at this time will not be necessary. Patients are contacted by phone two to three days prior to the appointment to remind them of the upcoming appointment. You believe that having a patient phone list for this process would be helpful. One way to prepare a phone list is through the creation of a report. You will create a report based on the Patients table that includes the patient's first and last name and the telephone number. Sort the list by last name in ascending order. Save the report as Phone List. Also, prepare mailing labels for each of the patients for use when sending out letters. Save and print the labels.

To visually enhance the report, you decide to add a graphic. Use the Help feature to learn more about adding a picture or graphic to a report. Then add an appropriate picture or graphic to the phone list created in the first part of the Chapter Challenge. Save the report again and print it.

Create a business letter in Word that will be sent to patients thanking them for choosing Tri-State Vision Care Center for their eye care. Include any other information in the body of the letter that you feel appropriate. Save the main document of the letter as **ThankYou**. Merge this letter with the Patients table used in the first part of the Chapter Challenge. After merging, print one copy of the letter.

IMPORTING AND EXPORTING DATA

PERFORMANCE OBJECTIVES

Upon successful completion of Chapter 7, you will be able to:
- ➤ Export Access data to Excel
- ➤ Export Access data to Word
- ➤ Merge Access data with a Word document
- ➤ Import data to a new table
- ➤ Link data to a new table
- ➤ Use the Office Clipboard
- ➤ Display database contents
- ➤ View object dependencies

ACCESS

Microsoft Office 2003 is a suite of programs that allows easy data exchange between programs. In this chapter you will learn how to export data from Access to Excel and Word, merge Access data with a Word document, import and link data to a new table, and copy and paste data between programs. You will also learn how to display database contents and view database object dependencies.

Using OfficeLinks

One of the advantages of a suite of programs like Microsoft Office is the ability to exchange data from one program to another. Access, like the other programs in the suite, offers a feature to export data from Access into Word and/or Excel. Exporting data can be easily accomplished with the OfficeLinks button on the Database toolbar.

Exporting Data to Excel

Access data saved in a table, form, or report can be exported to Excel. Use an option from the OfficeLinks drop-down list to export data from Access to Excel. The data is saved as an Excel file in the folder where Access is installed. Excel is automatically started when the file is opened.

OfficeLinks

QUICK STEPS

Export Data to Excel
1. Click the desired table, query, form, or report.
2. Click down-pointing arrow on OfficeLinks button.
3. Click Analyze It with Microsoft Office Excel.

To export data to Excel, open the database file, and then click the name of the database table, query, form, or report you want saved in Excel. With the file selected, click the down-pointing arrow at the right side of the OfficeLinks button on the Database toolbar, and then click Analyze It with Microsoft Office Excel at the drop-down list. The data is converted to an Excel worksheet, Excel is opened, and the data is displayed in a worksheet. The worksheet is automatically saved with the same name as the name in the database file, except the Excel extension of *.xls* is added to the name.

exercise 1

SAVING A DATABASE TABLE AS AN EXCEL WORKSHEET

(Note: Delete any database files from your disk.)

1. Copy the **Hilltop** database file from the CD that accompanies this textbook to your disk and then remove the read-only attribute.
2. Open the **Hilltop** database file and then click the Tables button on the Objects bar.
3. Save the Invoices database table as an Excel worksheet and format the worksheet by completing the following steps:
   a. Click once on *Invoices* in the list box. (This selects the database table.)
   b. Click the down-pointing arrow at the right side of the OfficeLinks button on the Database toolbar.
   c. At the drop-down list that displays, click Analyze It with Microsoft Office Excel.

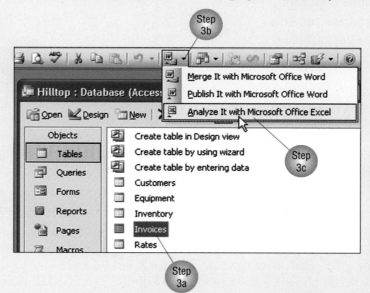

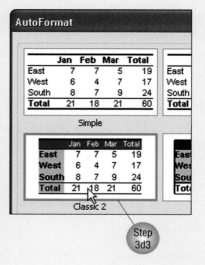

   d. When the data displays on the screen in Excel as a worksheet, make the following changes:
      1) Select cells A1 through F15.
      2) Click Format on the Menu bar and then click AutoFormat.
      3) At the AutoFormat dialog box, double-click the *Classic 2* autoformat.

4) With cells A1 through F15 still selected, click the Center button on the Formatting toolbar.
5) Deselect the cells.
e. Click the Save button on the Standard toolbar.
f. Click the Print button on the Standard toolbar.
g. Close the worksheet and then exit Excel.
4. Close the **Hilltop** database file.

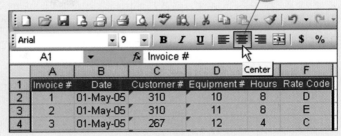

When you use the Analyze It with Microsoft Office Excel option from the OfficeLinks drop-down list, the table becomes an Excel worksheet. All Excel editing capabilities are available for changing or modifying the worksheet. A form can also be converted to a worksheet with the Analyze It with Microsoft Office Excel option.

exercise 2

SAVING A FORM AS AN EXCEL WORKSHEET

1. Open the **Hilltop** database file.
2. Create a form with fields in the Inventory table by completing the following steps:
   a. At the Hilltop : Database window, click the Forms button on the Objects bar.
   b. Double-click *Create form by using wizard*.
   c. At the first Form Wizard dialog box, click the down-pointing arrow at the right of the *Tables/Queries* option box, and then click *Table: Inventory* at the drop-down list. Click the button containing the two greater than symbols (>>) to insert all of the *Available Fields* in the *Selected Fields* list box.
   d. After entering the fields, click the Next button.
   e. At the second Form Wizard dialog box, click the Next button.
   f. At the third Form Wizard dialog box, click *Blueprint* in the format style list box, and then click the Next button.

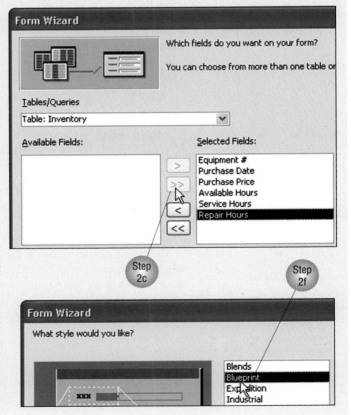

g. At the fourth Form Wizard dialog box, type **Equipment Inventory**, and then click the Finish button.

h. When the first record displays, click the Close button.

3. Save the Equipment Inventory form as an Excel worksheet and format the worksheet by completing the following steps:

a. Click once on *Equipment Inventory* in the list box. (This selects the form.)

b. Click the down-pointing arrow at the right side of the OfficeLinks button on the Database toolbar.

c. At the drop-down list that displays, click Analyze It with Microsoft Office Excel.

d. When the data displays on the screen in Excel as a worksheet, make the following changes:

1) Select cells A1 through F11.

2) Click Format on the Menu bar, and then click AutoFormat.

3) At the AutoFormat dialog box, double-click the *Colorful 1* autoformat.

4) Select cells A2 through B11 and then click the Center button on the Formatting toolbar.

5) Select cells D2 through F11 and then click the Center button on the Formatting toolbar.

6) Deselect the cells.

e. Click the Save button on the Standard toolbar.

f. Print and then close the worksheet.

g. Exit Excel.

4. Close the **Hilltop** database file.

Exporting Data to Word

Export data from Access to Word in the same manner as exporting to Excel. To export data to Word, open the database file, select the table, query, form, or report you want to export to Word, and then click the down-pointing arrow on the OfficeLinks button on the Database toolbar. At the drop-down list that displays, click Publish It with Microsoft Office Word. Word is automatically opened and the data is inserted in a Word document. The Word document is automatically saved with the same name as the database table, form, or report you selected, except the file extension *.rtf* is added to the name. An *rtf* file is saved in "rich-text format," which preserves formatting such as fonts and styles. A document saved with the *.rtf* extension can be opened with Microsoft Word and other Windows word processing or desktop publishing programs.

exercise 3

1. Open the **Hilltop** database file.
2. At the Hilltop : Database window, click the Tables button on the Objects bar.
3. Save the Invoices database table as a Word table and then add additional text to the Word document by completing the following steps:
   a. Click once on *Invoices* in the list box.
   b. Click the down-pointing arrow at the right side of the OfficeLinks button on the Database toolbar.
   c. At the drop-down list that displays, click Publish It with Microsoft Office Word.
   d. When the data displays on the screen in Word as a table, add text to the document (not the table) by completing the following steps:

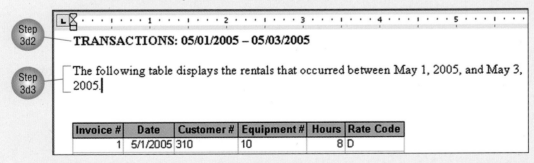

   1) Press the Enter key three times. (This inserts blank lines above the table.)
   2) Move the insertion point to the beginning of the document, turn on bold, type TRANSACTIONS: 05/01/2005 - 05/03/2005, and then turn off bold.
   3) Press the Enter key twice, and then type the following text:

      The following table displays the rentals that occurred between May 1, 2005, and May 3, 2005.

TRANSACTIONS: 05/01/2005 – 05/03/2005

The following table displays the rentals that occurred between May 1, 2005, and May 3, 2005.

Invoice #	Date	Customer #	Equipment #	Hours	Rate Code
1	5/1/2005	310	10	8	D

   e. Click the Save button on the Standard toolbar.
   f. Print the document.
   g. Close the document and then exit Word.
4. Close the **Hilltop** database file.

exercise 4

1. Open the **Hilltop** database file.
2. At the Hilltop : Database window, click the Reports button on the Objects bar.
3. Create a report with the Report Wizard by completing the following steps:
   a. Click the New button on the window toolbar.
   b. At the New Report dialog box, double-click *Report Wizard* in the list box.
   c. At the first Report Wizard dialog box, insert the following fields in the *Selected Fields* list box:

       From the Customers table:

           Customer

       From the Equipment table:

           Equipment

       From the Invoices table:

           Date
           Hours

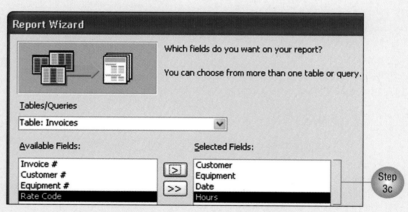

   d. After inserting the fields, click the Next button.
   e. At the second Report Wizard dialog box, make sure *by Customers* is selected in the list box in the upper left corner, and then click the Next button.
   f. At the third Report Wizard dialog box, click the Next button.
   g. At the fourth Report Wizard dialog box, click the Next button.
   h. At the fifth Report Wizard dialog box, click *Align Left 1*, and then click the Next button.
   i. At the sixth Report Wizard dialog box, click *Corporate* in the list box, and then click the Next button.
   j. At the seventh Report Wizard dialog box, type Customer Report, and then click the Finish button.
   k. When the report displays in Print Preview, view the report, and then click the Print button that displays on the Print Preview toolbar.
   l. Click the Close button that displays at the right side of the Customer Report title bar.

4. Save the Customer Report as a Word document by completing the following steps:
   a. Click once on *Customer Report* in the list box.
   b. Click the down-pointing arrow at the right side of the OfficeLinks button on the Database toolbar.
   c. At the drop-down list that displays, click Publish It with Microsoft Office Word.

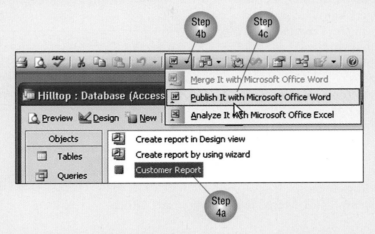

   d. When the data displays on the screen in Word, print the report by clicking the Print button on the Standard toolbar.
   e. Click the Save button (to save the document with the default name of Customer Report).
   f. Close the document and then exit Word.
5. Close the **Hilltop** database file.

Merging Access Data with a Word Document

Data from an Access database table can be merged with a Word document. When merging data in an Access table with a Word document, the data in the Access table is considered the data source and the Word document is considered the main document. When the merge is completed, the merged documents display in Word.

When merging Access data, you can either type the text in the main document or merge Access data with an existing Word document. In Exercise 5, you will merge Access data with an existing Word document and in Exercise 6, you will type the main document.

Merge Data with Word
1. Click the desired table or query.
2. Click down-pointing arrow on OfficeLinks button.
3. Click Merge It with Microsoft Office Word.
4. Make desired choices at each of the wizard dialog boxes.

exercise 5

1. Open the **Hilltop** database file.
2. At the Hilltop : Database window, click the Tables button on the Objects bar.
3. Merge data in the Customers database table with a Word document by completing the following steps:

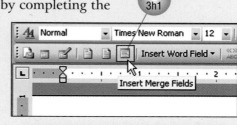

   a. Click once on *Customers* in the list box.
   b. Click the down-pointing arrow at the right side of the OfficeLinks button on the Database toolbar.
   c. At the drop-down list that displays, click Merge It with Microsoft Office Word.
   d. At the Microsoft Word Mail Merge Wizard dialog box, make sure *Link your data to an existing Microsoft Word document* is selected, and then click OK.
   e. At the Select Microsoft Word Document dialog box, make the AccessChapter07S folder on your disk the active folder, and then double-click the document named *HilltopLetter*.
   f. Click the Maximize button located at the right side of the HilltopLetter title bar.
   g. Press the Down Arrow key six times (not the Enter key), and then type the current date.
   h. Press the Down Arrow key five times, and then insert fields for merging from the Customers database table by completing the following steps:

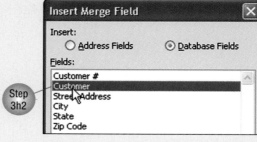

      1) Click the Insert Merge Fields button located toward the left side of the Merge toolbar.
      2) At the Insert Merge Field dialog box, double-click *Customer* in the *Fields* list box. (This inserts the *«Customer»* field in the document.)
      3) Click the Close button to close the Insert Merge Field dialog box.
      4) Press Enter, click the Insert Merge Fields button, and then double-click *Street Address* in the *Fields* list box of the Insert Merge Field dialog box.
      5) Click the Close button to close the dialog box.
      6) Press Enter, click the Insert Merge Fields button, and then double-click *City* in the *Fields* list box.

7) Click the Close button to close the dialog box.
8) Type a comma (,) and then press the spacebar.
9) Click the Insert Merge Fields button and then double-click *State* in the *Fields* list box.
10) Click the Close button to close the dialog box.
11) Press the spacebar, click the Insert Merge Fields button, and then double-click *Zip Code* in the *Fields* list box.
12) Click the Close button to close the dialog box.
13) Replace the letters *XX* that display toward the bottom of the letter with your initials.

i. Click the Merge to New Document button located toward the right side of the Merge toolbar.

j. At the Merge to New Document dialog box, make sure *All* is selected, and then click OK.

k. When the merge is completed, save the new document as **Wordsac7x05** in the AccessChapter07S folder on your disk.

l. Print just the first two pages (two letters) of **Wordsac7x05**.

m. Close **Wordsac7x05** and then close HilltopLetter, without saving the changes.

n. Exit Word.

4. Close the **Hilltop** database file.

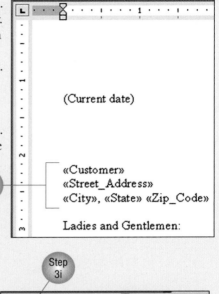

Step 3h

(Current date)

«Customer»
«Street_Address»
«City», «State» «Zip_Code»

Ladies and Gentlemen:

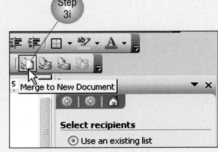

Step 3i

exercise 6

MERGING ACCESS DATA WITH A NEW WORD DOCUMENT

1. Open the **Hilltop** database file.
2. At the Hilltop : Database window, click the Tables button on the Objects bar.
3. Merge data in the Customers database table to a new Word document by completing the following steps:

   a. Click once on *Customers* in the list box.

   b. Click the down-pointing arrow at the right side of the OfficeLinks button on the Database toolbar.

   c. At the drop-down list that displays, click Merge It with Microsoft Office Word.

   d. At the Microsoft Word Mail Merge Wizard dialog box, click the *Create a new document and then link the data to it* option, and then click OK.

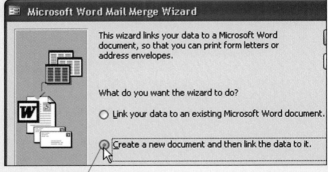

Step 3d

e. Click the Maximize button located at the right side of the Document1 title bar.
f. Complete the following steps to type text and insert fields in the blank Word document:
   1) Press Enter six times.
   2) Type the current date.
   3) Press Enter five times.
   4) Insert the following fields at the left margin in the order shown below (start by clicking the Insert Merge Fields button located toward the left side of the Mail Merge toolbar).

   «Customer»
   «Street_Address»
   «City», «State» «Zip_Code»

   5) Press Enter twice, and then type the salutation Ladies and Gentlemen:.
   6) Press Enter twice, and then type the following paragraph of text. (After typing the Hilltop e-mail address, Word will convert it to a hyperlink. Immediately click the Undo button to remove the hyperlink and then continue typing the remainder of the paragraph.)

   We have installed a new computer system for receiving rental equipment requests electronically. If you are interested in requesting equipment online, you may contact us at hilltop@emcp.com or visit our Web site at www.hilltop.emcp.com. If you need assistance with an online request, please contact us at (303) 555-9066.

   7) Press Enter twice, and then type the following complimentary close (at the left margin):

   Sincerely,

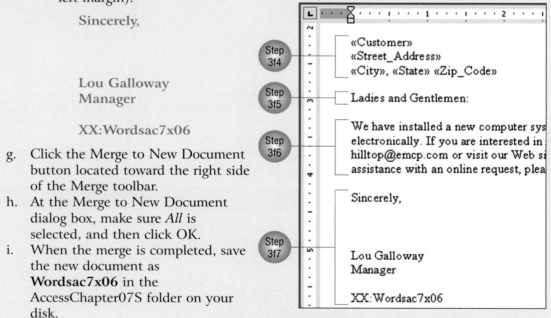

   Lou Galloway
   Manager

   XX:Wordsac7x06

g. Click the Merge to New Document button located toward the right side of the Merge toolbar.
h. At the Merge to New Document dialog box, make sure *All* is selected, and then click OK.
i. When the merge is completed, save the new document as **Wordsac7x06** in the AccessChapter07S folder on your disk.
j. Print the first two pages (two letters) of **Wordsac7x06**.
k. Close **Wordsac7x06**.
l. Save the main document as **WordHilltopLetter** in the AccessChapter07S folder on your disk and then close **WordHilltopLetter**.
m. Exit Word.
4. Close the **Hilltop** database file.

Merging Query Data with a Word Document

A query performed in Access can be saved, and then data from that query can be merged with a Word document. To do this, you would open the database file, complete the query, and then save the query. With the query name selected in the database file, you would click the OfficeLinks button on the Database toolbar and then click the Merge It with Microsoft Office Word option. You would specify whether you want to merge with an existing Word document or create a new document and then insert the appropriate fields.

exercise 7

PERFORMING A QUERY AND THEN MERGING WITH A WORD DOCUMENT

1. Open the **Hilltop** database file.
2. Perform a query with the Simple Query Wizard and modify the query by completing the following steps:
   a. Click the Queries button on the Objects bar.
   b. Double-click *Create query by using wizard* in the list box.
   c. At the first Simple Query Wizard dialog box, click the down-pointing arrow at the right of the *Tables/Queries* text box, and then click *Table: Customers*.
   d. Click the button containing the two greater than symbols (>>) to insert all of the fields in the *Selected Fields* list box.

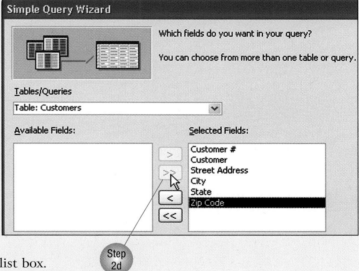

   e. Click the Next button.
   f. At the second Simple Query Wizard dialog box, click the *Modify the query design* option, and then click the Finish button.
   g. At the Customers Query : Select Query window, insert the query criterion by completing the following steps:
      1) Click in the *Criteria* text box in the *City* column.
      2) Type **Denver** and then press Enter.

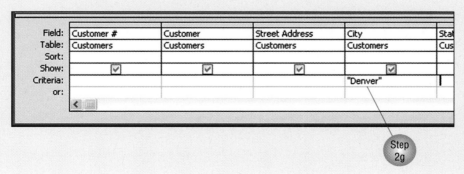

h. Click the Run button on the Query Design toolbar. (Those customers located in Denver will display.)

i. Save the query as Denver Query by completing the following steps:
   1) Click File and then Save As.
   2) At the Save As dialog box, type **Denver Query**, and then press Enter or click OK.

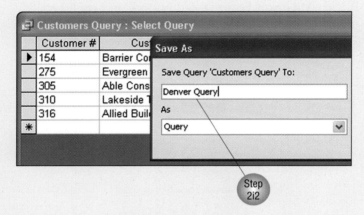

Step 2i2

j. Close the Denver Query by clicking the Close button at the right side of the Query title bar.

3. Merge the Denver Query to a new Word document by completing the following steps:
   a. Click *Denver Query* in the Hilltop : Database window list box.
   b. Click the down-pointing arrow at the right side of the OfficeLinks button on the Database toolbar.
   c. At the drop-down list that displays, click Merge It with Microsoft Office Word.
   d. At the Microsoft Word Mail Merge Wizard dialog box, click the *Create a new document and then link the data to it* option, and then click OK.
   e. Click the Maximize button located at the right side of the Document1 title bar.
   f. Complete the following steps to type text and insert fields in the blank Word document:
      1) Press Enter six times.
      2) Type the current date.
      3) Press Enter five times.
      4) Insert the following fields at the left margin in the order shown below (start by clicking the Insert Merge Fields button at the left side of the Mail Merge toolbar).

         «Customer»
         «Street_Address»
         «City», «State» «Zip_Code»

      5) Press Enter twice, and then type the salutation Ladies and Gentlemen:.
      6) Press Enter twice, and then type the following paragraphs of text.

         We have just opened a new branch office in downtown Denver to better serve our Denver customers. The branch office hours are 7:30 a.m. to 7:00 p.m. Monday through Friday, 8:00 a.m. to 5:00 p.m. Saturday, and 9:00 a.m. to 3:30 p.m. Sunday.

         Our new branch is located at 7500 Alameda Avenue. Stop by during the next two weeks and receive a 10% discount on your next equipment rental.

7) Press Enter twice, and then type the following complimentary close (at the left margin):

Sincerely,

Lou Galloway
Manager

XX:Wordsac7x07

   g. Click the Merge to New Document button located toward the right side of the Mail Merge toolbar.

   h. At the Merge to New Document dialog box, make sure *All* is selected, and then click OK.

   i. When the merge is completed, save the new document as **Wordsac7x07** in the AccessChapter07S folder on your disk.

   j. Print and then close **Wordsac7x07**.

   k. Save the main document and name it **WordBranchLetter**.

   l. Close **WordBranchLetter** and then exit Word.

4. Close the **Hilltop** database file.

Importing and Linking Data to a New Table

In this chapter, you learned how to export Access data to Excel and Word. Data from other programs, such as Excel and Word, can also be imported into an Access table. For example, you can import data from an Excel worksheet and create a new table in a database file. Data in the original program is not connected to the data imported into an Access table. If you make changes to the data in the original program, those changes are not reflected in the Access table. If you want the imported data connected to the original program, link the data.

Importing Data to a New Table

To import data, open the database file, click File, point to Get External Data, and then click Import. At the Import dialog box that displays, double-click the desired file name. This activates the Import Wizard and displays the first Wizard dialog box. The appearance of the dialog box varies depending on the file selected. Complete the steps of the Import Wizard specifying information such as the range of data, whether or not the first row contains column headings, whether you want to store the data in a new table or store it in an existing table, the primary key, and the name of the table.

QUICK STEPS

Import Data to a New Table
1. Open database file.
2. Click File, Get External Data, Import.
3. Double-click desired file name.
4. Make desired choices at each of the wizard dialog boxes.

exercise 8

(Note: Before completing this exercise, open Excel and then open ExcelWorksheet01 [located in your AccessChapter07S folder]. Save the worksheet with Save As and name it Excelsac7. Close Excelsac7 and then exit Excel.)

Step 3a

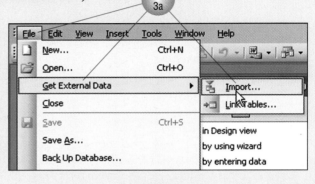

1. Copy the **SouthwestInsurance** database file from the CD that accompanies this textbook to your disk and then remove the read-only attribute.
2. Open the **SouthwestInsurance** database file and click the Tables button on the Objects bar.
3. Import an Excel worksheet into a new table in the **SouthwestInsurance** database file by completing the following steps:

   Step 3c

   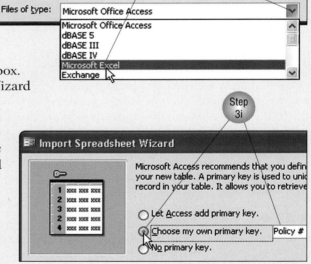

   a. Click File, point to Get External Data, and then click Import.
   b. At the Import dialog box, make the AccessChapter07S folder on your disk the active folder.
   c. Change the *Files of type* option to *Microsoft Excel*.
   d. Double-click *Excelsac7* in the list box.
   e. At the first Import Spreadsheet Wizard dialog box, click the Next button.
   f. At the second Import Spreadsheet Wizard dialog box, make sure the *First Row Contains Column Headings* option contains a check mark, and then click the Next button.
   g. At the third Import Spreadsheet Wizard dialog box, make sure the *In a New Table* option is selected, and then click the Next button.

   Step 3i

   h. At the fourth Import Spreadsheet Wizard dialog box, click the Next button.
   i. At the fifth Import Spreadsheet Wizard dialog box, click the *Choose my own primary key* option (this inserts *Policy #* in the text box located to the right of the option), and then click the Next button.
   j. At the sixth Import Spreadsheet Wizard dialog box, type Policies in the *Import to Table* text box, and then click the Finish button.
   k. At the message saying the data was imported, click OK.

4. Open the new Policies table in Datasheet view.
5. Print and then close the Policies table.
6. Close the **SouthwestInsurance** database file.

Step 3j

Linking Data to a New Table

Imported data is not connected to the source program. If you want the data to be connected, link the data. When the data is linked, changes made to the data in the source program are reflected in the data in the destination program and changes made in the destination program are reflected in the source program.

To link data to a new table, open the database file, click File, point to Get External Data, and then click Link Tables. At the Link dialog box, double-click the desired file name. This activates the Link Wizard and displays the first Wizard dialog box. Complete the steps of the Link Wizard specifying the same basic information as the Import Wizard.

QUICK STEPS

Link Data to a New Table
1. Open database file.
2. Click File, Get External Data, Link Tables.
3. Double-click desired file name.
4. Make desired choices at each of the wizard dialog boxes.

exercise 9

LINKING AN EXCEL WORKSHEET WITH AN ACCESS TABLE

1. Open the **SouthwestInsurance** database file and then click the Tables button on the Objects bar.
2. Link an Excel worksheet with a new table in the **SouthwestInsurance** database file by completing the following steps:
   a. Click File, point to Get External Data, and then click Link Tables.
   b. At the Link dialog box, make sure the AccessChapter07S folder on your disk is the active folder, and then change the *Files of type* option to *Microsoft Excel*.
   c. Double-click *Excelsac7*.
   d. At the first Link Spreadsheet Wizard dialog box, make sure *Show Worksheets* is selected, and that *Sheet1* is selected in the list box, and then click the Next button.
   e. At the second Link Spreadsheet Wizard dialog box, make sure the *First Row Contains Column Headings* option contains a check mark, and then click the Next button.
   f. At the third Link Spreadsheet Wizard dialog box, type Linked Policies (in the *Linked Table Name* text box), and then click the Finish button.
   g. At the message stating the linking is finished, click OK.
3. Open the new Linked Policies table in Datasheet view.

Step 2a

Step 2f

4. Change the number *745* in the *Premium* column to *850*.
5. Add the following new record in the specified fields:

Policy #	=	227-C-28
Client #	=	3120
Premium	=	685

6. Save, print, and then close the Linked Policies table.
7. Open Excel and then open **Excelsac7**. Notice that the information in this table contains the changes made to the Linked Policies table in Access.
8. Close **Excelsac7** and then exit Excel.
9. In Access, close the **SouthwestInsurance** database file.

Linked Policies : Table

Policy #	Client #	Premium
110-C-39	9383	$ 1,450
122-E-30	7335	$ 850
143-D-29	3120	$ 920
192-C-29	7335	$ 1,390
201-E-91	4300	$ 1,525
215-W-32	4300	$ 734
227-C-28	3120	$ 685

Step 4

Step 5

QUICK STEPS

Using the Office Clipboard

Display Clipboard Task Pane
1. Open database file.
2. Click Edit, Office Clipboard.

Use the Office Clipboard to collect and paste multiple items. You can collect up to 24 different items in Access or other programs in the Office suite and then paste the items in various locations. To copy and paste multiple items, display the Clipboard task pane shown in Figure 7.1 by clicking Edit and then Office Clipboard.

FIGURE 7.1 *Clipboard Task Pane*

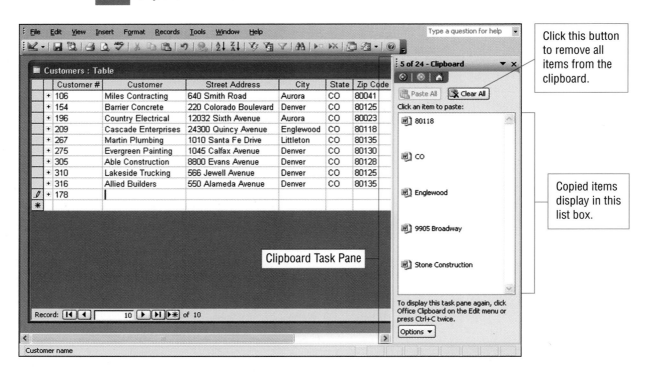

Click this button to remove all items from the clipboard.

Copied items display in this list box.

Select data or an object you want to copy and then click the Copy button on the toolbar. Continue selecting text or items and clicking the Copy button. To insert an item from the Clipboard task pane into a field in an Access table, make the desired field active, and then click the button in the Clipboard task pane representing the item. If the copied item is text, the first 50 characters display. When all desired items are inserted, click the Clear All button to remove any remaining items from the Clipboard task pane.

You can copy data from one table to another in an Access database file or from a file in another program to an Access database file. In Exercise 10, you will copy data from a Word document and paste it into a database table. Data can also be collected from documents in other programs such as PowerPoint and Excel.

exercise 10

| COLLECTING DATA IN WORD AND PASTING IT IN AN ACCESS DATABASE TABLE |

1. In Access, open the **Hilltop** database file.
2. Open the Customers table in Datasheet view.
3. Copy data from Word and paste it into the Customers table by completing the following steps:
    a. Open Word, make the AccessChapter07S folder on your disk the active folder, and then open **HilltopCustomers**.
    b. Display the Clipboard task pane by clicking Edit and then Office Clipboard.
    c. Select the first company name, *Stone Construction*, and then click the Copy button on the Standard toolbar.

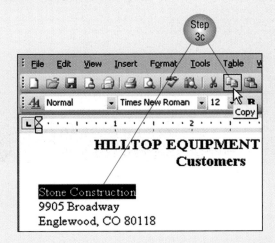

Step 3c

    d. Select the street address, *9905 Broadway*, and then click the Copy button.
    e. Select the city, *Englewood*, and then click the Copy button.
    f. Select the state, *CO*, and then click the Copy button.
    g. Select the Zip Code, *80118*, and then click the Copy button.
    h. Click the button on the Taskbar representing the Access Customers table. (Make sure you are in Datasheet view.)

i. Click in the first empty cell in the *Customer #* field, and then type 178.
j. Display the Clipboard task pane by clicking Edit, and then Office Clipboard.
k. Click in the first empty cell in the *Customer* field, and then click *Stone Construction* in the Clipboard task pane.

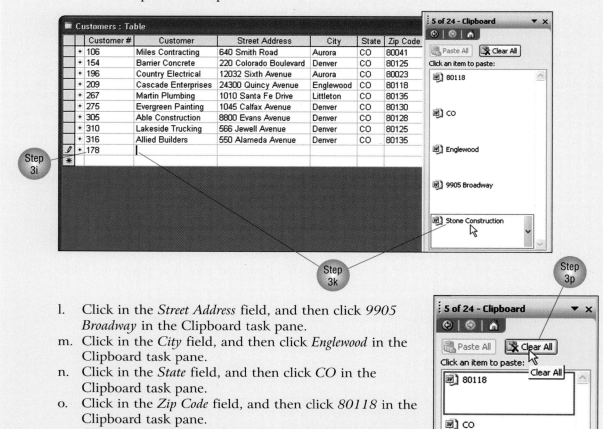

l. Click in the *Street Address* field, and then click *9905 Broadway* in the Clipboard task pane.
m. Click in the *City* field, and then click *Englewood* in the Clipboard task pane.
n. Click in the *State* field, and then click *CO* in the Clipboard task pane.
o. Click in the *Zip Code* field, and then click *80118* in the Clipboard task pane.
p. Click the Clear All button on the Clipboard task pane.

4. Complete steps similar to those in Steps 3c through 3p to copy the information for Laughlin Products and paste it into the Customers table. (The Customer # is 225.)
5. Close the Clipboard task pane by clicking the Close button (contains an *X*) located in the upper right corner of the task pane.
6. Save and then print the Customers table.
7. Close the Customers table and then close the **Hilltop** database file.
8. Make Word the active program, close **HilltopCustomers**, and then exit Word.

Viewing Objects and Object Dependencies

As you have learned throughout this book, the structure of a database is comprised of table, query, form, and report objects. Tables are related to other table(s) by creating relationships. Queries, forms, and reports draw the source data from records in the tables to which they have been associated and forms and reports can include subforms and subreports which further expand the associations between objects. A database with a large number of interdependent objects is more complex to work with. Viewing a list of the objects within a database and viewing the

ACCESS

dependencies between objects can be beneficial to ensure an object is not deleted or otherwise modified causing an unforeseen effect on another object. Access provides two features that provide information on objects—database properties and the Object Dependencies task pane.

Displaying Database Contents

The database Properties dialog box contains information about the database file. Display the Properties dialog box by opening the database file, clicking File, and then clicking Database Properties. Click each tab at the dialog box to display different information about the database file. Click the Contents tab and information displays about the contents of the database file including all objects such as tables, queries, forms, and reports. Figure 7.2 displays the Properties dialog box for the Hilltop database file.

Display Properties Dialog Box
1. Open database file.
2. Click File, Database Properties.

FIGURE

7.2 *Hilltop Properties Dialog Box with Contents Tab Selected*

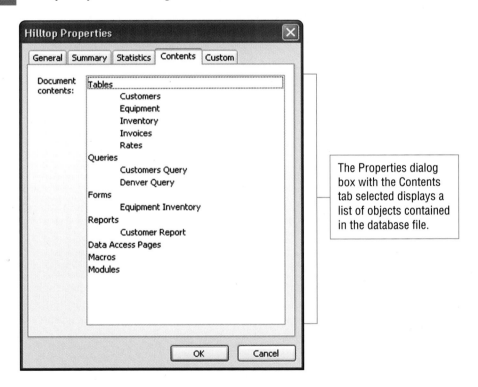

The Properties dialog box with the Contents tab selected displays a list of objects contained in the database file.

Viewing Object Dependencies

Display the structure of a database table, including tables, queries, forms, and reports objects as well as relationships at the Object Dependencies task pane. Display this task pane by opening the database file, clicking View, and then clicking Object Dependencies. The Object Dependencies task pane in Figure 7.3 displays the objects for the Hilltop database file.

7.3 Object Dependencies Task Pane

Display Object Dependencies Task Pane
1. Open database file.
2. Click desired table.
3. Click View, Object Dependencies.

HINT
Clicking an object name in the Object Dependencies task pane opens the object in Design view so that you can remove the dependency by deleting bound fields, controls, or otherwise changing the source from which the data is obtained.

By default, *Objects that depend on me* is selected in the Object Dependencies task pane and the list box displays the names of objects for which the Employee Dates and Salaries table is the source. Next to each object in the task pane list is an expand button (plus symbol). Clicking the expand button will show objects dependent at the next level. For example, if a query is based upon the Employee Dates and Salaries table and the query is used to generate a report, clicking the expand button next to the query name would show the report name.

Clicking an object name in the Object Dependencies task pane opens the object in Design view so that you can remove the dependency by deleting bound fields, controls, or otherwise changing the source from which the data is obtained. Relationships between tables are deleted by opening the Relationships window (as you learned in Chapter 2).

exercise 11

VIEWING DATABASE CONTENTS AND OBJECT DEPENDENCIES

1. Open the **Hilltop** database file.
2. Display file properties by completing the following steps:
   a. Click File and then Database Properties.
   b. At the Hilltop Properties dialog box, click the General tab.
   c. Read the information that displays in the dialog box, and then click the Summary tab.

d. Read the information that displays in the dialog box and then click the Statistics tab.

e. Read the information that displays in the dialog box and then click the Contents tab. Notice that the list box displays all objects in the database file.

f. Click the Cancel button to remove the Hilltop Properties dialog box.

3. Display the structure of the database file by completing the following steps:

a. At the Hilltop database file window, click the Tables button on the Objects bar.

b. Click once on the *Customers* table name.

c. Click View and then Object Dependencies. (If a message displays telling you that the dependency information needs to be updated, click OK. The Object Dependencies task pane displays. By default, *Objects that depend on me* is selected and the task pane lists the names of objects for which the Customers table is the source. Next to each object in the task pane list is an expand button (plus symbol). Clicking the expand button will show objects dependent at the next level.

d. Click the expand button (plus symbol) to the left of *Invoices* in the Tables section. (This displays the tables, queries, and reports that are dependent on the Invoices table. See figure at the far right.)

e. Click the *Objects that I depend on* option located toward the top of the Object Dependencies task pane.

f. Click the *Invoices* table in the Hilltop : Database window.

g. Click View and then Object Dependencies. (This displays the objects dependent on the Invoices table. The Object Dependencies task pane does not automatically update when you click a different table name. To update the task pane, you must click View and then Object Dependencies.)

h. Click the *Objects that depend on me* option located toward the top of the Object Dependencies task pane. Notice the objects that are dependent on the Invoices table.

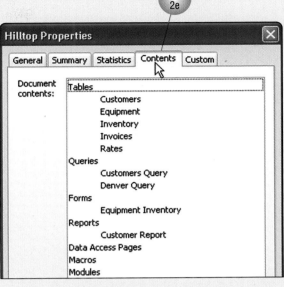

Step 2e

Hilltop Properties

General | Summary | Statistics | Contents | Custom

Document contents:

Tables
    Customers
    Equipment
    Inventory
    Invoices
    Rates
Queries
    Customers Query
    Denver Query
Forms
    Equipment Inventory
Reports
    Customer Report
Data Access Pages
Macros
Modules

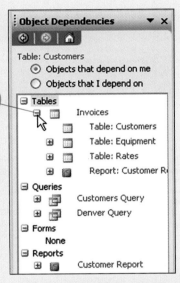

Step 3d

Object Dependencies

Table: Customers
◉ Objects that depend on me
○ Objects that I depend on
⊟ Tables
    Invoices
      Table: Customers
      Table: Equipment
      Table: Rates
      Report: Customer R
⊟ Queries
    Customers Query
    Denver Query
⊟ Forms
    None
⊟ Reports
    Customer Report

Object Dependencies

Step 3e

Table: Customers
○ Objects that depend on me
◉ Objects that I depend on
⊟ Tables
    Invoices
⊟ Queries
    None
⊟ Forms
    None
⊟ Reports
    None

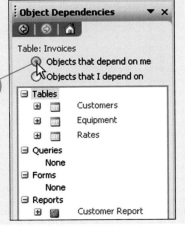

Step 3h

Object Dependencies

Table: Invoices
◉ Objects that depend on me
○ Objects that I depend on
⊟ Tables
    Customers
    Equipment
    Rates
⊟ Queries
    None
⊟ Forms
    None
⊟ Reports
    Customer Report

    i.   Close the Object Dependencies task pane.
4.   Delete the relationship between the Invoices table and
    the Rates table by completing the following steps:
    a.   Click the Relationships button on the
        Database toolbar.
    b.   Right-click the black join line between
        the Invoices and Rates tables.
    c.   At the shortcut menu that displays,
        click Delete.
    d.   At the message asking if you are sure
        you want to permanently delete the
        relationship, click Yes.
    e.   Close the Relationships window.

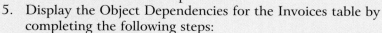

5.   Display the Object Dependencies for the Invoices table by
    completing the following steps:
    a.   Click once on the *Invoices* table in the Hilltop: Database window with the Tables
        button selected on the Objects bar.
    b.   Click View and then Object Dependencies. (Notice that the Rates table is no
        longer listed in the Tables section of the Object Dependencies task pane.)
6.   Close the Object Dependencies task pane.
7.   Close the **Hilltop** database file.

CHAPTER summary

➤   A database table, form, or report can be exported to Excel with the Analyze It with Microsoft Office Excel option at the OfficeLinks drop-down list.

➤   When data is exported to Excel, the data becomes an Excel worksheet with all Excel editing capabilities available.

➤   A database table, form, or report can be exported to Word with the Publish It with Microsoft Office Word option from the OfficeLinks drop-down list.

➤   An Excel worksheet or a Word document created from Access data is automatically saved with the same name as the database table, form, or report selected. A different file extension, however, is added to the document name.

➤   Access data can be used to merge with a Word document. Access uses the data from the database table as the data source and merges the data with a Word document.

➤   Access data can be merged with an existing Word document or merged with a new document.

➤   A query performed in Access can be saved, and then data from that query can be merged with a Word document.

➤   Data from another program can be imported into an Access database table. Access contains an Import Wizard that guides you through the importing data steps.

➤   Data from another program can be linked to an Access table. Changes made to the data in the source program are reflected in the data in the destination program and changes made in the destination program are reflected in the source program.

➤   Use the Clipboard task pane to collect up to 24 different items in Access or other programs and paste them in various locations.

➤ The database Properties dialog box contains information about the open database file. Display this dialog box by clicking File and then Database Properties.

➤ Display the structure of a database table at the Object Dependencies task pane. Display this task pane by opening a database file, clicking a table name, clicking View, and then clicking Object Dependencies.

FEATURES summary

FEATURE	BUTTON	MENU
OfficeLinks drop-down list	[icon]	Tools, Office Links
Import Wizard		File, Get External Data, Import
Link Wizard		File, Get External Data, Link Tables
Clipboard task pane		Edit, Office Clipboard
Properties dialog box		File, Database Properties
Object Dependencies task pane		View, Object Dependencies

CONCEPTS check

Completion: On a blank sheet of paper, indicate the correct term, symbol, or command for each description.

1. Click this option from the OfficeLinks drop-down list to export the selected database table, form, or report to Excel.
2. Click this option from the OfficeLinks drop-down list to export the selected database table, form, or report to Word.
3. Click this option from the OfficeLinks drop-down list to merge Access data with a Word document.
4. Access data exported to Excel is saved with this file extension.
5. Access data exported to Word is saved with this file extension.
6. If you want imported data connected to the original program, do this to the data.
7. Display this task pane to collect up to 24 different items in Access or other programs and then paste them in various locations.
8. Click this option on the Menu bar, and then click Database Properties to display the Properties dialog box.
9. This task pane displays the structure of a table including the objects that are dependent on the table and upon which the table is dependent.

SKILLS check

Assessment 1

1. Copy the database file named **LegalServices** from the CD that accompanies this textbook to your disk. Remove the read-only attribute from the **LegalServices** database file.
2. Open the **LegalServices** database file.
3. Create a form named Billing using the Form Wizard with the following fields:

   From the Billing table:

   > *Billing #*
   > *Client ID*
   > *Date*
   > *Hours*

   From the Rates table:

   > *Rate*

4. When the form displays, close it.
5. At the LegalServices : Database window, create an Excel worksheet with the Billing form.
6. Make the following changes to the *Billing* worksheet:
   a. Select cells A1 through E22 and then apply the Classic 2 autoformat.
   b. Select cells A1 through E1 and then click the Center button on the Formatting toolbar.
   c. Select cells A2 through B22 and then click the Center button on the Formatting toolbar.
   d. Save the *Billing* worksheet.
   e. Print and then close the *Billing* worksheet.
   f. Exit Excel.
7. Close the **LegalServices** database file.

Assessment 2

1. Open the **LegalServices** database file.
2. Create a report named Client Billing using the Report Wizard with the following fields:

   From the Clients table:

   > *First Name*
   > *Last Name*

   From the Billing table:

   > *Date*
   > *Hours*

   From the Rates table:

   > *Rate*

3. When the report displays, print and then close the report.

4. At the LegalServices : Database window, create a Word document with the Client Billing report form. In the Word document, add the following text *above* the report data:

> LEGAL SERVICES
> 330 Jackson Street
> Kent, WA 98043
> (253) 555-3490
>
> CLIENT BILLING INFORMATION

5. Select the text you just typed and then apply a typeface, type size, and font color that closely matches the existing text in the report.
6. Save the Word document with Save As and name it **Wordsac7Report**.
7. Print **Wordsac7Report**, close it, and then exit Word.
8. Close the **LegalServices** database file.

Assessment 3

1. Open the **LegalServices** database file.
2. Merge data in the Clients database table to a new Word document using the Merge It with Microsoft Office Word option from the OfficeLinks drop-down list.
3. Click the Maximize button located at the right side of the Document1 title bar.
4. Compose a letter with the following elements:
   a. Press Enter six times, type the current date, and then press Enter five times.
   b. Insert the proper field names for the inside address. *(Hint: Use the Insert Merge Fields button on the Mail Merge toolbar.)*
   c. Insert a proper salutation.
   d. Compose a letter to clients that includes the following information:

   > The last time you visited our offices, you may have noticed how crowded we were. To alleviate the overcrowding we are leasing new offices in the Meridian Building and will be moving in at the beginning of next month.
   >
   > Stop by and see our new offices at our open house planned for the second Friday of next month. Drop by any time between 2:00 and 5:30 p.m. We look forward to seeing you.

   e. Include an appropriate complimentary close for the letter. Use the name and title *Marjorie Shaw, Senior Partner* for the signature and add your reference initials and the document name (**Wordsac7sc03**).
5. Merge to a new document and then save the document with the name **Wordsac7sc03**.
6. Print only the first two letters in the document and then close **Wordsac7sc03**.
7. Close the main document without saving it and then exit Word.
8. Close the **LegalServices** database table.

Assessment 4

1. Open the **LegalServices** database file.
2. Extract records from the Clients database table of those clients located in Kent and then name the query Kent Query.
3. Merge the Kent Query to a new Word document using the Merge It with Microsoft Office Word option from the OfficeLinks drop-down list.

4. Click the Maximize button located at the right side of the Document1 title bar.
5. Compose a letter with the following elements:
   a. Press Enter six times, type the current date, and then press Enter five times.
   b. Insert the proper field names for the inside address.
   c. Insert a proper salutation.
   d. Compose a letter to clients that includes the following information:

   > The City of Kent Municipal Court has moved from 1024 Meeker Street to a new building located at 3201 James Avenue. All court hearings after the end of this month will be held at the new address. If you need directions to the new building, please call our office.

   e. Include an appropriate complimentary close for the letter. Use the name *Thomas Zeiger* and the title *Attorney* in the complimentary close and add your reference initials and the document name (**Wordsac7sc04**).
6. Merge to a new document and then save the document with the name **Wordsac7sc04**.
7. Print only the first two letters in the document and then close **Wordsac7sc04**.
8. Close the main document without saving it and then exit Word.
9. Close the **LegalServices** database table.

Assessment 5

1. Open the **LegalServices** database file and click the Tables button on the Objects bar.
2. Import **ExcelWorksheet02** into a new table named Cases. (Use the Import Spreadsheet Wizard to do this.)
3. Open the Cases table in Datasheet view.
4. Print and then close the Cases table.
5. Close the **LegalServices** database file.

Assessment 6

1. Open the **LegalServices** database table.
2. Use the Access Help feature to learn how to change the font, font style, size, and color in a datasheet.
3. Open the Clients table and then make the following changes:
   a. Change the font to Times New Roman.
   b. Change the font size to 9.
   c. Change the font color to Maroon.
4. Change the page orientation to landscape and then print the table in datasheet view.
5. Close the table without saving the changes.
6. Close the **LegalServices** database table.

CHAPTER challenge

You work in the customer relations department at Molly's Museum and Memories. Currently, a simple tracking system of customers is being used and maintained in Excel. The information is very beneficial, but you see where it could be more easily managed if it were in Access. Import the worksheet named *Tracking* in the Excel file named **Molly'sMuseum** into a new database table named **Molly's Museum and Memories**. *(Hint: Prepare the Excel file for import.)* Do not import the *Distance Traveled* field. Use the *Customer Number* field as the primary key. Once the table has been imported, be sure to assign appropriate data types to each field.

Once tables have been created in Access, renaming the tables to better identify the information in the table may be necessary. Use the Help feature to learn about renaming tables. Then rename the Tracking table imported in the first part of the Chapter Challenge to Statistics.

You decide that the information being gathered in the Statistics table may be of interest to others. To share the information with others, you will post it to the museum's intranet on a monthly basis and possibly to the museum's Web site. Export the Statistics table as an HTML file to prepare it for posting. Save the HTML file as **Statistics**.

CHAPTER 8

CREATING WEB PAGES AND USING DATABASE WIZARDS

PERFORMANCE OBJECTIVES

Upon successful completion of Chapter 8, you will be able to:
➤ Save a table as a Web page
➤ Apply a theme to a Web page
➤ Create hyperlinks in a Web page
➤ Create a database with sample data using a Database Wizard
➤ Manipulate data within the database file

In previous chapters, you learned to use wizards to organize fields in a variety of formats including queries, forms, reports, mailing labels, and charts. Access also includes a wizard that walks you through the steps for creating a data access page along with a number of database wizards you can use to create an entire database file. In this chapter, you will use the Page Wizard to create a data access page from data in a table and you will also create a database file using a database wizard.

Creating a Data Access Page

HINT
A data access page is stored in a separate file in HTML format.

Make Access data available for viewing on the Internet or on a company's intranet by saving the data as a data access page. A data access page is a special type of Web page designed for viewing and working with data from the Internet or intranet. Data saved as a Web page can be viewed in the default browser, formatting can be applied to the Web page, and hyperlinks can be inserted in the Web page.

Saving a Table as a Web Page

HINT
Other users on the Internet or on a company intranet can work with a data access page.

Access contains a wizard that walks you through the steps for creating a data access page. To use this wizard, open the desired database file, click the Pages button on the Objects bar, and then double-click *Create data access page by using wizard* in the list box. Complete the Page Wizard steps to create the data access page. The Page Wizard steps are similar to the wizard steps for creating a form or report.

When you create a data access page, the Page Wizard specifies a folder and subfolders for Web page files. This is because a Web page generally consists of a variety of items that are inserted in individual files. For example, each bullet image and clip art image or picture in a Web page is saved in a separate image file. Inserting all of these files into folders makes it easier for you to take this information to another location. For example, you can copy the contents of a Web page folder and all of its subfolders to another computer or onto a disk.

Another method for creating a data access page is to create the page in Design view. To do this, open the desired database file, click the Pages button on the Objects bar, and then double-click *Create data access page in Design view*. This displays the Design grid where you can create the form with the desired objects. Use the Toolbox to add control objects to the grid. With buttons on the Toolbox, you can also add Web page features such as hyperlinks and scrolling text.

Applying a Theme to a Web Page

Some interesting and colorful formatting can be applied to a Web page with options at the Theme dialog box shown in Figure 8.1. To display this dialog box, click Format, and then click Theme. Click a theme in the *Choose a Theme* list box and a preview displays at the right side. Click OK to close the dialog box and apply the theme to the page. (You can also double-click a theme at the Theme dialog box.)

FIGURE

8.1 **Theme Dialog Box**

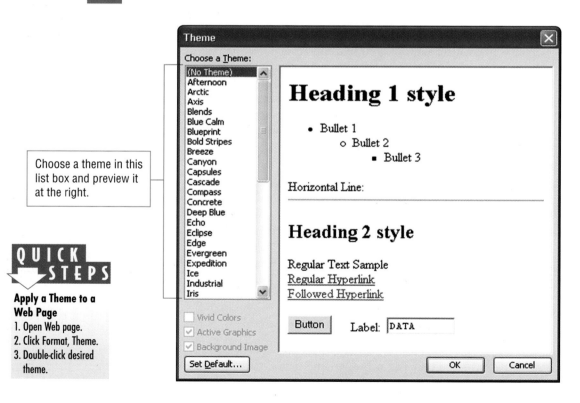

Choose a theme in this list box and preview it at the right.

Previewing a Web Page in Web Page Preview

When creating a Web page, you may want to preview it in your default Web browser. Depending on the browser you are using, some of the formatting may not display in the browser. To preview a Web page in your default Web browser, click File and then Web Page Preview.

(Note: Delete any database files from your disk.)

1. Copy the **OutdoorOptions** database file from the CD that accompanies this textbook to your disk and then remove the read-only attribute from **OutdoorOptions**.
2. Create a Web page by completing the following steps:
   a. At the OutdoorOptions : Database window, click the Pages button on the Objects bar.
   b. Double-click *Create data access page by using wizard* in the list box.

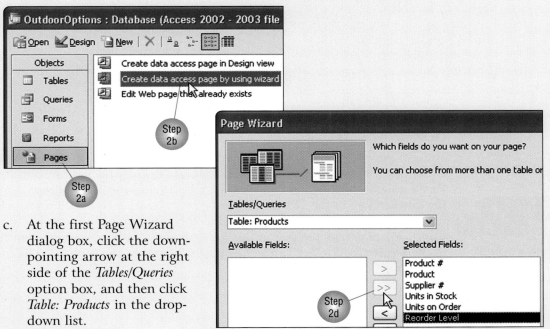

c. At the first Page Wizard dialog box, click the down-pointing arrow at the right side of the *Tables/Queries* option box, and then click *Table: Products* in the drop-down list.
d. Click the button containing the greater than symbols (>>) (this inserts all of the fields in the *Selected Fields* list box).
e. Click the Next button.
f. At the second Page Wizard dialog box, click the button containing the less than symbol (<) to reduce the priority of *Supplier #*.

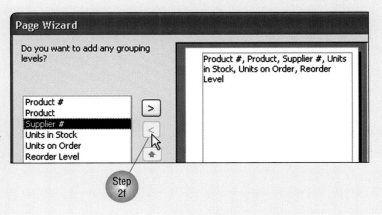

g. Click the Next button.

h. At the third Page Wizard dialog box, click the Next button.

i. At the fourth Page Wizard dialog box, make sure the *Modify the page's design* option is selected, and then click the Finish button. (The completed data access page displays on the screen in Design view.)

3. Click the text *Click here and type title text*, and then type Outdoor Options – Products.

4. Apply a theme to the page by completing the following steps:

a. Click Format and then Theme.

b. At the Theme dialog box, click *Blends* in the *Choose a Theme* list box, and then click OK.

5. Click the View button to change to the Page view.

6. Save the access data page and name it **ProductsWebPage**.

7. Make sure you are connected to the Internet and then view the page in the default Web browser by clicking File and then Web Page Preview. (If you are not connected to the Internet, a message may display telling you that the page might not be able to connect to data. At this message, click OK.)

8. In Web Page Preview, use the navigation buttons along the bottom of the form to display various records.

9. Close the browser by clicking File and then Close.

10. Close the data access page and then close the **OutdoorOptions** database file.

Toolbox

Create a Hyperlink
1. Open Web page in Design view.
2. Click Toolbox button to display Toolbox.
3. Click Hyperlink button on Toolbox.
4. Drag to create hyperlink text box.
5. At Insert Hyperlink dialog box, type desired text in *Text to display* text box, type Web address in the *Address* text box, then click OK.

Creating Hyperlinks

You can create a hyperlink in your Web page. To do this, display the Web page in Design view and then display the Toolbox by clicking the Toolbox button on the Page Design toolbar. Click the Hyperlink button on the Toolbox and then, using the mouse, drag in the Design view window to create a box. When you release the mouse button, the Insert Hyperlink dialog box displays as shown in Figure 8.2. At this dialog box, type the text in the *Text to display* text box that you want to display in the Design view. Click in the *Address text* box, type the Web site URL, and then click OK.

FIGURE

8.2 *Insert Hyperlink Dialog Box*

In this text box, type the text you want to display in the page.

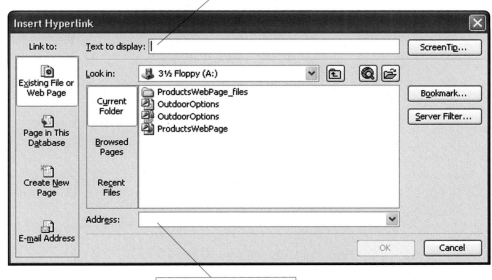

Type the Web site address in this text box.

HINT

A hyperlink is a pointer from one object to another. A hyperlink generally points to a Web page but it can also point to a file, a program, a picture, or an e-mail address.

Another method for creating a hyperlink is to type the URL in a label in the Design view. When you type the complete URL, Access automatically converts the URL to a hyperlink and changes the color of the URL.

exercise 2

SAVING A TABLE AS A WEB PAGE

1. Open the **OutdoorOptions** database file.
2. Create a Web page by completing the following steps:
   a. At the OutdoorOptions : Database window, click the Pages button on the Objects bar.
   b. Double-click *Create data access page by using wizard* in the list box.
   c. At the first Page Wizard dialog box, click the down-pointing arrow at the right side of the *Tables/Queries* option box, and then click *Table: Suppliers* at the drop-down list.
   d. Click the button containing the two greater than symbols (>>). (This inserts all of the fields in the *Selected Fields* list box.)
   e. Click the Next button.
   f. At the second Page Wizard dialog box, click the Next button.
   g. At the third Page Wizard dialog box, click the Next button.
   h. At the fourth Page Wizard dialog box, make sure the *Modify the page's design* option is selected, and then click the Finish button. (The completed data access page displays on the screen in Design view.)

3. Click the text *Click here and type title text*, and then type OUTDOOR OPTIONS. (You may need to drag up the top of the data access page window to see this text.)
4. Apply a theme to the page by completing the following steps:
   a. Click Format and then Theme.
   b. At the Theme dialog box, click *Blends* in the *Choose a Theme* list box, and then click OK.
5. Add two hyperlinks to the page that will allow the user to jump to the Parks Canada site and the United States National Park Service site by completing the following steps:

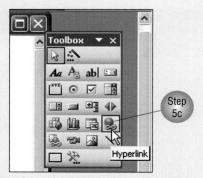

Step 5c

   a. Increase the size of the page window by dragging down the bottom border of the window. (This gives you space to create the hyperlinks.)
   b. Click the Toolbox button on the Page Design toolbar to turn on the display of the Toolbox. (Skip this step if the Toolbox is already displayed.)
   c. Click the Hyperlink button on the Toolbox.
   d. Position the crosshair pointer with the hyperlink icon attached to it toward the bottom of the window. Drag the mouse down to the approximate height and width shown at the right and then release the mouse button.
   e. At the Insert Hyperlink dialog box, make the following changes:
      1) Click in the *Text to display* text box, and then type Parks Canada.
      2) Click in the *Address* text box, and then type http://parkscanada.gc.ca.
      3) Click OK.
   f. Click the Hyperlink button on the Toolbox.
   g. Position the crosshair pointer with the hyperlink icon attached to it to the right of the Parks Canada hyperlink, and then drag to create a box.
   h. At the Insert Hyperlink dialog box, make the following changes:
      1) Click in the *Text to display* text box, and then type National Parks Service.
      2) Click in the *Address* text box, and then type http://www.nps.gov.
      3) Click OK.

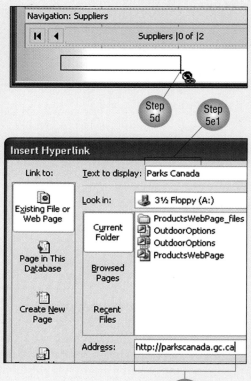

Step 5d

Step 5e1

Step 5e2

6. Click the View button to change to the Page view.
7. Save the access data page and name it **SuppliersWebPage**.
8. View the page in the default Web browser by clicking File and then Web Page Preview.
9. In Web Page Preview, complete the following steps:
   a. Click the Parks Canada hyperlink.
   b. At the Parks Canada home page, navigate to a particular page that interests you.
   c. Close the page by clicking File and then Close.
   d. At the Suppliers Web Page, click the National Parks Service hyperlink.

ACCESS

e. At the National Parks Service home page, navigate to a particular page that interests you.

f. Close the page by clicking File and then Close.

10. Close the browser by clicking File and then Close.

11. Close the data access page, and then close the **OutdoorOptions** database file.

Creating a Database with a Wizard

Access provides numerous database wizards you can use to create database files. These wizards include all of the fields, formatting, tables, and reports needed to manage data. Most of the work of creating the database file is done for you by the wizard. In Exercise 3, you will be using the Contact Management Database Wizard to create a contact management database file.

To see a list of available database wizards, click the New button on the Database toolbar (first button from the left). This displays the New File task pane. Click the <u>On my computer</u> hyperlink in the New File task pane and the Templates dialog box displays. Click the Databases tab and the dialog box displays as shown in Figure 8.3.

Create a Database Using a Wizard
1. Click New button.
2. Click <u>On my computer</u> hyperlink at New File task pane.
3. Click Databases tab at Templates dialog box.
4. Double-click desired template.
5. Complete database wizard steps.

New Database

FIGURE

8.3 *Templates Dialog Box with Databases Tab Selected*

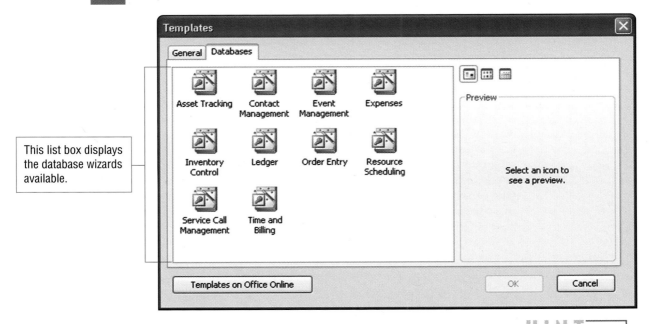

This list box displays the database wizards available.

If your dialog box displays with fewer wizards than what you see in Figure 8.3, not all components of the Access program were installed. You may need to run the Microsoft Installation process again to include the database wizards.

At the Templates dialog box with the Databases tab selected, double-click the

HINT
Choose the wizard that creates the database that most closely meets your needs.

desired wizard. This displays the File New Database dialog box. At this dialog box, type a new name for the database or accept the default name provided by Access, and then press Enter or click Create.

After a few moments, the first Database Wizard dialog box displays as shown in Figure 8.4. This dialog box shows information about the Contact Management database you will create in Exercise 3. Depending on the database you choose, this information will vary. After reading the information in the dialog box, click the Next button.

FIGURE

8.4 *First Database Wizard Dialog Box (for Contact Management)*

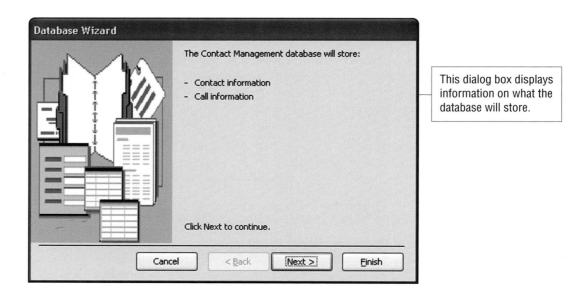

This dialog box displays information on what the database will store.

At the second Database Wizard dialog box, shown in Figure 8.5, notice how the wizard provides predesigned tables displayed in the *Tables in the database* list box and also fields displayed in the *Fields in the table* list box. Most field names in the *Fields in the table* list box are preceded by a check mark. Some database tables may include fields in the *Fields in the table* list box that display in italics with no check mark in the check box. These are additional fields that are not included as part of the table. If you want one of these extra fields included in a table, click the check box to insert a check mark. When all changes are made to this dialog box, click the Next button.

HINT

Optional fields display in italics.

8.5 *Second Database Wizard Dialog Box*

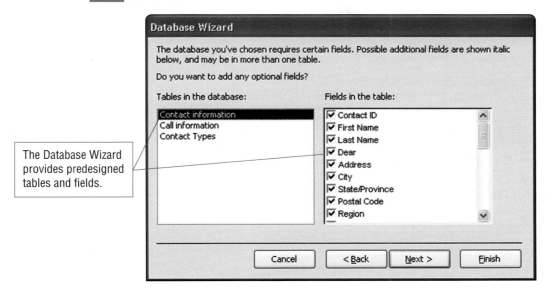

The Database Wizard provides predesigned tables and fields.

Choose a screen display at the third Database Wizard dialog box, shown in Figure 8.6. A sample displays at the left side of the dialog box. After choosing the screen display, click the Next button.

8.6 *Third Database Wizard Dialog Box*

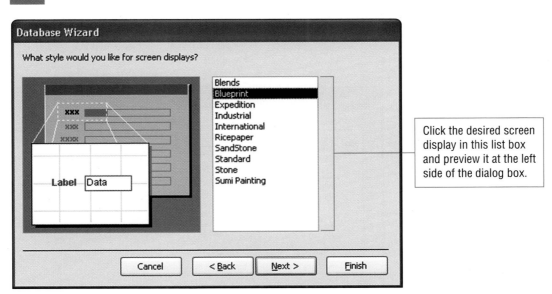

Click the desired screen display in this list box and preview it at the left side of the dialog box.

The fourth Database Wizard dialog box, shown in Figure 8.7, asks you to choose a style for printed reports. Like the previous dialog box, a sample displays at the left side of the dialog box. After choosing the style, click the Next button.

8.7 **Fourth Database Wizard Dialog Box**

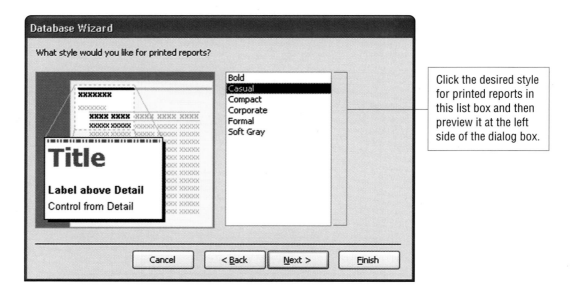

Click the desired style for printed reports in this list box and then preview it at the left side of the dialog box.

Type a name for the database or accept the default at the fifth Database Wizard dialog box shown in Figure 8.8. At this dialog box, you can also choose to include a picture in all reports. After making these decisions, click the Next button.

8.8 **Fifth Database Wizard Dialog Box**

Type a title for the database in this text box or accept the default title offered by Access.

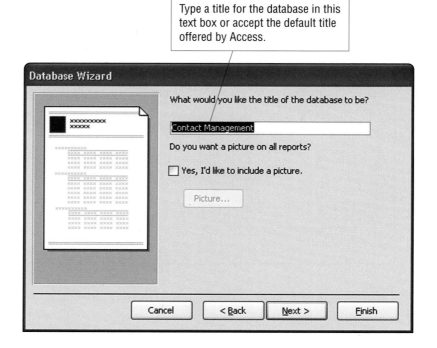

The sixth (and last) Database Wizard dialog box tells you that the wizard has all of the information it needs to build the database. By default, the database will start when the database is completed. Remove the check mark from this option if you do not want the database to start when completed. Click the Finish button and the wizard builds the database. This process can take several minutes.

When the database is completed, a Main Switchboard displays as shown in Figure 8.9, and the Database window is minimized and displays in the bottom left corner of the Access window. With options on the Switchboard, you can choose to enter or view products, enter or view other information in the database, preview reports, change the switchboard items, or exit the database. The Switchboard is intended for people who use the database rather than work on the design of the database. To bypass the Switchboard, click the Minimize button located in the upper right corner of the Switchboard title bar. Display the Database window by clicking the Maximize button located on the Database title bar.

Minimize   Maximize

F I G U R E

8.9   *Main Switchboard*

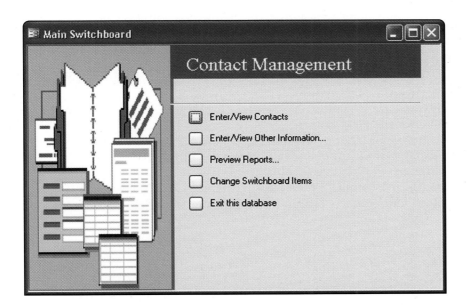

In Exercise 3, you will be creating a contact management database. When the database is completed, you will enter two records and then view some of the different database tables and forms contained in the database.

exercise 3

(Before beginning Exercise 3, delete the OutdoorOptions database file from your disk.)

1. Create a contact management database by completing the following steps:
   a. At the blank Access screen, click the New button on the Database toolbar.
   b. Click the <u>On my computer</u> hyperlink in the New File task pane.
   c. At the Templates dialog box, click the Databases tab.
   d. Double-click *Contact Management* in the list box.
   e. At the File New Database dialog box, type **Contacts**, and then press Enter or click the Create button.
   f. At the first Database Wizard dialog box (see Figure 8.4), read the information, and then click the Next button.
   g. At the second Database Wizard dialog box (see Figure 8.5), click the Next button. (This tells the wizard to use all default tables and fields.)
   h. At the third Database Wizard dialog box (see Figure 8.6), click *Blueprint* in the list box, and then click the Next button.
   i. At the fourth Database Wizard dialog box (see Figure 8.7), click *Casual* in the list box, and then click the Next button.
   j. At the fifth Database Wizard dialog box (see Figure 8.8), click Next.
   k. At the sixth Database Wizard dialog box, click the Finish button.
   l. After a few minutes, the Main Switchboard displays.

2. At the Main Switchboard, complete the following steps:
   a. Click the Enter/View Contacts button and then enter the following information in the specified fields:

First Name	=	Robin	*Contact ID*	=	(AutoNumber)
Last Name	=	Osborn	*Title*	=	Manager
Company	=	Westside Storage	*Work Phone*	=	(612) 555-4550
Dear	=	Ms. Osborn	*Work Extension*	=	245
Address	=	403 West 22nd	*Mobile Phone*	=	(612) 555-1209
City	=	St. Cloud	*Fax Number*	=	(612) 555-4590
State/Province	=	MN			
Postal Code	=	55200			
Country/Region	=	U.S.A.			

   b. Click the 2 button that displays toward the bottom of the record. (This displays page 2 of the record.) Enter the following information in the specified fields:

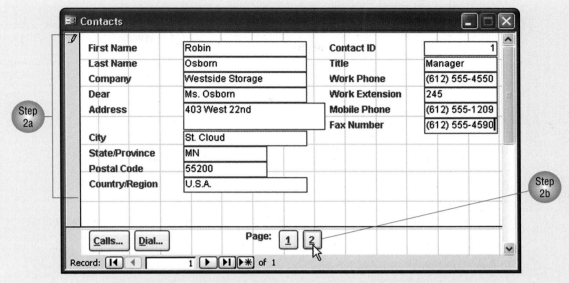

Step 2a

Step 2b

First Name	Robin	Contact ID	1
Last Name	Osborn	Title	Manager
Company	Westside Storage	Work Phone	(612) 555-4550
Dear	Ms. Osborn	Work Extension	245
Address	403 West 22nd	Mobile Phone	(612) 555-1209
		Fax Number	(612) 555-4590
City	St. Cloud		
State/Province	MN		
Postal Code	55200		
Country/Region	U.S.A.		

Calls...   Dial...   Page: 1 2

Record: |◄ ◄ 1 ► ►| ►* of 1

Contact Name = (Access automatically inserts *Robin Osborn*)
Contact Type = (skip this field)
Email Name = rosborn@emcp.net
Referred By = Samuel Eldred
Notes = (skip this field)

c. Click the New Record button, click the 1 button, and then type the following information in the specified fields:

First Name	=	Carol	*Contact ID*	=	(AutoNumber)
Last Name	=	Hoyt	*Title*	=	Owner
Company	=	Hoyt Construction	*Work Phone*	=	(612) 555-4322
Dear	=	Ms. Hoyt	*Work Extension*	=	10
Address	=	900 North 21st	*Mobile Phone*	=	(612) 555-4100
City	=	St. Cloud	*Fax Number*	=	(612) 555-4201
State/Province	=	MN			
Postal Code	=	55200			
Country/Region	=	U.S.A.			

d. Click the 2 button that displays toward the bottom of the record. (This displays page 2 of the record.) Enter the following information in the specified fields:

Contact Name = (Access automatically inserts *Carol Hoyt*)
Contact Type = (skip this field)
Email Name = choyt@emcp.net
Referred By = Jared Snyder
Notes = (skip this field)

3. Click the Save button on the toolbar to save the records.
4. Close the Contacts form.
5. Close the Main Switchboard and display the Contacts : Database window by completing the following steps:
   a. With the Main Switchboard displayed, click the Close button that displays at the right side of the dialog box title bar. (This closes the Main Switchboard and displays the minimized Contacts.)

b. Click the Restore button on the minimized Contacts title bar. (This displays the Contacts : Database window with the Forms button selected.)

6. View various tables, forms, and reports in the database file by completing the following steps:

   a. Click the Tables button on the Objects bar.

   b. Double-click *Calls* in the list box (this opens the Calls table), look at the fields in the table, and then close the table.

   c. Double-click *Contact Types* in the list box, look at the fields in the table, and then close the table.

   d. Double-click *Contacts* in the list box, look at the fields in the table, and then close the table.

   e. Click the Forms button on the Objects bar.

   f. Double-click *Contacts* in the list box, look at the layout of the form, and then close the form.

   g. Click the Reports button on the Objects bar.

   h. Double-click *Alphabetical Contact Listing* in the list box.

   i. When the report displays, print it by clicking the Print button.

   j. Close the report.

7. Investigate the relationship between tables created by the wizard by completing the following steps:

   a. With the Contacts : Database window displayed, click the Relationships button on the Database toolbar.

   b. At the Relationships window, notice the one-to-many relationship created by the wizard. View information about the relationship by completing the following steps:

      1) Position the arrow pointer on the black join line connecting *ContactID* in the Contacts table with *ContactID* in the Calls table and then click the *right* mouse button.

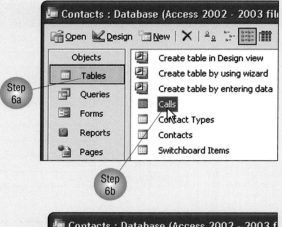

Step 6a
Step 6b

Step 6e
Step 6f

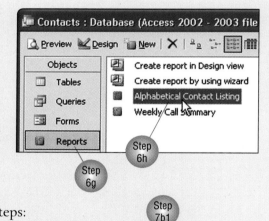

Step 6g
Step 6h
Step 7b1

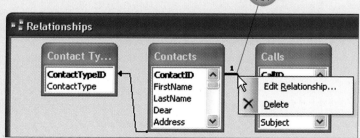

2) At the shortcut menu that displays, click Edit Relationship. This displays the Edit Relationships dialog box, which displays information on the type of relationship created between the tables.
3) After viewing the information in the Edit Relationships dialog box, click the Cancel button.
c. Click the Close button at the right side of the Relationships window title bar.
8. Close the **Contacts** database file.

Viewing a database file created by the database wizard provides you with an example of what can be included in a database file. Consider using some of the other wizards displayed in the Templates dialog box with the Databases tab selected. Each database is set up differently with different tables, forms, and reports. The sample Contacts database you created in Exercise 3 is fairly large—it will probably occupy over 1,000 kilobytes of space on your disk. For this reason, you will delete the Contacts database table.

exercise 4

DELETING THE CONTACTS DATABASE FILE

1. At the blank Access screen, click the Open button on the Database toolbar.
2. At the Open dialog box, click *Contacts* in the list box, and then click the Delete button on the dialog box toolbar.
3. At the message asking if you are sure you want to delete the database file, click Yes.
4. Click Cancel to close the Open dialog box.

CHAPTER summary

➤ Make Access data available for viewing on the Internet or on a company's intranet by saving the data as a data access page.

➤ Data saved as a Web page can be viewed in the default browser, formatting can be applied to a data access page, and hyperlinks can be inserted.

➤ Apply theme formatting to a Web page with options at the Theme dialog box.

➤ Preview a Web page in the default browser by clicking File and then Web Page Preview.

➤ One method for displaying the Insert Hyperlink dialog box is to click the Hyperlink button on the Toolbox and then drag to create a box.

➤ Access provides numerous database wizards that will create a variety of database files including all of the fields, formatting, tables, and reports needed to manage the data.

➤ Database wizards are displayed in the Templates dialog box with the Databases tab selected.

➤ A database file created with a wizard can be modified.

FEATURES summary

FEATURE	BUTTON	MENU	KEYBOARD
New File task pane	📄	File, New	Ctrl + N
Templates dialog box		File, New, <u>On my computer</u>	
Theme dialog box		Format, Theme	
Preview Web page		File, Web Page Preview	
Hyperlink dialog box	🌐	Insert, Hyperlink	Ctrl + K

CONCEPTS check

Completion: On a blank sheet of paper, indicate the correct term, symbol, or command for each description.

1. Make Access data available for viewing on the Internet or on a company's intranet by saving the data as this.
2. Review a Web page in the default browser by clicking File and then this.
3. Display a list of database wizards by displaying the Templates dialog box with this tab selected.
4. To display the New File task pane, click this button on the Database toolbar.
5. When a database wizard is done creating a database, this displays giving you options for entering or viewing information in the database, previewing reports, changing items, or exiting the database.
6. Delete a database file at this dialog box.
7. List the steps you would complete to create a sample database with the Ledger Database Wizard.

SKILLS check

Assessment 1

1. Copy the **Hilltop** database file from the CD that accompanies this textbook to your disk and then remove the read-only attribute from **Hilltop**.
2. Create a Web page using the data access Page Wizard with the fields from the Inventory table. (You determine the title of the page.)
3. Apply a theme of your choosing to the page.
4. Change to the Page view.
5. Save the data access page and name it **InventoryWebPage**.
6. View the page in the default Web browser, use navigation buttons along the bottom of the window to display various records, and then close the browser.
7. Close the data access page and then close the **Hilltop** database file.

Assessment 2

1. Open the **Hilltop** database file.
2. Create a Web page using the data access Page Wizard with the fields from the Customers table. (You determine the title of the page.)
3. Apply a theme of your choosing to the page.
4. Add a hyperlink to the page that will allow the user to jump to the City of Denver Web site at www.denvergov.org. (You determine the location of the hyperlink.)
5. Add a hyperlink to the page that will allow the user to jump to the State of Colorado Web site at www.state.co.us. (You determine the location of the hyperlink.)
6. Change to the Page view.
7. Save the access data page and name it **CustomersWebPage**.
8. View the page in the default Web browser, use navigation buttons along the bottom of the window to display various records, and then click each hyperlink to jump to the specified Web site.
9. Close the browser, close the data access page, and then close the **Hilltop** database file.

Assessment 3

1. Use the Expenses Database Wizard to create a database with the following specifications:
   a. At the File New Database dialog box, type **Expenses** as the database file name.
   b. At the third Database Wizard dialog box, you determine the type of screen display.
   c. At the fourth Database Wizard dialog box, you determine the style for reports.
2. When the database file is completed and the Main Switchboard displays, enter information on expenses for one employee by completing the following steps:
   a. Click the Enter/View Expense Reports by Employee button that displays in the Main Switchboard.
   b. At the Expense Reports by Employee dialog box, type the following in the specified fields (you will be skipping many of the fields):

First Name	=	Nina
Last Name	=	Schueller
Title	=	Manager
Employee #	=	210

   c. Click the Expense Report Form button that displays in the lower left corner of the dialog box.

d. At the Expense Reports dialog box, type the following in the specified fields (you will be skipping fields):

Exp Rpt Name	=	Marketing Seminar
Exp Rpt Descr	=	Two-day Marketing Seminar
Dept Charged	=	Marketing Department
Date Submitted	=	5/14/05

e. Create three expense categories by completing the following steps:
   1) Double-click in the first box below the *Expense Category* heading (located toward the bottom of the dialog box). (This displays the Expense Categories dialog box.)
   2) At the Expense Categories dialog box, enter the following three records:

Expense Category	=	Airfare
Expense Account#	=	10
Expense Category	=	Meals
Expense Account#	=	20
Expense Category	=	Lodging
Expense Account#	=	30

f. After entering the third record, click the Close button to close the Expense Categories dialog box.

g. At the Expense Reports dialog box, enter the following in the specified fields (located toward the bottom of the dialog box):

Expense Date	=	05/10/05
Expense Category	=	Airfare
Description	=	Airline ticket
Amount	=	850
Expense Date	=	05/11/05
Expense Category	=	Meals
Description	=	Daily meals
Amount	=	52
Expense Date	=	05/12/05
Expense Category	=	Meals
Description	=	Daily meals
Amount	=	48
Expense Date	=	05/12/05
Expense Category	=	Lodging
Description	=	Hotel
Amount	=	220

h. Click the Preview Report button located in the lower left corner of the dialog box.
i. When the report displays, print the report by clicking the Print button on the Print Preview toolbar.
j. Close the Expense Report report.
k. Close the Expense Reports form.
l. Close the Expense Reports by Employee form.

3. View the relationships between tables by completing the following steps:
   a. Close the Main Switchboard.
   b. Click the Restore button on the minimized **Expenses** database file.
   c. With the Expenses : Database window displayed, click the Relationships button on the Database toolbar.
   d. After viewing the relationships between tables, click the Close button to close the Relationships window.
   e. Display a few tables and forms to see how the data is organized.
4. Close the **Expenses** database file.
5. Delete the **Expenses** database file.

Assessment 4

1. You can get help for Microsoft Office 2003 programs, such as Access, using the Help feature. Assistance is also available from resources on the Web. Use the Access Help feature to learn about the Help resources available on the Web.
2. After reading the information on Web resources, make sure you are connected to the Internet and then visit at least one Web site that provides information on Microsoft Office 2003. Print at least one page from a site you visit.
3. Create a Word document explaining the resources available. Save the document and name it **WebResources**. Print and then close **WebResources**.

CHAPTER challenge

You work in the business department at a large computer corporation, Computers R Us. Sales representatives from various departments within the corporation are responsible for completing their own expense reports. To ensure consistency and increase efficiency, you decide to create a database that contains expense reports that could be used by these sales reps. Create a new database based on the Expenses Wizard. Choose appropriate fields for each of the tables and select styles and formats of your own. Enter information about yourself in the expense report and then print it. To give sales reps easier access to these forms, you decide to post the expense report to the company's intranet. To do this, you will create a data access page based on the Expense Reports table. Format the data page so that it is attractive and easily understood.

In the database created in the first part of the Chapter Challenge, a switchboard was generated as well. You decide that one of the titles on the switchboard could be better identified. Use the Help feature to learn about customizing switchboards. Then customize the switchboard created in the Expenses database by changing the text of item 4, "Change Switchboard Items" to "Modify Switchboard Items".

One of the supervisors has requested an expense report for a particular sales rep in the software department. Send the expense report created in the first part of the Chapter Challenge as an attachment to the supervisor (your professor). Provide the necessary information in the subject line and in the message of the e-mail.

WORKPLACE Ready

Creating Forms and Reports

ASSESSING proficiency

In this unit, you have learned to create forms and reports in Access. You also learned how to use Access wizards, export Access data to Word and Excel, import and link data, display object dependencies, and create data access pages and insert hyperlinks.

Assessment 1

1. Use Access to create a database for clients of a mental health clinic. Name the database file **LancasterClinic**. Create a database table named Clients that includes the following fields (you determine the data type, field size, and description):

> *Client #* (primary key)
> *Client Name*
> *Street Address*
> *City*
> *State*
> *ZIP Code*
> *Telephone Number*
> *Date of Birth*
> *Diagnosis ID*

2. After creating the database table, save it, switch to Datasheet view, and then enter the following data in the appropriate fields:

> *Client #:* 1831
> George Charoni
> 3980 Broad Street
> Philadelphia, PA 19149
> (215) 555-3482
> *Date of Birth:* 04/12/1958
> *Diagnosis ID:* SC

> *Client #:* 3219
> Marian Wilke
> 12032 South 39th
> Jenkintown, PA 19209
> (215) 555-9083
> *Date of Birth:* 10/23/1981
> *Diagnosis ID:* OCD

> *Client #:* 2874
> Arthur Shroeder
> 3618 Fourth Avenue
> Philadelphia, PA 19176
> (215) 555-8311
> *Date of Birth:* 03/23/1953
> *Diagnosis ID:* OCD

> *Client #:* 1583
> Roshawn Collins
> 12110 52nd Court East
> Cheltenham, PA 19210
> (215) 555-4779
> *Date of Birth:* 11/03/1963
> *Diagnosis ID:* SC

Client #: 4419
Lorena Hearron
3112 96th Street East
Philadelphia, PA 19132
(215) 555-3281
Date of Birth: 07/02/1984
Diagnosis ID: AD

Client #: 1103
Raymond Mandato
631 Garden Boulevard
Jenkintown, PA 19209
(215) 555-0957
Date of Birth: 09/20/1974
Diagnosis ID: MDD

3. Adjust the column widths and then save the Clients database table.
4. Change the page orientation to landscape, print, and then close the Clients database table.
5. Create a database table named Diagnoses that includes the following fields (you determine the data type, field size, and description):

    Diagnosis ID (primary key)
    Diagnosis

6. After creating the database table, save it, switch to Datasheet view, and then enter the following data in the appropriate fields:

Diagnosis ID	=	AD
Diagnosis	=	Adjustment Disorder
Diagnosis ID	=	MDD
Diagnosis	=	Manic-Depressive Disorder
Diagnosis ID	=	OCD
Diagnosis	=	Obsessive-Compulsive Disorder
Diagnosis ID	=	SC
Diagnosis	=	Schizophrenia

7. Adjust the column widths, print, and then close the table.
8. Create a database table named Fees that includes the following fields (you determine the data type, field size, and description):

    Fee Code (primary key)
    Hourly Fee

9. After creating the database table, save it, switch to Datasheet view, and then enter the following data in the appropriate fields:

Fee Code	=	A
Hourly Fee	=	$75.00
Fee Code	=	B
Hourly Fee	=	$80.00
Fee Code	=	C
Hourly Fee	=	$85.00
Fee Code	=	D
Hourly Fee	=	$90.00
Fee Code	=	E
Hourly Fee	=	$95.00
Fee Code	=	F
Hourly Fee	=	$100.00

ACCESS

Fee Code	=	G
Hourly Fee	=	$105.00
Fee Code	=	H
Hourly Fee	=	$110.00

10. Save, print, and then close the Fees table.
11. Create a database table named Employees that includes the following fields (you determine the data type, field size, and description):

> *Provider #* (primary key)
> *Provider Name*
> *Title*
> *Extension*

12. After creating the database table, save it, switch to Datasheet view, and then enter the following data in the appropriate fields:

> *Provider #:* 29
> *Provider Name:* James Schouten
> *Title:* Psychologist
> *Extension:* 399
>
> *Provider #:* 15
> *Provider Name:* Lynn Yee
> *Title:* Child Psychologist
> *Extension:* 102
>
> *Provider #:* 33
> *Provider Name:* Janice Grisham
> *Title:* Psychiatrist
> *Extension:* 11
>
> *Provider #:* 18
> *Provider Name:* Craig Chilton
> *Title:* Psychologist
> *Extension:* 20

13. Adjust the column widths and then save the Employees database table.
14. Print and then close the Employees database table.
15. Create a database table named Billing that includes the following fields (you determine the data type, field size, and description):

> *Billing #* (primary key; identify the data type as *AutoNumber*)
> *Client #*
> *Date of Service*
> *Insurer*
> *Provider #*
> *Hours*
> *Fee Code*

16. After creating the database table, save it, switch to Datasheet view, and then enter the following data in the appropriate fields:

> *Client #:* 4419
> *Date of Service:* 03/01/2005
> *Insurer:* Health Plus
> *Provider #:* 15
> *Hours:* 2
> *Fee Code:* B
>
> *Client #:* 1831
> *Date of Service:* 03/01/2005
> *Insurer:* Self
> *Provider #:* 33
> *Hours:* 1
> *Fee Code:* H
>
> *Client #:* 3219
> *Date of Service:* 03/02/2005
> *Insurer:* Health Plus
> *Provider #:* 15
> *Hours:* 1
> *Fee Code:* D
>
> *Client #:* 2874
> *Date of Service:* 03/02/2005
> *Insurer:* Penn-State Health
> *Provider #:* 18
> *Hours:* 2
> *Fee Code:* C

Client #: 4419	Client #: 1103
Date of Service: 03/03/2005	Date of Service: 03/04/2005
Insurer: Health Plus	Insurer: Penn-State Health
Provider #: 15	Provider #: 18
Hours: 1	Hours: 0.5
Fee Code: A	Fee Code: A
Client #: 1831	Client #: 2874
Date of Service: 03/04/2005	Date of Service: 03/04/2005
Insurer: Self	Insurer: Penn-State Health
Provider #: 33	Provider #: 18
Hours: 1	Hours: 0.5
Fee Code: H	Fee Code: C

17. Adjust the column widths and then save the Billing database table.
18. Print and then close the Billing database table.

Assessment 2

1. With the **LancasterClinic** database file open, create the following one-to-many relationships (enforcing referential integrity and cascading fields and records):
    a. *Client #* in the Clients table is the "one" and *Client #* in the Billing table is the "many."
    b. *Diagnosis ID* in the Diagnoses table is the "one" and *Diagnosis ID* in the Clients table is the "many."
    c. *Provider #* in the Employees table is the "one" and *Provider #* in the Billing table is the "many."
    d. *Fee Code* in the Fees table is the "one" and *Fee Code* in the Billing table is the "many."
2. Use the AutoForm feature to create a form with the data in the Clients database table.
3. After creating the form, add the following record to the Clients form:

   Client #: 1179
   Timothy Fierro
   1133 Tenth Southwest
   Philadelphia, PA 19178
   (215) 555-5594
   Date of Birth: 12/07/1987
   Diagnosis ID: AD

4. Save the form as Clients, print the form, and then close the form.
5. Add the following records to the Billing database table:

Client #: 1179	Client #: 1831
Date of Service: 03/08/2005	Date of Service: 03/09/2005
Insurer: Health Plus	Insurer: Self
Provider #: 15	Provider #: 33
Hours: 0.5	Hours: 1
Fee Code: C	Fee Code: H

6. Save and then print the Billing database table.
7. Close the Billing database table.

Assessment 3

1. With the **LancasterClinic** database file open, create a form with fields from related database tables using the Form Wizard with the following specifications:
   a. At the first Form Wizard dialog box, insert the following fields in the *Selected Fields* list box:

   From the Clients database table:

   > *Client #*
   > *Date of Birth*
   > *Diagnosis ID*

   From the Billing database table:

   > *Insurer*
   > *Provider #*

   b. Do not make any changes at the second Form Wizard dialog box.
   c. Do not make any changes at the third Form Wizard dialog box.
   d. You determine the format style at the fourth Form Wizard dialog box.
   e. At the fifth Form Wizard dialog box, type the name ProviderInformation.
2. When the first record displays, print the form.
3. Close the record that displays.

Assessment 4

1. With the **LancasterClinic** database file open, create a query in Design view with the following specifications:
   a. Add the Billing, Employees, and Clients tables to the design grid.
   b. Add the following fields from the specified tables:

Date of Service	=	Billing table
Provider #	=	Employees table
Client #	=	Clients table
Hours	=	Billing table

   c. Run the query.
   d. Save the query and name it ProviderHours.
2. Display the query in PivotTable view.
3. At the PivotTable layout, drag and drop the fields as follows:
   a. Drag the *Provider #* field to the *Drop Row Fields Here* section.
   b. Drag the *Client #* field to the *Drop Column Fields Here* section.
   c. Drag the *Hours* field to the *Drop Totals or Detail Fields Here* section.
   d. Drag the *Date of Service* field to the *Drop Filter Fields Here* section.
4. Remove the PivotTable Field List box from the screen.
5. Click the Print button to print the query in PivotTable view.
6. In the *Provider #* field, display only the hours for provider number 15.
7. Print the PivotTable and then redisplay all providers.
8. In the *Date of Service* field, display only hours for provider hours for March 1, 2005.
9. Print the PivotTable and then redisplay all rental dates.
10. Switch to Datasheet view, save, and then close the query.

Assessment 5

1. Open the **LancasterClinic** database file.
2. Use the Label Wizard to create mailing labels (you determine the label type) with the client names and addresses and sorted by ZIP Code. Name the mailing label file **ClientMailingLabels**.
3. Print the mailing labels.
4. Close the mailing labels file and then close the **LancasterClinic** database file.

Assessment 6

1. Open the **LancasterClinic** database file.
2. Create an Excel worksheet with the Billing database table, with the following specifications:
   a. In Excel, select the cells in the worksheet containing data and then apply an autoformat of your choosing.
   b. Print the worksheet centered horizontally and vertically on the page.
   c. Save the worksheet. (Excel will automatically name it **Billing**.)
3. Exit Excel.
4. Close the **LancasterClinic** database file.

Assessment 7

1. Open the **LancasterClinic** database file.
2. Merge data in the Clients database table to a blank Word screen. *(Hint: Use the Merge It with Microsoft Office Word option from the OfficeLinks drop-down menu.)* You determine the fields to use in the inside address and an appropriate salutation. Type March 10, 2005 as the date of the letter and type the following text in the body of the document:

   The building of a new wing for the Lancaster Clinic will begin April 1, 2005. We are excited about this new addition to our clinic. With the new facilities, we will be able to offer additional community and group services along with enhanced child-play therapy treatment.

   During the construction, the main entrance will be moved to the north end of the building. Please use this entrance until the construction of the wing is completed. We apologize in advance for any inconvenience this causes you.

   Include an appropriate complimentary close for the letter. Use the name and title *Marianne Lambert, Clinic Director* for the signature and add your reference initials and the document name (Wordsau2pa07).
3. Merge to a new document and then save the document with the name **Wordsau2pa07**.
4. Print the first two letters of the document and then close **Wordsau2pa07**.
5. Save the main document as **ConstructionLetter** and then close **ConstructionLetter**.
6. Exit Word and then close the **LancasterClinic** database file.

Assessment 8

1. Open the **LancasterClinic** database file.
2. Click the Tables button on the Objects bar.
3. Import **ExcelWorksheet03** into a new table named StaffHours. (Use the Import Spreadsheet Wizard to do this.)
4. Open the StaffHours table in Datasheet view.
5. Print and then close the StaffHours table.
6. Use the Form Wizard to create a form with the following specifications:
   a. Use all of the fields from the StaffHours table.
   b. You determine the layout and the style of the form.
   c. Name the form StaffWages.
   d. When the form is completed, change to Design view and add the following:
      1) Add a calculated control that multiplies the Hours by the Rate. (Name this calculated control Wages.)
      2) Format the calculated control text box so that the format is changed to *Currency* and the decimal places option is set to 2.
      3) Insert the company name, *Lancaster Clinic*, in the Form Header and increase the size of the company name (you determine the size).
      4) Make any other changes you feel are necessary to create an attractive form.
   e. Change to the Form view.
   f. Print only the first record in the form.
   g. Close the StaffWages form.
7. Close the **LancasterClinic** database file.

Assessment 9

1. Open the **LancasterClinic** database file.
2. Create a Web page using the data access Page Wizard with the fields from the Billing table. (You determine the title of the page.)
3. Apply a theme of your choosing to the page.
4. Change to the Page view.
5. Save the data access page and name it **BillingWebPage**.
6. View the page in the default Web browser, use navigation buttons along the bottom of the window to display various records, and then close the browser.
7. Close the data access page and then close the **LancasterClinic** database file.

WRITING activities

The following activities give you the opportunity to practice your writing skills along with demonstrating an understanding of some of the important Access features you have mastered in this unit. Use correct grammar, appropriate word choices, and clear sentence constructions.

Activity 1

The director at Lancaster Clinic has asked you to add information to the **LancasterClinic** database file on insurance companies contracted by the clinic. You need to create another database table that will contain information on insurance companies. The director wants the database table to include the insurance company name, address, city, state, and ZIP Code along with a telephone number and a name of a representative. You determine the field names, data types, field sizes, and description for the database table and then include the following information (in the appropriate fields):

Health Plus
4102 22nd Street
Philadelphia, PA 19166
(212) 555-0990
Representative: Byron Tolleson

Penn-State Health
5933 Lehigh Avenue
Philadelphia, PA 19148
(212) 555-3477
Representative: Tracey Pavone

Quality Medical
51 Cecil B. Moore Avenue
Philadelphia, PA 19168
(212) 555-4600
Representative: Lee Stafford

Delaware Health
4418 Front Street
Philadelphia, PA 19132
(212) 555-6770
Representative: Melanie Chon

Print the insurance company database table. Create a form with the insurance company database table and then print the form.

Open Word and then write a report to the clinic director detailing how you created the database table. Include a title for the report, steps on how the database table was created, and any other pertinent information. Save the completed report and name it **sau2act01**. Print and then close **sau2act01**.

Activity 2

Merge data in the insurance company database table to a blank Word screen. You determine the fields to use in the inside address and an appropriate salutation. Compose a letter to the insurance companies informing them that Lancaster Clinic is providing mental health counseling services to people with health insurance through their company. You are sending an informational brochure about Lancaster Clinic and are requesting information from the insurance companies on services and service limitations. Include an appropriate complimentary close for the letter. Use the name and title *Marianne Lambert, Clinic Director* for the signature and add your reference initials. When the merge is completed, name the document containing the merged letters **sau2act02**. Print the first two letters in the merged document and then close **sau2act02**. Close the main document without saving it and then exit Word. Close the insurance company database table and then close the **LancasterClinic** database file.

ACCESS

INTERNET project

Health Information Search

In this activity, you will search the Internet for information on a health concern or disease that interests you. You will be looking for specific organizations, interest groups, or individuals who are somehow connected to the topic you have chosen. It may be an organization that raises money to support research, it may be a support group that posts information or answers questions, or you may find information about clinics or doctors who specialize in your topic. Try to find at least ten different groups that support the health concern you are researching.

Record information about the organizations you found in your database. Create a database file in Access and create a table in that file to store the results of your search. Design the table so that you can store the name, address, phone number, and Web address of the organizations you find. You will also want to identify the connection the group has to your topic (supports research, interest group, treats patients, etc.). Create a report to summarize your findings. In Microsoft Word, create a letter that could be used to write for further information about the organization. Then use the names and addresses in your database to merge with the letter. Select and then print the first two letters that result from the merge. Finally, write a paragraph describing information you found out about the health concern while searching the Web that you previously did not know.

JOB study

City Improvement Projects

In this activity, you are working with the city council in your area to keep the public informed of the progress being made on improvement projects throughout the city. These projects are paid for through tax dollars voted on by the public, and the city council feels that an informed public leads to a good voter turnout when it is time to make more improvements.

Your job is to create a database file and a table in the database that will store the following information for each project: a project ID number, a description of the project, the budgeted dollar amount to be spent, the amount spent so far, the amount of time allocated to the project, and the amount of time spent so far. Enter five city improvement projects into the table (sample data created by you). Create a query based on the table that calculates the percent of budgeted dollars spent so far and the percent of budgeted time spent so far. Generate a report that will include a chart showing the percentages of dollars and time spent so far for each project. Finally, save the report as a Web page to be viewed by the public. Include an attractive theme and a link to your city's home Web site (or a city of your choice).

INDEX

reports, 174
Less than symbol (<), 71, 96, 173
Link dialog box, 223
Linking
  data to Access table, 230
  data to new table, 223
Lookup Wizard, 27-28, 35
Lookup Wizard dialog boxes, 28

M

Mailing labels
  creating, 202
  features summary, 203
  preparing, 186-190
Mailing Label Wizard, 186
Main Switchboard, 247
Margins: changing, 21, 34
Mathematical equations: and calculated fields, 105
Max function, 108, 125
Maximize button, 247
Min function, 108, 125
Minimize button, 247
Minus symbol (-)
  and data display in PivotTable, 197
  turning off subatasheet display with, 61

N

Naming: fields, 8, 34
New File task pane, 243
New Form dialog box, 145, 146
New Object button, 142
New Query dialog box, 101, 116, 119
New Record button, 24, 144, 164
New Report dialog box, 172, 186
Null value, 43

O

Object dependencies: viewing, 227-230
Object Dependencies task pane, 227, 228, 231
Objects bar, 94
  Pages button on, 237
  Queries button on, 101, 116
  Reports button on, 172, 179
Office Assistant, 85
Office Clipboard: using, 224-225
Office Clipboard task pane, 224, 230
OfficeLinks: using, 209-221
OfficeLinks button, 209
One-to-many relationships, 49, 61
  creating, 47-50
  creating additional ones in database files, 53-54
  related tables and, 47
  tables joined by, 178
Open button, 17
Open dialog box, 34
Options dialog box: with General tab selected, 81
Orders: Filter By Form window, 122, 123
Orders table: form created from data in, 142

P

Page Design toolbar: Toolbox button on, 240
Page Footer section, 179, 181, 202
Page Header section, 179, 181, 202
Page orientation: changing, 34
Pages button, 237
Page setup: changing, 21-22
Page Setup dialog box, 34, 142, 164
  with Margins tab selected, 21, 22
  with Page tab selected, 22
Page Wizard, 237, 238
Paper size: changing, 34
Pasting
  data in Access database table, 225-226

with Office Clipboard, 224, 230
PivotChart: creating, 199, 203
PivotChart view, 171, 194, 203
  data summarized with, 199-202
PivotTable: creating, 194, 203
PivotTable Field List box, 194, 195
PivotTable toolbar: AutoCalc button on, 194
PivotTable view, 171
  changing to, 203
  data analyzed in, 197-199
  data summarized in, 194-197
Plus symbol (+)
  and data display in PivotTable, 197
  as expand button in Object Dependencies task pane, 228
  before records in related tables, 58
Portrait orientation, 21
Pound symbols (#): around dates, 96, 124
PowerPoint: data collected from documents in, 225
Premium: Database window, 17
Premium database: Employees table in, 18
Premium database file, 14, 15
Previewing: Web pages, 251
Primary fields: creating, 43
Primary Key button, 43, 61
Primary key fields
  defining, 61
  identifying, 41
Primary keys, 43, 44-46, 60
Primary table, 47, 49, 50
Print button, 20, 34
Printing
  database relationships, 50
  database tables, 20-21, 34
  forms, 142, 164
Print Preview toolbar, 175
Print Relationships Wizard, 50, 61
Products: Table window, 71